The Women's Institutes' Book of
Gardening
for the Kitchen

Sheila Chase

Rosemary Kenrick

Peggy Fonge

Consultant: Arthur Organ
Head of Horticulture
Nottingham College of Agriculture

Macdonald Educational in association with WI Books Ltd.

© WI Books Ltd. 1980

First published 1980
Macdonald Educational Ltd.
Holywell House
Worship Street
London EC2A 2EN
in association with
WI Books Ltd.
39 Eccleston Street
London SW1W 9NT

Editorial manager
Chester Fisher
Publishing co-ordinator
Robin Cross
Production manager
Eva Wrennall

Designed and created by
Berkeley Publishers Ltd.
9 Warwick Court
London WC1R 5DJ

Editor: Gaynor Cauter
Design: Keith Worthington
Picture research:
 Julia Schottlander
Special photography:
 Chris Ridley
Illustrations: David Parr
 Gabrielle Stoddart
Photographs supplied by:
A–Z Botanical Collection
 Ltd.
Bodleian Library, Colour
 Film Strip
Brian Furner
The National Trust,
 Hardwick Hall
Harry Smith Horticultural
 Photographic Collection

Our thanks to:
Access Irrigation Ltd.
Fisons Limited
Hozelock Ltd.
Murphy Chemical Ltd.
Norlett Ltd.
Ocean Spray J. O. Sims Ltd.
Templar Tillers Ltd.

Made and printed by
Purnell & Sons Ltd.
Paulton

ISBN 0 356 07040 9

Contents

Introduction

Most people do some gardening at some stage in their lives, either for sheer pleasure and satisfaction or simply to maintain the value of their property by ensuring that the garden looks reasonably neat and trim. Gardening is either loved, or hated as a tedious chore that has to be done. Keen gardeners find their hobby a calming therapy and the people to whom the whole process is a tiresome bore usually know very little about the subject. Not surprisingly, their rewards are small compared with the efforts they put in.

This book is designed to take the pain out of gardening. It explains basic things in simple and straightforward terms and is a refreshing change from that often unintelligible jargon with which the 'expert' has surrounded himself. These sensible and practical contributors have made a powerful contribution towards dispelling that aura of secrecy and mystique with which gardening is too often associated.

Every page of this book is the result of practical experience. The contributors will readily admit that they, too, have known the pangs of failure as well as the thrill of success.

The book not only contains the cultural details concerning the growing of vegetables, fruit and herbs. It is also full of those personal and very practical tips which are the result of long experience. They are the sort of hints that are usually passed on from person to person over a pint in a pub or at a local village show. They are all too rarely put down on permanent record in print.

There are many references to the historical background of many of the plants mentioned and to growing techniques. All this makes splendid background material. This book is not a text book for gardeners and was not intended to be one. It is a book written by ordinary but good gardeners and is designed to meet the needs of the gardener who enjoys pottering around his or her garden and dabbling in all sorts of different 'bits and pieces'.

The material covered is wide in scope and a great deal of knowledge is presented in a simple and very readable way. To the gardener whose efforts often end in failure the book will prove a blessing—a practical demonstration of that old adage 'If at first you don't succeed, try, try again'.

I thoroughly recommend it.

A. A. Organ
Head of Horticulture
Nottingham College of Agriculture

Planning Your Kitchen Garden

Make your garden work for you

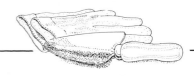

The kitchen garden

Keen gardeners would all agree that fruit and vegetables from their own gardens taste far better than any bought over the counter. But to-day's garden seldom has enough space to grow sufficient to meet a family's needs throughout the year. The answer is either to acquire an allotment or to be selective, grow-ing only those things which the family particularly enjoy or out-of-season crops when prices are high in the shops. Whether a whole allot-ment is being cultivated or only a small bed of salad crops, the same care and attention must be given to ensure success.

Some people object to the look of vegetables in a small garden, and ad-mittedly a row of rotting cabbages is not particularly attractive. But a productive plot of well-tended crops has its attractions. Careful planning can provide a screen to hide the plot. Even a small garden can be productive and remain at-tractive. In a larger garden the vegetables and fruit plots are separ-ate units to be fitted into the overall plan. Whichever is the case, some thought must be given to the siting of these units.

Site and aspect

It is particularly handy to have the herbs and vegetables near the kitchen door. For best results, food crops re-quire a site in full light, not shaded by trees. It is important that they should be well beyond the reach of any roots of trees or shrubs nearby. These deprive the soil of much valu-able food and moisture and this should be carefully considered when planning a new garden.

The ideal aspect is on a slight slope to the south. The north side of a building is not a good place except for certain wall fruit. In winter the sun is very low in the sky and build-

Top left Melon plants in fruit under low barn cloches.
Left A modern frame with glass removed to allow for plant growth.

ings and trees cast more shade during this period.

A warm, sheltered border, facing south, is good for early fruit and vegetables. Where space limits the amount to be grown, this site may be used for producing crops such as early salads when the prices are high in the shops.

If the garden is sloping, the bot-tom of the slope may well be prone to frost damage. This is bad for vegetables and disastrous for fruit. Shelter from wind is also an advan-tage. Too often the limited size of the garden means there is no choice of site or aspect. However, when-ever possible, these considerations should be made, especially when planning a new garden.

Use of glass

Greenhouses, frames or cloches may be used to extend the season or to grow out-of-season vegetables and fruit. The greenhouse is a permanent fixture. The larger it is, the greater the benefit derived from it because it will hold more warmth. The sit-ing of the greenhouse is important. It should be sheltered but away from buildings and trees which might shade it. To obtain maximum light

in the winter months it should run east to west with the door on the sheltered side.

The use of frames is limited by their height, but they are ideal for early salads and strawberries or tender crops like cucumbers. Glass cloches retain less warmth than frames. Because they are easily moved, they can be used for more than one crop during the year. As the crop need not be protected for the whole of its life, the height re-striction does not apply. However, a rigid plan is needed to give the crops maximum protection, to en-sure that the cloches are used all the year round and to avoid moving them from one part of the garden to another unnecessarily. Polythene tunnel cloches are easier to move, but their use is limited to short-term protection such as finishing lettuces and ripening strawberries.

Tools and equipment

As every practical person knows, good tools are a joy to use. They will last a lifetime if well cared for and it is worth buying the best one can

Siting the greenhouse to give maximum light for winter crops.

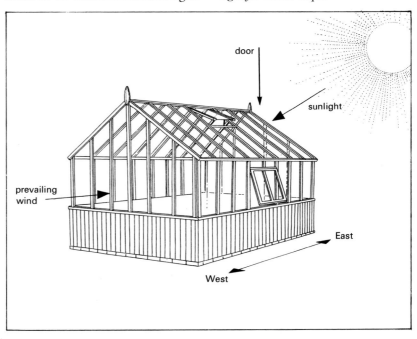

afford to ensure the best quality.

Stainless steel tools will need no more than a wipe after use to maintain them but they are the most expensive to buy. Other tools must be cleaned after use and wiped over with an oily rag to prevent them from rusting. It is astonishing how much harder it is to dig with a dirty spade than a clean one so it is always worth keeping them clean.

The basic tools required for the garden are:

Spade for digging and preparing planting holes.

Digging fork for light cultivation and aerating the soil; and for lifting plants and crops. A potato fork with flat prongs is an advantage if a lot of potatoes are grown.

Rake for breaking down lumps in the soil; for levelling; for producing a fine tilth for the seedbed; and removing weeds and surface stones.

Hoe A draw hoe is needed for taking out drills and a dutch hoe or a modern-type of double-edged hoe for weeding and loosening the soil in summer. An onion hoe or small hand cultivator is useful for working between plants, in frames or under cloches.

Garden line A good strong line with no knots in it is vital for drawing straight drills. A fancy reel makes the job of winding it up easy and neat but is not essential. What is needed is a strong stake at each end, long enough to anchor it firmly in the ground.

Trowel for planting small plants. The style should suit the individual—some prefer a long handle, some a short one.

Measuring rod Useful for marking out distances for sowing and planting. It is quite simple to make one from a light strip of wood, marking it off at 10-cm (3-in) intervals. A suitable size would be 2m (2 yd) but a longer one would be needed when planting fruit trees.

Dibber A dibber is needed for planting brassicas and other plants.

Wheelbarrow Consider the capacity, the weight when empty and

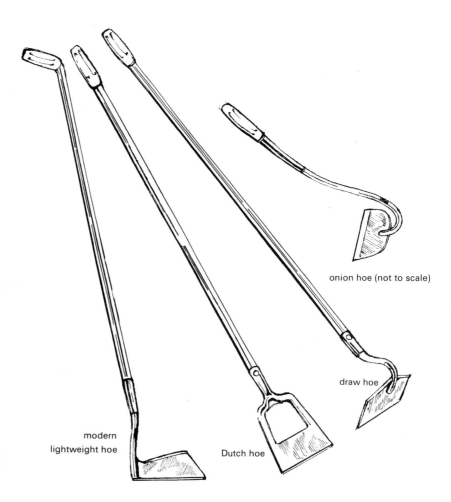

onion hoe (not to scale)

draw hoe

modern lightweight hoe

Dutch hoe

Above *Different types of hoe*. Below *Pruning tools*.

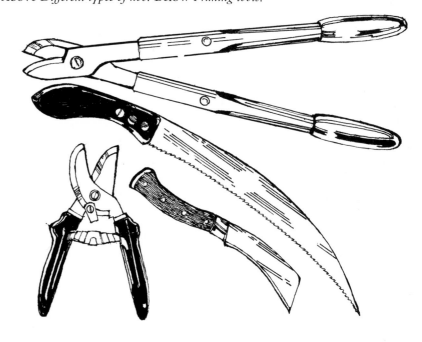

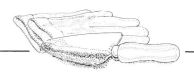

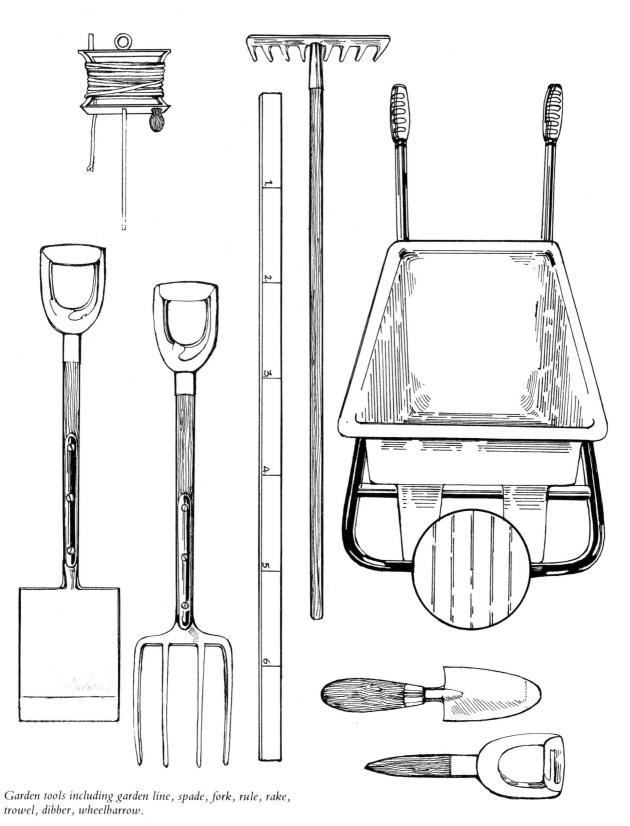

Garden tools including garden line, spade, fork, rule, rake, trowel, dibber, wheelbarrow.

the ease with which it can be emptied and moved in awkward places. Small wheels make hard work on soft ground. The new light-weight plastic barrows are easy to manage, whilst those with a ball-wheel are to be preferred for use on soggy ground.

Pruning tools A good pair of secateurs is needed for pruning both soft fruit and top fruit. Long-handled pruners will cut slightly larger branches and are useful for reaching awkward places A pruning saw is useful for top fruit. This is also designed to cut in awkward places and overhead. A sharp knife is needed to clean up the saw cuts. All cutting and pruning tools should be carefully maintained and kept sharp. Modern pruning tools often have Teflon-coated blades which are easier to clean and less likely to become rusty.

Pest control
Some form of sprayer is needed for pest and disease control and there is a wide selection available. Aerosol cans of spray are not really the answer, although they are useful for prompt action when a pest is discovered unexpectedly. The size of the sprayer depends on the amount of use it will get. It is important that it should be capable of producing a fine spray. If top fruit is being grown, ensure that the spray will reach the necessary height. Many sprayers are sold with an extension lance for this purpose. Also make sure that the sprayer can be filled easily without spilling the spray. Pressure sprayers, which are pumped up beforehand, are easy to use and are available in a conveniently wide range of sizes.

Sprayers should always be well rinsed out with clean water after use. It is vital that this is done very thoroughly after using weedkiller. If possible, it is better to keep a separate sprayer for weedkiller. Any chemical can corrode the sprayer itself or leave residues which could react with other solutions.

The easiest way to apply a dust (insecticide or fungicide) is to buy it in a puffer pack. It is not usually necessary to buy special dusting equipment for the home garden.

Machinery for the small garden
Machines are not really justified in a small garden. If the ground being cultivated is more than 2,000 m² (½ acre), then a small mechanical cultivator will save time for summer cultivation and control weeds.

For winter cultivation, the use of mechanical means must be considered carefully. Most of these cultivators work by a rotary action. A number of hoe blades rotate at speed through the soil, turning it over and breaking it up. They work to a standard depth and continued use may result in a hard pan forming below that depth which eventually impedes the drainage. They tend to destroy the structure of the soil, reducing it to a dust-like consistency

The majority of powered cultivators work by a rotary action with a number of hoe blades rotating at high speed.

and leaving it in a very loose, puffy state which takes time to settle. Perennial weeds will be chopped up and increased.

Cultivators seldom work the soil as deeply as a spade and they are not suitable for cultivating before growing deep-rooted crops. Stony ground causes hard wear on the blades.

For summer cultivation, machines are not set so deeply and the rotary hoes simply chop up the annual weeds and maintain the surface tilth. If mechanical cultivation is to be used, then the garden must be planned for it. Rows must be spaced to allow the machine to get between the plants. Headlands must be left to allow adequate space to turn the machine. Rows should be long to avoid having to turn the machine too often.

Before purchasing a machine it is

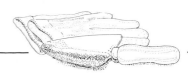

Cultivators must be chosen with care and, when used, sufficient headland left for turning the machine after each row.

best to ask for a trial in one's own garden. Try it out for balance and manoeuvrability in the space available and check the performance on sloping or stony ground. Small cultivators are usually run on petrol but there are one or two electrically driven machines available. For these it is essential that the plot to be cultivated is reasonably close to a source of power. The advantage of machinery powered by electricity is that it is relatively quiet.

Wheeled push hoes have a pair of hoe blades or other tools mounted on a wheeled frame. These are quite effective but need a lot of energy and muscle-power to push them. It is essential to have a good tilth for them to run easily through the soil.

Soil types

There are seldom two soils which are exactly alike. In fact, the soil can even vary within one plot or garden. Soils are derived from rocks and retain the characteristics of the rock from which they originated. It is vital for the gardener to understand the material with which he or she is working. The soil may be improved to make it more fertile and so produce better crops. Fertility must be maintained. Improvement of the soil will, in addition, make it easier to work.

It is quite simple to make a general assessment of the soil in a garden. First, look at it. Is it dark or light in colour? A dark soil is warmer, therefore good for early crops. A light soil probably lacks organic matter; lumps of chalk indicate a very alkaline soil. Secondly, feel its texture by running it between thumb and forefinger.

A greasy feel indicates a clay soil; a gritty feeling, a sandy soil. Very spongy or peaty soils contain a large amount of organic matter derived from rotting vegetation. In fact, soils occur in every possible combination of these three substances, clay, sand and organic matter, hence the variation in their physical character.

Soil analysis

A rough visual analysis of the soil can be made by shaking up a small handful of soil with 500 ml (1 pint) of water in a tall, narrow jar. An old sauce bottle is ideal. Leave it for about one hour until the constituents of the soil have settled in different layers. The heaviest particles of sand will fall to the bottom, while the finer particles will settle in layers on top. Clay, the finest of all, will remain suspended in the liquid while organic matter floats on the top. By gauging the proportions of sand and clay an indication of soil type is given.

The chemical character also varies and it is this that affects plant growth. The plant obtains much of its food from the soil. The only way to discover the chemical content is by analysis, which is really a professional job. There is a soil testing set available for those who are interested, but much can be learnt purely by observation of plant growth and the type of weeds which grow on it. The amount of lime in the soil affects the availability of plant foods and it is worth finding out how acid or alkaline it is with a soil test.

The soil is also teeming with life, not just visible insects and worms, but millions of microscopic plants and animals. These work in the soil, aerating it, decomposing organic matter and converting it for plant use. Without this life the soil would be sterile. The active part of the soil is in the top 25 cm (10 in). This is known as the top soil. Below this is the sub-soil, and the life in it diminishes as it gets deeper. Top soil and sub-soil should always remain in their same relative positions. The top soil must never be removed altogether. When levelling, the top soil should be removed, the sub-soil levelled, and then the top soil can once more be replaced.

Clay soils

Where there is a high percentage of clay particles, the soil is termed 'heavy'. This means it is hard to work because it is sticky. The small particles cling together and hold a lot of water. In all soils the individual particles are coated with a film of moisture and between the particles there are air spaces. The smaller the particles, the more moisture and the less air there is in a given amount of soil.

Treating clay soils

To improve a clay soil the stickiness must be broken up and the air allowed in. Frost can be a great help in doing this. The addition of lime and organic matter, especially peat, is also beneficial. Organic matter in the form of rotted animal and vegetable matter contains an important substance called humus which is especially good for the soil. It breaks

Ridging exposes the maximum surface of the soil to the weather.

up the stickiness of the clay, causing the particles to separate.

It is possible to buy conditioners which help to improve the physical nature of soils, particularly clay. Although there is no doubt that they do have the beneficial effect claimed by the manufacturers, they are expensive and the first time the soil is turned over to expose fresh soil from below the surface benefit is lost and more conditioner must be used.

Cultivating clay soils

The procedure with heavy clay soils is to dig them in autumn, leaving the surface rough or thrown up in ridges to gain maximum effect from attack by winter frosts. After digging, lime should be applied to the surface, if required. Organic matter, such as manure, compost, leaf mould or peat, should be worked into the surface soil. Do not work the soil whilst it is too wet. In particular, it should not be walked upon as this compacts it. When it dries out it will set like concrete.

If the condition of the soil is doubtful, it may be possible to carry out some work by standing on a board. Because of their wetness, clay soils are cold and it is not always possible to get early crops from them. Sometimes this difficulty can be overcome by using raised beds for early sowings and crops which over-winter outside. Make the beds approximately 90 cm (3 ft) wide by throwing up the soil from the paths on either side. The beds should be no more than 6-10 cm (3-4 in) above the normal level of the ground. This is enough to allow surplus moisture to drain away from the plants. In spite of its difficult physical properties, clay soil is usually fertile and produces good results.

Sandy soils

Sandy soils tend to be poor, lacking in nourishment for plants. They also dry out quickly. They are warm and can be worked very soon after wet weather, making them good for producing early crops. However, maincrops tend to suffer from lack of moisure.

Organic matter is beneficial to sandy soils for the opposite reason to clay soils. In sandy soils humus helps to bind the particles together, making the soil more retentive of moisture and less likely to dry out. Mulching with a layer of organic matter on the surface of the ground helps to conserve moisture and it can be dug in at the end of the season to increase the organic matter in the soil. Because this type of soil has low nutritive value, crops grown on it are likely to need extra feeding. It is often acid, requiring regular liming.

Peat soils

This type of soil does not suffer from lack of organic matter, but it is acid and often wet. Particular attention must be paid to drainage and acidity. This is also a hungry soil needing regular feeding to make it productive. It is not difficult to work because of the high organic content.

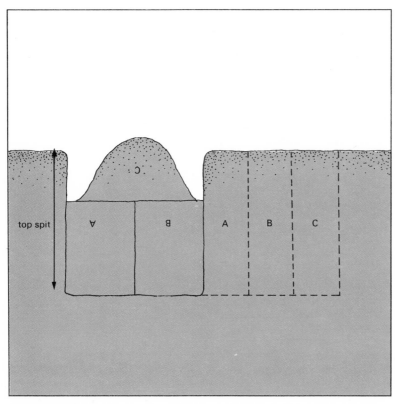

top spit   A   B   A   B   C

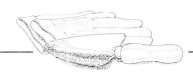

Alkaline and chalk soils

Alkaline soils are derived from limestone or chalk. Some have only 7-10 cm (3-4 in) of soil on top of pure chalk. Water drains through the chalk very quickly, making them dry. They are so alkaline that some plant foods are rendered unavailable to plants. This causes a condition known as lime-induced chlorosis, which produces yellow, sickly leaves. These soils need adequate organic matter to make them more retentive and feeding to give balanced growth. Trees need special care in the early years to establish a good root system and to promote balanced growth.

Stony soils

An excessive number of stones in a soil is extremely annoying and can cause problems when preparing a seedbed. Do not remove all the stones as they are necessary to the structure of the soil. This type of soil is often dry and moisture will collect around a stone lying on the surface and aid germination. Rake off only the large stones which impede the drawing of the drill. In some ways the stones act as a mulch, conserving moisture.

Loamy soils

The ideal soil is a medium loam, a mixture of sand and clay with a high proportion of organic matter. It is the type of soil that everybody wants and hardly anybody has. It should be easy to handle and fertile. The gardener must maintain that fertility by regular and adequate use of manure or compost.

Drainage

A complicated drainage scheme is not usually necessary in the home garden. However, no plant will grow in ground that is perpetually waterlogged. Fruit trees in particular are virtually doomed in such conditions. From the point of view of drainage, it is never a good plan to put vegetables or fruit in the lowest part of the garden. If drainage is found to be a problem, some levelling or terracing of the ground may solve it. If the problem is acute and a system of land drains has to be considered, it is best to consult an expert. It is important to have some outlet, such as a ditch, into which to drain the water. If waterlogging is suspected, dig a hole about 45 cm (18 in) deep and observe what happens after heavy rain.

Digging

The ground is dug to aerate it and improve drainage, to incorporate organic matter and to clear weeds and spent crops. When a fairly large piece of ground is to be dug, the easiest way is to divide the plot in two. At one end of one half take out a trench 30 cm (1 ft) wide and deposit the soil from the trench at the same end of the other half. Proceed digging down the first half by filling in the first trench to form the second and so on to the bottom of the first half of the plot. Then take the soil from the bottom of the second half of the plot to fill the last trench on the first half. Work back until the soil from the first trench is reached and use this to fill in the last trench.

Soil test.

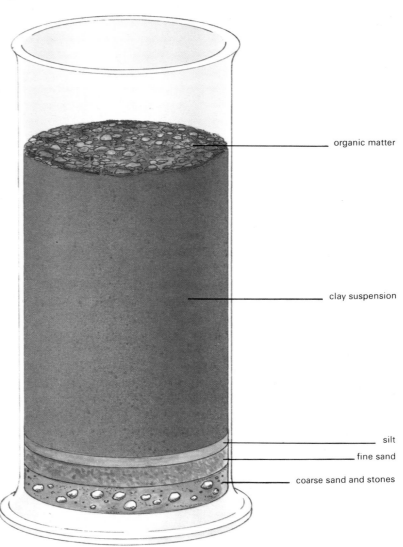

organic matter

clay suspension

silt

fine sand

coarse sand and stones

This is called single digging—one spit deep or one spade's depth. It is important to insert the blade of the spade absolutely vertical to get the full depth. The removal of the soil to form a trench makes it easy to incorporate manure which is laid in the bottom of each trench as the work proceeds. It also makes it easier to extract a spadeful of soil because there is nothing to press against it as it is lifted. The amount or weight of soil taken at each spadeful determines the amount of strain on the back and each individual must gauge his or her own capabilities. It is also wise to dig slowly and build up a rhythm rather than to rush into it for a short time and retire exhausted.

Double digging

If deeper cultivation is required, the ground is dug two spits deep or double-dug. Divide the plot in the same way as for single digging but take out a wider trench, 60 cm (2 ft)

wide. Break up the bottom of the trench with a fork. With both single and double digging it is important to keep the freshly dug ground level. This is not difficult providing each trench is measured accurately. When grassland is being freshly dug, it is best to double dig it. The turf is skimmed off each trench and placed face down on the broken-up bottom of the trench and chopped up before covering in.

Ridging

When digging heavy soil, place it in a ridge to expose the maximum surface to frost.

Sowing

Seed sowing should only be carried out when the soil is sufficiently dry. This is when it does not stick to the boots when walked on. It should be hoed or lightly forked to let the air and sun dry out the surface soil. It will then rake down to a fine tilth, reducing the lumps of soil to fine

When digging it is wise to build up a comfortable rhythm slowly and steadily rather than rush and become exhausted.

crumbs of even texture. It is an important stage in the preparation of the seedbed because a fine texture enables each seed to be in close contact with the soil. Lumpy soil leaves some seeds high and dry in a pocket of air.

If the ground has not settled, this is the stage at which to tread it firm. The position of the rows should be marked with canes and a tight line put down to ensure straight rows. To do this, push the stakes to which the line is fixed well down into the soil and put the second stake in at an angle to pull it taut. The seed drills are drawn using a draw hoe with the long cutting face held vertically against the line. Aim to make the drill even in depth. Shallow drills can be made with a stick. The depth depends on the size of the seed.

In dry weather the drill should be

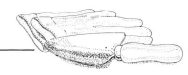

taken out the night before sowing and watered thoroughly. Alternatively, a lining of moist peat can be put along the drill and the seeds sown in this. After sowing as thinly as possible, the drills are filled in with a rake and lightly firmed using the head of the rake. Remove the line but leave the marker canes and rake tidy.

Planting

The art of planting is to move a plant from one place to another with the minimum check to growth. If it is at all dry, water the plants thoroughly the night before transplanting. If the soil is too wet, it is not fit for planting and the operation should be delayed. Lift the plants carefully with a fork so as not to damage the roots. If there is any delay before replanting, take care to prevent the roots from drying out by covering them with a damp sack or a loose covering of soil.

The ground should be well prepared for planting. This is especially important for fruit trees and bushes which remain in the ground for a very long time.

When planting, there are basic guidelines which should be fol-
lowed. Set the plant at the same depth as it was in the nursery. The planting hole should be big enough to accommodate the roots when they are spread out. Replace the soil and firm it so that the roots are in full contact with the particles of soil. It is helpful to put peat around the roots, particularly in poor soil. Bonemeal, added to the soil as it is returned to the planting hole, encourages new root growth.

Thinning out

Small seeds cannot be sown at definite intervals, therefore the seedlings must be thinned out so that each stands alone with adequate space to allow it to develop. The first thinning should be carried out as soon as possible, usually when the seedling forms its first true leaf. This is best carried out by hand, but with later thinnings the seedlings can be chopped out with a hoe for final spacing. Thinning by stages ensures against loss through attack by pests or diseases. Gaps can be filled by transplanting. Thinnings may be used for further rows with crops like lettuce, although rootcrops rarely transplant well. Transplanting by thinning will extend the season of cropping.

Weed control

Wherever possible, ground should be cleared of perennial weeds before attempting to grow crops on it. If necessary, chemical means can be used before cropping begins. When the ground is dug, watch out for the roots of dandelion, docks, bindweed and other perennial weeds. Pick them out and burn them. Annual weeds should be destroyed by regular hoeing and on no account should they be allowed to seed.

There is a lot of truth in the saying that one year's seeding gives seven years' weeding. Modern chemical

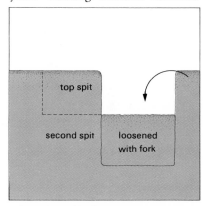

Above *Double digging*
Below *Plan for single-digging a plot of ground.*

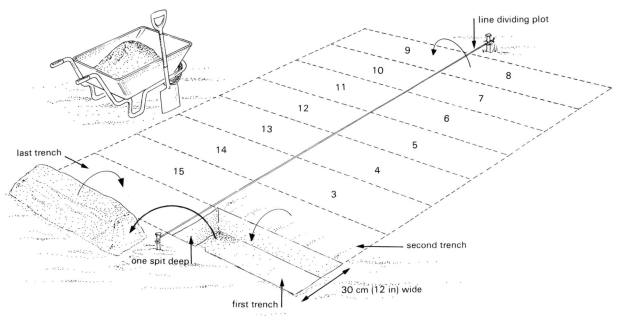

Above *Planting sweet corn, using a trowel.*

Below *Use a garden line stretched between two stakes to draw drills.*

Below *Using a hoe to make a V-shaped drill for sowing.*

cane marking end of row

line taught against cane

rod pushed right down to soil level

half-hitch to prevent line unravelling

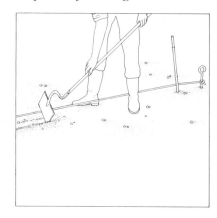

Above *Spreading manure around the base of a tree after planting. There are three types of manure, true, substitute and garden compost.*

One way to avoid the awkward job of mowing close to the trunks of fruit trees is to spray weeds with a contact weedkiller.

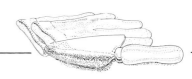

weedkillers can be used with care among growing crops, but cultural methods of weed control are preferable in the small garden. Where they are perhaps justified is in the area surrounding the garden, such as hedge bottoms. Contact weedkillers, such as paraquat and diquat, may safely be used at the base of trees and bushes providing the foliage is not splashed.

Spraying round the base of fruit trees with contact weedkillers at the beginning of the season saves the awkward job of mowing close round the trunks. They kill annual weeds and the tops of perennial weeds. Residual weedkillers, such as propachlor and simazine, control the germination of weed seeds, although they do not kill existing weeds and are therefore quite good for treating the seedbed. If these weedkillers are used, the instructions should be read carefully. It may be necessary to keep pets away when they have been used and they should *never* be transferred for storage from the containers in which they were purchased.

Watering

Lack of watering during the growing season causes a check to growth. This is followed by delay and reduction in cropping as well as susceptibility to disease, notably mildew. By watering in dry weather these disadvantages can be avoided and it will be possible to carry out those operations, such as transplanting, which would be impossible in dry conditions. For individual plants or small areas like the seedbed, use a watering can with a rose for seedlings; dispense with the rose for bigger plants.

For larger areas a hose will be needed with some form of sprinkler to imitate, as closely as possible, natural rainfall. The water must not

Top right *A rotary sprinkler covering a circular area.*
Right *An oscillating sprinkler being used to water a flower bed.*

be applied with too much force. Large drops may batter the plants and the soil. There are three types of equipment: a rotary sprinkler will cover a circular area and may therefore leave patches unwatered or under-watered; an oscillating fan sprayer covers a square area; and a perforated hose will cover two or three rows at a time.

It is important to give a good soaking when watering. Once watering is begun during a dry spell it should be continued or the plants will suffer more than if they had not been watered at all. The amount of water needed to produce the equivalent of 25 mm (1 in) of rain is 25 litres ($4\frac{1}{2}$ gall) per 1 m² (1 sq yd), which is 2·5 litres ($\frac{1}{2}$ gall) per 30 cm² (1 sq ft). By finding out the time it takes to fill a 5-litre (1-gall) bucket from the hose and by measuring the area to be covered, it is possible to calculate how long it will take the equipment to give the equivalent of 25 mm (1 in) of rain. This should be given approximately every ten days in dry weather.

Mulching

Mulching has already been described as a means of conserving moisture in the soil and of adding organic matter to it. It also plays a part in the control of weeds. A mulch consists of a layer of loose material such as compost, manure, leaf mould, lawn mowings, peat or pulverised bark fibre. These act as an insulating layer keeping the soil cool, preventing the evaporation of moisture from the soil and preventing the germination of weed seeds by excluding the light from them. Black polythene has a similar effect. It may feed the plants at the same time, as in the case of compost and manure, or simply have a physical effect on the soil. A mulch should be applied in the late spring when the soil is moist. Do not put it on too early in the case of tender plants. By insulating the soil it prevents the reflection of heat from the soil at night which can be important in preventing frost damage. At the end of the season the mulch is simply worked into the soil during autumn digging.

Plant foods

The needs of the plant are the most important consideration when gardening. It must be well fed and healthy in order to give maximum production. Probably the most important consideration are the roots. Not only do they anchor the plant in the ground, but they also spread through the soil searching out moisture and food. The food is dissolved in the moisture in the soil and is absorbed by the plant through the hairs at the tips of the roots. Encouraging root growth will ensure both that the plant has a greater capacity to take in food from the soil and that it grows better.

The shoot or above-ground part of the plant also functions to increase growth. The leaves are the manufacturing department of the plant. Not only do they breathe oxygen from the air, but they also take in carbon dioxide. Using energy from

Tomato plants with a peat mulch—a mulch can consist of compost, manure, leaf mould, lawn mowings or peat.

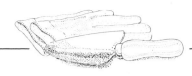

the sunlight, they manufacture carbohydrates which are used in the process of growth. Encourage good leafy growth and the plant has a greater growth potential.

Finally, the plant loses moisture from the leaves. This is the water taken in at the root which passes right through the plant, making it turgid. There must be a balance between the water taken in at the root and that lost from the leaves. Excessive loss from the leaves when the soil is dry cuts the intake from the roots and results in wilting and a check to growth.

The practical applications of these plant functions are simple. The gardener should maintain a fertile soil with a good moisture-holding capacity and give adequate light and moisture when necessary. Observation and experience will tell when supplementary feeding or watering is needed to improve growth.

Spring cabbage with a mulch of black polythene, which retains moisture in the soil and discourages weed growth.

The soil

Gardening involves the constant removal of material: gathering crops; clearing spent crops; and removing dead leaves and weeds. In nature all this lies where it falls, rots and returns to the soil. Therefore, something must be done to compensate for the removal of plant material and to maintain the fertility of the soil. Plant foods can be given in the form of chemicals but these do nothing to improve the physical character of the soil. For this, bulky manures must be used. These provide organic matter or humus which is vital for the aeration and moisture-holding capacity of the soil.

Bulky manures

These are divided into three types. The true manures, of which there is seldom enough, compost made from garden waste and manure substitutes. Manures, when well rotted, provide balanced plant food and bulky organic matter. In the less rotted state they produce more nitrogen, which causes soft growth.

Very fresh manure may produce ammonia which can scorch the foliage of plants when used as a mulch. It is best to stack fresh manure for a month or two before use.

Farm and stable manures should contain plenty of litter, preferably straw. They can be dug in or used as a mulch, feeding gradually as they break down.

Cow and pig manures are known as cold manures.

Poultry manure should always be stored in the dry for some months before use. It is not as balanced nutritionally as the others mentioned. It is better as a feed during growth and applied to the surface of the soil. Horse manure is best for heavy soils, cow and pig manure for light soils. An average dressing is a good barrow-load to 8 m² (10 sq yd).

Compost made from garden waste is an excellent material for improving the soil and feeding the plants. Unfortunately there is seldom enough waste to make sufficient compost, although material can be sought from elsewhere. The greengrocer's trimmings or a farmer's damaged straw bales would be useful.

Mulching conserves the moisture in the soil and is also a means of adding organic matter at the same time. It is useful in controlling weed growth by excluding them from the light. A layer of loose material such as compost or peat forms the mulch or, alternatively, a sheet of black polythene.

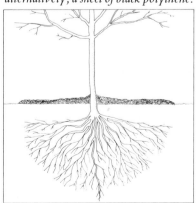

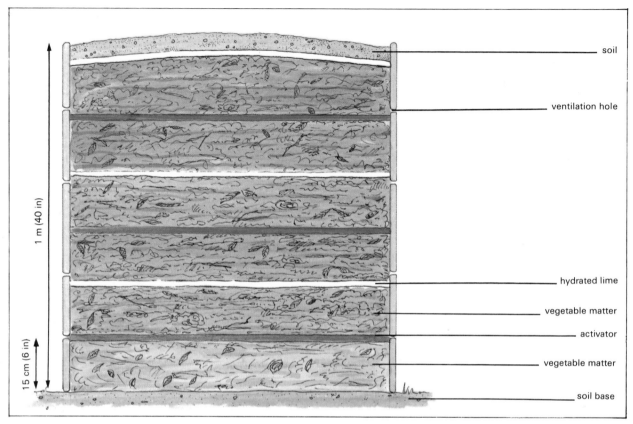

soil

ventilation hole

1 m (40 in)

hydrated lime

vegetable matter

activator

vegetable matter

15 cm (6 in)

soil base

Above *There is more to making a compost heap than just piling up any garden rubbish in a heap. It should be built up in layers on a proper soil base.*

Below *An open bin-type compost heap lined with polythene.*

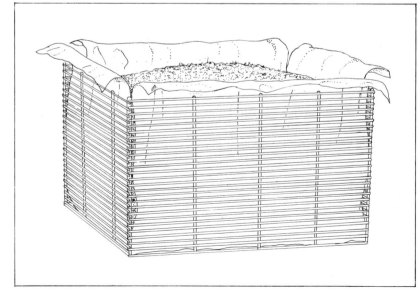

Making a compost heap

Any haphazard heap of weeds and leaves will eventually rot down, but by making a proper compost heap, the material will be ready to use more quickly and will be more uniform. Any garden rubbish that can be chopped up with a spade is suitable. It is best to keep autumn leaves, especially beech and oak, separate as they are tougher and slower to rot. The secret is to mix soft and hard materials as much as possible—do not put a thick layer of lawn mowings by itself. Tougher things, such as cabbage stalks, should always be chopped or cut up roughly if they are to be used.

Make the heap on a soil base. A compost bin can be used from a choice of several on the market. A wooden bin can be made or a polythene dustbin sack used. Whatever type is used, it must have ventilation holes in the sides. A bin helps to prevent the heap from drying out. Experience has shown that the most convenient size for a compost bin is about 1 × 1 m (3 × 3 ft).

The mixed material is put in layers about 15 cm (6 in) thick and then sprinkled with an activator. This can be a little manure, a proprietary compost activator or a handful of

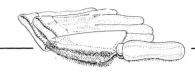

sulphate of ammonia or nitrate of chalk fertiliser. If there is not much soil with the weeds and plant matter, a sprinkling could also be added. If the material is dry, it should be watered.

This is followed by another layer of vegetable matter and then a sprinkling of hydrated lime. These layers are then repeated until the heap is about 1 m (3-3½ ft) high. It may then be capped with a thin layer of soil and covered to retain the moisture. A damp sack is ideal.

Boards or a sheet of polythene will do, but must not be so tightly fitted that they prevent aeration.

Exposed to sufficient air and moisture, vegetable matter is decomposed by bacteria and converted to humus, which is so beneficial to the soil. The use of an activator provides food for the bacteria to do the job.

The quicker the heap is made, the quicker it will rot down. This happens most quickly in late spring. During spring and summer it will take about three months. It is always best to have a succession of small heaps so that there is one heap in the making, one completed and rotting down and one available for use.

Other bulky materials
Old mushroom compost is often available. It is a good source of humus but not very high in food value. Nevertheless, it is a very useful addition to the soil. It is better for neutral and acid soils because it is

Left *A closed bin-type compost heap with ventilation holes in the sides.* Below *A natural compost heap (left) and an enclosed heap (right). The quicker a heap is made, the quicker it will rot down. This happens most quickly during the late spring.*

usually very alkaline in nature.

Leaf mould is made up of rotted or part-rotted leaves and is probably best for mulching. It is good for working into the top 5-10 cm (2-4 in) of the soil. There is not much food value in it but it is high in humus.

Peat is an excellent soil conditioner. Moss peat is good on light soil for increasing the moisture-holding capacity, but sedge peat is probably better for general use as it rots down more quickly.

Pulverised bark fibre is new to most gardeners. Its action is similar to peat and it is very good for breaking up clay.

Green manuring If land is vacant in late summer, this is a good way of adding organic matter. A special crop such as rape or mustard is sown broadcast in August to September and then dug in early in the new year. It is advisable to broadcast sulphate of ammonia or nitrate of soda at 66 g (2 oz) per 1 m² (1 sq yd) before digging in to compensate for the nitrogen used up in the rotting process in the soil.

Seaweed is only available to people living near the sea. It is as good as farmyard manure. It should either be dug in in autumn or composted for use later.

Above *Applying a foliar feed.*

Nitrogen deficiency in any plant can be detected by stunted growth and pale leaves.

A shortage of potash is shown by marginal scorching of the leaves and poor resistance to disease.

Failure to become established because of poor root development often indicates a lack of phosphate.

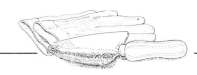

Fertilisers

By using fertilisers it is possible to give a balanced plant food or a single substance for a specific purpose. The three basic plant foods are:

Nitrogen which promotes leafy growth.

Potash for good fruit production and for hardiness.

Phosphate to encourage root growth.

There are also certain minor elements which effect plant growth. Magnesium, for example, has a noticeable effect on tomatoes and is therefore included in specialised fertilisers. The plant will show marked symptoms when these foods are in short supply. Lack of nitrogen is shown by stunted growth and pale leaves. Too much nitrogen promotes a lush soft growth that is susceptible to disease. Potash shortage is shown by marginal scorching of the leaves, poor disease resistance and undersized fruit. Failure to become established because of poor roots and slow development of seedlings is often the result of a shortage of phosphate.

Fertilisers may either be of chemical (inorganic) or organic origin. Usually those of organic origin are slower acting and only gradually become available to the plant.

Nitrogenous fertilisers

Sulphate of ammonia is readily soluble in water so that it may be given as a liquid fertiliser. It is quick acting and good as a tonic for green crops in spring, applied at the rate of 33 g (1 oz) per 1 m^2 (1 sq yd).

Nitrate of soda and nitro-chalk are similar to sulphate of ammonia and should both be applied in the same way.

Hoof and horn is a slow-acting organic fertiliser. The coarser grades are slower to release nitrogen than fine grades. Apply 66 g (2 oz) per 1 m^2 (1 sq yd).

Dried blood is an expensive form of organic nitrogen which is faster acting than hoof and horn. Apply 16 g ($\frac{1}{2}$ oz) per 1 m^2 (1 sq yd).

A solid fertiliser being applied to pea plants.

Potash fertilisers

Sulphate of potash and muriate of potash are the only sources of potash and should be given at the rate of 33 g (1 oz) per 1 m^2 (1 sq yd).

Phosphate fertilisers

Superphosphate is an inorganic source of phosphate. Use on the seed bed at the rate of 50 g ($1\frac{1}{2}$ oz) per 1 m^2 (1 sq yd).

Bone meal is a slow acting organic phosphate. The coarser grades are the slowest to become available. Bone flour is finer and therefore quicker acting. Apply 66 g (2 oz) per 1 m^2 (1 sq yd).

General fertilisers

These are mixtures of the three basic plant foods, made up by the manufacturer to form a balanced feed for general use. It is easier to purchase such a fertiliser rather than to make up one's own. General fertilisers are usually of chemical origin but there are some good liquid ones based on seaweed.

Fertilisers should always be applied when the plant is in active growth and not when it is dying down or dormant. The period from March to April is the best time for feeding fruit trees and bushes, perennial crops such as asparagus and perennial herbs such as fennel.

Where annual crops are concerned fertilisers may be applied when preparing the ground before sowing or later during growth. They can be given in solid form, scattered to cover the full extent of the roots and hoed in or in liquid form, dissolved in water and watered in. Obviously the liquid fertiliser will reach the roots of the plant more quickly than a dry fertiliser when the weather is dry.

A third way to apply fertiliser is as a foliar feed. This is sprayed on to the foliage where it is absorbed by the leaves. All proprietary fertilisers should be used as directed by the manufacturer.

Lime

Lime is necessary in most soils to counteract acidity which results from decaying vegetation in the soil. It renders plant foods more readily available to the growing plants, whether they are natural foods or fertilisers. Lime should never be applied to chalk soils which are already very alkaline. It is possible to buy a small kit for testing the acidity of the soil which is measured as pH, indicating the amount of lime required. This is particularly worth doing in a new garden. Average soils require lime once in three years. It may be given as ground limestone or chalk. An average dressing is 200 g (6 oz) per 1 m² (1 sq yd).

Planning and crop rotation

The layout of the vegetable garden should be planned carefully each year, both to the advantage of the vegetables being grown and to the soil, so that it is well cultivated and the fertility is maintained. Vegetables can be divided into four groups according to their cultural requirements.

A Peas, beans and other gross feeders which need the soil liberally manured.

Below *An immaculately-tended vegetable garden.*
Right *Vegetables at peak production.*

B Brassicas (cabbage family) which need lime.
C Root crops which are fed with fertilisers.
D Perennial or permanent crops.

The vegetable garden should be divided into four plots and one group grown on each. Obviously the perennial crops in group D remain permanently on one section but the other three groups are rotated each year and only grown on the same ground every third year.

The rotation of crops, as it is called, makes it easier to prepare the soil, gives each vegetable the right growing conditions and prevents the carry-over of pests and diseases.

The basic layout for three years is shown in the chart, which covers the full range of vegetables. If not all of them are being grown, some adaptations will have to be made.

The average allotment is about 27 × 9 m (90 × 30 ft). If well planned and cropped, it should produce enough vegetables, including potatoes, for a family of four. Obviously, adjustments have to be made for smaller plots, different sized families and tastes in vegetables.

The tendency with a small plot is to crop more intensively, particularly if cloches are used, when two crops are taken from the ground in one year. Catch crops of lettuce are taken whilst taller crops of peas and beans are developing. The more intensive the cultivation, the more organic matter should be put into the soil to compensate.

By planning of crops, maximum use can be made of cloches at all times.

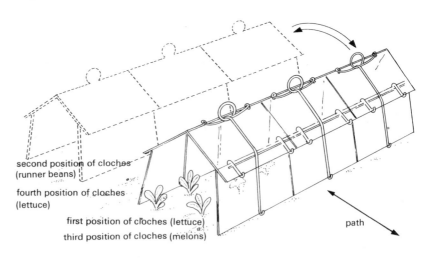

second position of cloches (runner beans)

fourth position of cloches (lettuce)

first position of cloches (lettuce)

third position of cloches (melons)

path

	Year 1	Year 2	Year 3
Plot 1	**A Manured** Peas, beans, onions leeks, spinach, celery	**B Limed** Cabbage, cauliflower, sprouts, kales, broccolis	**C Fertilisers** Potatoes, carrots, beet, turnips, parsnips, swedes
Plot 2	**B Limed** Cabbage, cauliflower, sprouts, kales, broccolis	**C Fertilisers** Potatoes, carrots, beet, turnips, parsnips, swedes	**A Manured** Peas, beans, onions, leeks, spinach, celery
Plot 3	**C Fertilisers** Potatoes, carrots, beet, turnips, parsnips, swedes	**A Manured** Peas, beans, onions, leeks, spinach, celery	**B Limed** Cabbage, cauliflower, sprouts, kales, broccolis
Plot 4	**D Permanent crops** Seedbed, herbs	**D Permanent crops** Seedbed, herbs	**D Permanent crops** Seedbed, herbs

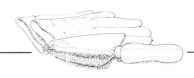

The following charts give some suggestions as to how the plot can be arranged:

Plot 1 *2 × 6 m (6½ × 20 ft)*

Year 1

Section A
1 row dwarf beans followed by spring cabbage.

Section B
1 row early carrots followed by November sown broad beans, 1 row beetroot.

Section C
1 row calabrese followed by 1 row carrots and 1 row beetroot. Later crop lettuce when space available.

Year 2

Section C
1 row calabrese followed by 1 row carrots and 1 row beetroot. Later crop lettuces when space available.

Section A
1 row dwarf beans followed by spring cabbage.

Section B
1 row early carrots followed by November sown broad beans, 1 row beetroot.

Year 3

Section B
1 row early carrots followed by November sown broad beans, 1 row beetroot.

Section C
1 row calabrese followed by 1 row carrots and 1 row beetroot. Later crop lettuce when space available.

Section A
1 row dwarf beans followed by spring cabbage.

Plot 2 *Sheltered plot 2 × 5 m (6½ × 16 ft)*

Year 1

Section A
1 row tomatoes

Section B
2 rows lettuce followed by 1 row Purple sprouting

Section C
2 rows root crops.

Year 2

Section B
2 rows lettuce followed by 1 row Purple sprouting

Section C
2 rows root crops

Section A
1 row tomatoes.

Year 3

Section C
2 rows root crops.

Section A
1 row tomatoes.

Section B
2 rows lettuce followed by 1 row Purple sprouting.

Plot 3 *2 × 5 m (6½ × 16 ft) using 1 row of glass cloches*

Row 1 October-sown lettuce, cloched October-April followed by June-planted cucumbers or melons, cloched June-September

Row 2 April-sown runner beans, cloched April-May followed by October-sown lettuce

Here a 60-cm (2-ft) path is allowed between cloche rows. In the second year the runner beans will be on Row 1.

Some vegetables do not look entirely out of place in the flower border when space is really short. Runner beans, especially those with pink or red and white flowers, can be grown on a wigwam of poles. Tomato plants will also fit in quite well. Two crops can occupy the space of one if a sweetcorn plant is used for a stake for either a tomato or a runner bean plant. Remember that a group of sweetcorn plants is needed to ensure good pollination.

This is unorthodox gardening but providing adequate food is given to carry a double crop, results can be surprisingly good. Another crop that does not look out of place amongst flowers is the beetroot, but it must not be sown in a straight line in the border. It should be sown either broadcast or in small drills to cover a circular area and then thinned.

Yet another way to get some return from the smallest garden is to use growbags. These can be placed on a path or paved area. Use a south-facing wall to grow peppers, aubergines or tomatoes.

Planning the fruit garden

The planning of the vegetable garden is an annual affair but the fruit garden is virtually permanent, therefore it is much more important not to make mistakes. Although it may appear to be a waste of a year, it is worth waiting to see just where the prevailing wind is in a new garden. Find out where water tends to lie in wet weather and if there is a frost pocket. It is then possible to site the fruit in the best position. The time may be usefully employed clearing pernicious perennial weeds which can be very troublesome with soft fruits.

The amount of space available rules the size of the fruit and the amount to be grown. This is a matter for the individual. It is not worth growing fewer than six black currant or gooseberry bushes, three red

or white currants and a 9-m (30-ft) row of raspberries. It is important to group together the same kinds of fruit when planning the layout, to facilitate spraying and manuring. In a small garden make use of any suitable wall or fence space. Cordon or other trained fruit is useful for providing a dividing screen between one part of the garden and another. Alternatively, they may be trained against boundary fences.

Where birds are a problem, a fruit cage may be necessary. This must be carefully sited, preferably where it is

not too visible from the house. Having decided which fruit to grow allow each tree or bush adequate space in which to grow.

Pest control

There are so many troubles which can beset garden crops that it is safe to say that they can never all occur in one garden in one year. If plants

Right *A beautiful fruit cage, as decorative as it is functional.*
Below *A neat line of gooseberry bushes grown as cordons.*

Month by month in the fruit garden

Top fruit	January	February	March	April	May	June
Apples and pears			Feed	Spray for scab, sawfly and codlin ●		Fruit thinning
Damsons, gages and plums		Spray bird deterrent	Feed	●	Spray for sawfly	Fruit thinning
Nectarines and peaches			Feed Spray for peach leaf curl	●	Spray for red spider	Fruit thinning
Cherries			Feed			
Quince						
Fig						
Cob nut						
Walnut						
Soft fruit						
Currants			Feed	Spray for big bud mite		
Gooseberry			Feed	Spray for sawfly Spray for mildew		
Strawberry			Feed Sow Alpine		Spray for mildew and botrytis	
Raspberry		Top canes	Feed Spray for cane spot		Mulch Spray for cane spot	Spray for raspberry beetle
Blackberry, loganberry, etc.						
Vines (outdoor)						
Medlar						
Mulberry						
Rhubarb						

28

...ly	August	September	October	November	December
	Apple sticky bands				
	Black currants		Take cuttings	Red and white currants	
			Take cuttings		
Take runners			Take runners		
Top layer					
...ray for mildew					
			Manure		

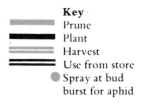

Key
Prune
Plant
Harvest
Use from store
● Spray at bud burst for aphid

Pest Control
Always spray promptly at onset of trouble

are well cultivated, they will not have to struggle for existence but will, on the contrary, be healthy and vigorous and better able to resist damage.

Plants can suffer from insect pests, fungal, bacterial or virus diseases or animals. They can also be affected by the weather. Wind, rain, drought or frost as well as faults in cultivation can all create problems.

Insect pests

The insects which attack plants can be divided into the biters and the suckers. The biters cause actual holes in leaves or tunnels in the leaves, stems and roots. They may even bite off a whole plant. The cutworm can do this to a lettuce. Biters include the soil pests which work unseen and are only discovered when a crop is lifted or the plant collapses through severe damage to the roots. Most of these insects are big enough to be seen easily with the naked eye. Slugs, caterpillars, leaf miners, root flies, wire worm, leatherjackets and weevils are just a few examples of the biting variety.

The sucking insects feed by penetrating the cells of the plant and sucking the sap. This causes distortion or discoloration of the leaves and stems. The brightly coloured blisters on the leaves of currants are an example of this sucking damage. They are caused by the currant blister aphid. Sucking insects are responsible for the spread of virus disease by carrying infected sap from plant to plant. Many of the insects in this group are minute, even microscopic. Examples are red spider mite, white fly, aphid, capsid and froghopper, which causes cuckoo spit.

Insecticides

Insect pests are controlled by the use of insecticides in the form of dusts and sprays or smokes for the greenhouse. Another form is the bait used for pests such as slugs. Sprays should be applied promptly as soon as the pest is seen and identified. Always use them according to the manufacturer's instructions. Store them out of reach of children and *never* transfer any form of insecticide to unmarked bottles or tins.

Some insecticides kill by actual contact with the insect, some by being poisonous to the insect when eaten. Contact insecticides should be applied so that they cover the whole plant and special care taken to cover the undersides of the leaves. Rain will, of course, wash off an insecticide. Systemic insecticides are sometimes watered at the base of the

Sow	Transplant	Distance in rows between plants	Cut	Varieties
March–April	June	45 × 45 cm (18 × 18 in)	mid July–September	Hispi F1 Hybrid Golden Acre Primo
May	July	60 × 45 cm (24 × 18 in)	November–December late December–February	Christmas Drumhead, January King
Early May	July	45 × 60 cm (18 × 24 in)	early November and store use November–February	Holland Late Winter (white storing cabbage)
Late July–early August	September	23 × 45 cm (9 × 18 in)	April–June	Harbinger, April, Wheelers Imperial, Durham Early
January–February under glass	March–April	30 × 45 cm (12 × 18 in)	April–May	Golden Acre, Hispi

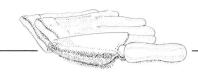

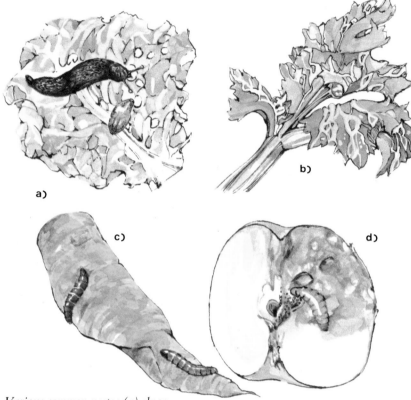

*Various common pests; (a) slug;
(b) leaf miner; (c) wireworm;
(d) caterpillar of codling moth.*

plants which absorb them through the roots. Sometimes they are sprayed directly on to the plants which then absorb them through the leaves. In this case it is only necessary to spray the upper sides of the leaves. In the case of soil pests a deterrent may be applied to the soil.

There are some insects which can actually prove useful as predators on insect pests. Among them are the ladybird, the lacewing, the centipede, the devil's coach horse beetle and the white fly parasite, which is used in glasshouses.

Fungus diseases
The most common fungus diseases are mildew, rust, grey mould (botrytis), potato blight, scab disease of fruit and brown rot of fruit. They are carried from one plant to another by wind or rain and attack often follows a check to growth. Control is by fungicide applied as a spray or

a dust. In the main, sprays are easier to apply effectively. In the greenhouse, however, it is not always wise to increase damp conditions by using a spray and it is better to obtain varieties which are resistant, although not immune, to certain fungus diseases.

Bacterial diseases
These are usually secondary in nature, following some physical damage to the plant. This damage may have been caused by the weather, particularly frost, insects or careless pruning. The effect causes a breakdown or rotting of the plant tissue, as in canker of tree fruit. The only remedy is to cut off the diseased tissue and burn it at once.

Virus diseases
These are caused by a substance actually in the cell sap and are most often transmitted by insects. They cause discoloration and distortion of the leaves, stunting of the plant and poor cropping. They occur par-

ticularly in soft fruits and there is no known cure. Infected plants should be lifted and burnt to prevent them being a source of further infection.

Animals
Birds, mice, moles, rabbits and deer can all cause trouble in the garden. Of these marauders, only the mole does not actually feed on the plants. It feeds on worms and unfortunately, if the soil has been well enriched with organic matter, this is where the worms are. Damage is only done when the mole erupts immediately under a plant, in the middle of a seedbed or if its tunnel leaves a plant high and dry with no soil round its roots. They are very difficult to eradicate. Any deterrent, such as moth balls or prickly twigs in the runs, simply moves them elsewhere and spreads the damage. Trapping is probably best.

Harvesting and storage

Home-grown fruit and vegetables must be harvested and stored properly for the winter if they are to last and keep well. It is especially important to store only those fruit and vegetables that are sound. Set aside any that are bruised or damaged by pests or careless harvesting, for immediate use.

Ladybirds are welcome as they feed on very unwelcome aphids.

31

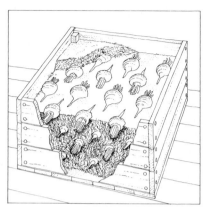

Root vegetables should be stored in sand or peat to prevent drying out.

Vegetables

Some vegetables can be used from the ground during the winter months. Others, like onions, need careful drying and ripening before storing in a dry, airy place, with a good circulation of air around them. Root crops need to be stored in conditions which will prevent them from drying out. The rest must be used fresh, pickled and preserved or stored away in the freezer for use later.

Vegetables should always be harvested at the peak of perfection and not left to get too old on the plant. Peas and beans need to be picked almost daily. Beans, in particular, are more tender if used at once and not left lying about. Roots should be lifted carefully with a fork so as not to damage them. They may be stored in a clamp outside or in boxes or containers in a frost-proof shed, using sand or peat to prevent them from drying out. Onions, shallots and garlic should be ripened and thoroughly dried off before hanging in a dry, airy shed.

Fruit

Apples and pears are the only fruits that will store. Others can be frozen, preserved or used in jam-making. To store successfully, apples and pears must be picked at the right time and handled very carefully. The ideal store is damp with an even temperature, such as a cellar. A dry loft is not suitable because the lack of humidity will cause shrivelling. To tell if an apple or pear is ready for picking it should be cupped in the hand and gently lifted. If it is ready, the stalk will part easily from the tree.

The fruit should be handled as carefully as eggs to prevent bruising. It may be stored on shelves or in boxes, preferably slatted to allow air to circulate. It is worth wrapping late-keeping varieties either in special oiled wraps or in newspaper. This way, if one rots, it will not infect the others surrounding it.

Another method is to store the fruit in polythene tubes. It is easy to see if one rots and it can be removed. Only sound fruit with the stalk intact should be stored. Different varieties are best kept separate.

Both fruit and vegetables in store should be inspected periodically and any that have rotted removed. Always keep a watch for damage by mice or rats and if necessary use traps or poison baits.

Soil and weather must work together

Everyday vegetables

The practice of grouping vegetables according to their habit and soil requirements, so that they can be rotated in the vegetable garden to the benefit of the soil, has long been in use. There are three groups including root crops, brassicas and peas and beans. Root crops do not require fresh manure—in fact it is harmful and causes forked roots. Brassicas require lime, while peas and beans need a richly manured soil. These three groups are rotated so that similar types of vegetable are grown in one place every third year. This avoids exhausting the soil by repeatedly growing the same thing in the same place and checks the pests which attack that crop.

Timing

In considering the culture of vegetables in this section, the dates suggested are for average gardens which do not suffer from extreme weather conditions. In more sheltered gardens sowings may be made a week or two earlier, while in exposed gardens and those liable to late spring frosts they must be a week or two later. Autumn sowings, such as broad beans, must be made earlier in cold gardens and later in warmer parts. Each gardener learns from experience the best timing for a particular site.

Varieties

The selection of suitable varieties or cultivars can be bewildering to the beginner. It is not just the geographical location of a garden that determines the success of a variety, but also the type of soil. One can only experiment or ask around in the neighbourhood to find the best varieties for that particular locality. In the seed catalogues there are many old and tested varieties as well as new ones to try. The seedsmen have the present trend of smaller gardens very much in mind when they offer

Before planting, treat the young seedling with insecticide.

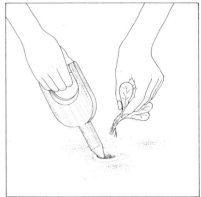

Planting a young seedling using a dibber to make the hole.

There is nothing more satisfying than a kitchen garden at the peak of production. The carrots in the foreground have just been thinned, while behind are rows of beetroots and potatoes. If well tended, they can look as good as flowers in a bed.

new varieties, so it is worth giving them a trial. For each vegetable just one or two suggestions are made here.

Seed
Two items listed in seed catalogues are worth mentioning—FI hybrids and pelleted seed.

FI hybrids
These are first-generation seeds produced as the result of crossing selected parents. They have hybrid vigour, producing excellent plants with increased yield. Seed should not be saved from FI hybrid plants but new seed bought each year. Because of the extra work needed in its production it is more costly.

Pelleted seed
Each seed is encased in a pellet, enabling it to be handled more easily and spaced more accurately when sown. The resulting seedlings are much better. They are not overcrowded, which makes thinning out much easier. When using pelleted seed great care should be taken to keep the soil thoroughly moist until the seedlings emerge, otherwise they may fail to germinate.

Brassicas
Most green crops in the vegetable garden belong to the botanical genus *Brassica*. This name is used as a blanket term for Brussels sprouts, cabbages, cauliflowers, kales, savoys and sprouting broccolis.

All the plants above are raised in a seed bed and then transplanted to their permanent site. They are encouraged to make leafy growth, although in the case of cauliflower and sprouting broccolis it is the young, immature flowering shoots

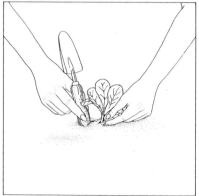

Ensure that plants are well firmed with no air pockets around the roots.

that are eaten while they are tender.

Kohl rabi, swede, turnip and radish, although members of the brassica genus, are not included in the group for the purposes of rotation.

All brassicas need an alkaline soil. The ground should be in good heart but using fresh manure is inadvisable because of its tendency to produce loose hearts when the soil is over-rich. Secondly, lime and fresh manure do not mix. In fact, if the two are applied together, there is a chemical reaction resulting in the release of ammonia, which is likely to scorch the foliage of any plants growing nearby. Thus brassicas are grown on ground manured for a previous crop. However, if the soil is in very poor heart, a little compost or very well-rotted manure can be incorporated. If the ground is not alkaline, it may be necessary to lime it the winter before growing brassicas. It is important that the ground should be allowed to settle after it is dug and before the brassicas are planted. Failure to do this can result in loose sprouts or cabbages with poor hearts.

Plant raising
The seedbed for brassicas needs careful preparation. It should not be hidden away in some corner where nothing else will grow, but situated in an open sunny position. A piece of ground about 1×2 m ($3 \times 6\frac{1}{2}$ ft) is adequate for an average garden. Small numbers of plants can be grown between other crops. The soil should be fertile but not over-rich. A little sifted compost worked into the top 5 cm (2 in) will improve the texture of the soil or, alternatively, a little moist peat can be used. If necessary, a dusting of hydrated lime will give the necessary alkalinity and a dressing of 50 g ($1\frac{1}{2}$ oz) per 1 m² (1 sq yd) of superphosphate encourages good root production. Careful preparation of the seedbed will ensure the production of good plants, although a poor seedling never makes a good plant.

Seed is sown at the appropriate time in drills 2 cm (½ in) deep and 15 cm (6 in) apart (see individual crops). If the soil is very dry, it should be watered thoroughly the day before sowing. Sometimes birds cause trouble by having dustbaths in the seedbed and scattering the seeds. This can be prevented either by netting it or laying pea sticks or a very thin sprinkling of lawn mowings over the seedbed. Lawn mowings are usually the most effective, if only because sparrows invariably find a space between the pea sticks.

The seedlings may be thinned to stand about 2·5 cm (1 in) apart. This will encourage sturdy plants. When they are ready for lifting, the plants should be watered the night before if the weather is at all dry. This will ensure turgid plants for transplanting. They should be lifted carefully with a fork and the roots protected from drying winds and sun. Before planting out, treat the plants with an insecticide to deter cabbage root fly. Plant out, using either a trowel or a dibber. Ensure that the plants are firm with no air pocket around the roots.

It is a good plan to draw a drill 5 cm (2 in) deep and plant in the drill. If it is dry, water the drill, as well as the plants, the night before. If subsequent watering is required, the drill will ensure that the water is channelled to the roots and does not run away from them. Later the cultivation of the soil will fill in the drill and provide further support to the plant. Newly planted brassicas are particularly vulnerable to pigeons and may need protection.

Some brassicas, particularly Brussels sprouts, need a lot of space. However, modern varieties, bred with the small garden in mind, make smaller plants which can be planted close together. If a mechanical cultivator is to be used, the plants should be set opposite each other in the rows to allow the machine to pass in both directions easily. It is important to allow sufficient space at the end of the rows to turn the machine. This is particularly important where there is a concrete path or brick edging, which may not only be damaged itself but also do considerable damage to the machine.

Brussels sprouts

Sow seeds in a prepared seedbed from mid-March to mid-April for transplanting at the end of May or early in June. For early crops, seed may be sown in a frame or under cloches, hardened off and planted out in April.

It is most important that the ground should be firm before planting Brussels sprouts. It should be dug well in advance of planting time. A few days before planting, it should be broken down and a general fertiliser raked in. A dressing of 100–133 g (3–4 oz) per 1 m² (1 sq yd) should be given.

Brussels sprouts should be planted in rows 75 cm (2–2½ ft) each way. Some of the new F1 hybrids, such as Peer Gynt, are smaller plants and may be planted at 60-cm (2-ft) intervals. Too much space may result in loose sprouts. Plant firmly.

If the weather is dry after planting, watering may be necessary until the plants are established. Weeds should be controlled by regular hoeing. In the autumn, remove the leaves as they become yellow.

Start picking from the bottom of the stem when the sprouts are ready, taking a few from each plant. When picking is almost finished, and not before, the tops may be picked and used as greens.

Varieties

Peer Gynt An F1 hybrid of dwarf habit. Ready from October to December. Suitable for freezing.

Citadel An F1 hybrid with medium-size sprouts. Ready in December. Suitable for freezing.

Noisette A dwarf variety of French origin.

Roodnerf Perfection (formerly known as Exhibition). Ready from November onwards.

Roodnerf Seven Hills A medium-sized late variety. Freezes well.

Fresh Brussels sprouts ready for cooking. When picking is almost over, the tops can be used as greens.

Cabbages

To ensure a succession of cabbage for cutting over as long a period as possible, three sowings should be made. The first sowing in spring will be ready for cutting in the summer. An early summer sowing will provide for autumn and winter, and an autumn sowing will produce for the spring.

An additional sowing can be made under glass in early spring if the winter proves severe and greens suffer damage. This will also provide an extra crop in early summer. If a white cabbage is required, there is a storable variety for use in late winter. Sow on a prepared seedbed, 2 cm ($\frac{1}{2}$–$\frac{3}{4}$ in) deep in rows 15 cm (6 in) apart.

Cabbages should follow a crop that has been manured, but if the ground is not in very good heart, well-rotted compost can be dug in. Before planting, rake the soil level and make it firm. Fertiliser is only used for spring-sown cabbage. Rake in a general fertiliser at the rate of 100 g (3 oz) per 1 m² (1 sq yd) before planting.

Hoe frequently during the summer months and at other times when the ground is in a suitable condition. Plants for over-wintering and cutting in spring should have soil drawn up around the stems for added protection. In early March put down a dressing of sulphate of ammonia or nitrate of soda hoed in at the rate of 33 g (1 oz) per 1 m² (1 sq yd).

Hispi cabbage with peat mulch.

Storage

Storable cabbage should be cut in early November. Remove the outer leaves and store the heads in a shed or outdoor heap covered with straw or bracken.

Savoys

The savoy is a very hardy form of cabbage suitable for standing through the winter. The soil requirements and preparation are the same as for broccoli.

Sow the seeds in a seedbed in May. Plant out in July or early August, putting the plants 45 cm (18 in) apart in rows 60 cm (2 ft) apart. Hoe during the summer and early autumn. Remove decaying leaves as they occur.

Varieties

Best of All (early); Dwarf Green Curled (January to March); Ormskirk Late (January to March).

Red cabbage

The red pickling cabbage is cultivated like the ordinary cabbage. It is usually sown in the spring. However, by sowing in late summer in frames or cloches and planting out in the spring, monster heads will be ready for cutting in the autumn.

Varieties

Early Blood Red; Red Drumhead.

Cauliflower

For the earliest cauliflowers, seed should be sown under cloches or in a frame in late September or early October. The young plants should be grown as hardy as possible, ventilating them whenever the weather permits. In severe weather they will need the protection of sacks or mats.

The practice of potting up the seedlings in 8-cm (3-in) pots produces excellent plants but entails more work. If they are left in position they must be lightly thinned to avoid overcrowding. A second sowing may be made under glass in January, to be followed by a sowing outdoors in March to April. Finally, varieties for autumn are sown in late April to mid-May.

Soil preparation

Cauliflowers, which mature in summer, need soil that is in good heart. Without adequate manuring the heads will be small and virtually useless. Therefore it is vital not to skimp the feeding. The ground for cauliflowers should be deeply dug and well manured. Before planting, a general fertiliser should be raked in at the rate of 100 g (3 oz) per 1 m^2 (1 sq yd).

Transplanting and cultivation

Summer-heading types should be planted out from March to June, 45-60 cm (1½-2 ft) each away. Autumn varieties are planted during June and July, more widely spaced at 60-75 cm (2-2½ ft) each way.

Hoe regularly to control weeds. If growth seems to be slow, a quick-acting nitrogenous fertiliser should be hoed in. Use a dressing of sulphate of ammonia or nitrate of soda at the rate of 33 g (1 oz) per 1 m^2 (1 sq yd). When the curds have formed, a leaf should be broken over them to preserve their whiteness.

Left Ice Queen *savoy cabbage with its distinctive leaves.*
Below Ruby Ball *cabbage.*

Varieties
All the Year Round Suitable for freezing.
Alpha
Snowball Suitable for freezing.
South Pacific Suitable for freezing.
Majestic Autumn-maturing and suitable for freezing.

Broccoli (winter cauliflower)

Broccoli is hardier than summer cauliflower. It does not need such rich soil, as it would produce growth too soft to withstand hard frost. The ground needs to be very firm so the best plan is to grow it on ground that has been well manured for the previous crop and which has not been disturbed since that crop was cleared. Before transplanting, hoe in a dressing of superphosphate at 50 g ($1\frac{1}{2}$ oz) per 1 m² (1 sq yd), sulphate of potash at 33 g (1 oz) per 1 m² (1 sq yd).

Sow seeds from mid-April to mid-May. Plant 60 cm (2 ft) each way during June and July. Cultivation is the same as for cauliflower, but do not feed them. They must be grown hard to withstand the winter weather.

Varieties
Adam's Early White; Snow's Winter White (January to February); St. George (April); Late Queen (May); Walcheren Winter (April to May).

Sprouting broccoli

The spring-sprouting broccoli also occupies the ground for a very long time. However, it provides green vegetable at a time when there is not much else about. The summer-sprouting broccoli (calabrese) has a shorter growing period and produces shoots that are particularly tender and well flavoured. They are an excellent vegetable for freezing.

The soil preparation, sowing and planting times are the same as for winter broccoli but calabrese may be sown direct and thinned to 37·5 cm (15 in) as an alternative to transplanting and produces shoots considerably earlier.

Keep picking the shoots to prevent flowering. In the case of calabrese, the plants produce a large central head which should be cut and eaten first. This is followed by smaller shoots.

Varieties
Purple Sprouting; White Sprouting; Italian Sprouting (calabrese); Express Corona (calabrese) F1 hybrid. All these varieties are suitable for freezing.

The whiteness of the cauliflower curd is preserved by breaking a leaf over to protect it from light and weather.

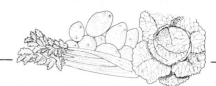

Kales

The kales are the hardiest of the brassicas and provide greens for the kitchen during the winter and spring. The young shoots are picked as they are produced. The soil requirements are as for broccoli.

Sow seed in late April or early May to produce plants for transplanting. Set the plants 60 cm (2 ft) each way in July or early August. An unorthodox crop of spring greens may be obtained from a sowing of kale in frames or cloches in February, to provide greens for picking in late spring. A close stand of plants is needed. They are sown broadcast or in drills 10 cm (4 in) apart and grown without transplanting.

Varieties

Dwarf Curled; Hungry Gap; Pentland Brig.

Pests and diseases

Flea beetles and turnip fly The little beetles feed on the seed-leaves, piercing them with tiny holes. The pest is most troublesome in dry weather. It can be checked by watering in the evenings until the plants are growing well. Spray with gamma-HCH or derris soon after germination and then at weekly intervals until the leaf stage is reached.

Cabbage caterpillar (large and small white butterflies and the cabbage moth). The caterpillars feed on the leaves and can cause extensive damage if not checked. On a small scale, hand picking the caterpillars and crushing the egg clusters on the undersides of the leaves will control them. Dusting with gamma-HCH or derris is effective. Do *not* use HCH within two weeks of picking.

Cabbage root fly The maggot of the fly feeds on the roots and tunnels in the stems, causing the plant to wilt. Infested plants should be dug up and burned. Control by treating plants as they are transplanted with 4% calomel.

Left *Purple Sprouting broccoli.*

Above *Dwarf Curled kale.*

Common garden pests and diseases:
(a) flea beetle; (b) club root;
(c) cabbage root fly; (d) white fly;
(e) cabbage caterpillar.

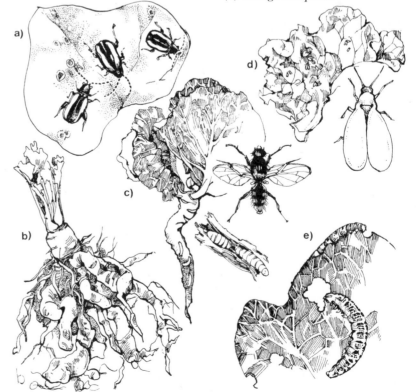

Grey cabbage aphid This is found on the underside of the leaves and causes blistering and distortion. As soon as it is identified spray with gamma-HCH or a systemic insecticide.

Whitefly If whitefly is also present the two sprays mentioned above will be effective and should be applied at seven-day intervals.

Club root disease (finger and toe) The extremities of the roots become swollen, eventually causing the death of the plant. These swellings are solid and should not be confused with the galls of the turnip gall weevil. These occur nearer ground level and are hollow, often containing a grub. Club root disease is extremely persistent in the soil and if it is badly infected, brassicas must not be grown at all for a number of years.

It is important to maintain the alkalinity of the soil by heavy liming. Use as much as 500 g (28 lb) per 1 m² (30 sq yd) of ground chalk and 260 g (20 lb) per 1 m² (3 sq yd) of hydrated lime, followed by annual light dressings thereafter. The drainage of the ground should be attended to if it becomes waterlogged. Good deep digging will help to improve it. Where club root disease is known to occur, it is a wise precaution to treat plants with 4% calomel before planting. It should be mixed into a thick cream with water and soil and the plant roots dipped in it.

Birds The plants can be protected by netting. Bird scarers are seldom effective for long, although they may act as a temporary deterrent.

Peas and beans

Peas and beans belong to the botanical family *Leguminoseae*, hence the name legumes. They all bear characteristic flowers. The seeds are carried in pods and the roots are capable of utilising nitrogen from the atmosphere and making it available to the plant. The vegetable gardener can put this function to good use for the benefit of the soil by digging in the roots of leguminous crops when the ground is being cleared.

All peas and beans need a thoroughly manured soil. They are deep rooting and therefore need soil that has been deeply dug. Without such soil preparation these crops will not give a satisfactory yield. The extra trouble needed to produce peas and beans is well worthwhile. They have far more flavour and tenderness than any bought in a greengrocer's.

Peas

Nowadays, with the freezer extending the season of each vegetable, there is a choice between growing a large quantity of one variety, which will involve a lot of freezing at once, or growing a number of different varieties for succession. The latter would supply fresh peas over a longer period and only small quantities for freezing at any one time. The space available will be the main factor in deciding how many rows of peas to grow as they take up a lot of space. The more dwarf varieties occupy the least space.

Soil preparation

The ground should be deeply dug in autumn and well manured. A generous dressing of manure or compost not only provides the necessary food for the crop but also helps the plants to withstand drought. Bulky manures hold water like a sponge and are slow to release it. When the roots of the plants can find their way into this water-retentive material, the growth receives less check in dry weather. If the manuring has been liberal, no further fertiliser is required. However, a light dressing of superphosphate at 33 g (1 oz) per 1 m² (1 sq yd), raked in before sowing, helps to produce good roots in the early stages of growth.

Seed sowing

Peas are usually sown in a flat-

Peas are usually sown in flat-bottomed drills drawn with a hoe. It should be 15–20 cm (6–8 in) wide and 5–7.5 cm (2–3 in) deep. The seeds are best placed singly in three rows down the drill although they can also be sown broadcast. The latter method is only recommended for the expert as it requires a certain amount of skill.

This cross-section shows clearly how the roots of a pea plant develop under the surface. The small growths which appear at intervals along the roots are nitrogen-fixing nodules.

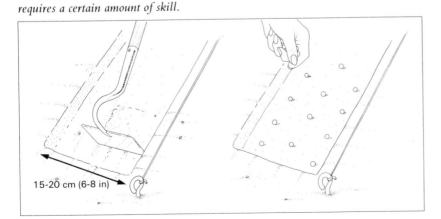

15-20 cm (6-8 in)

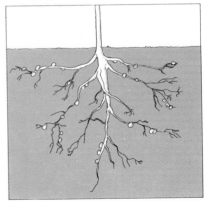

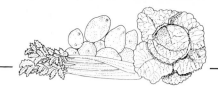

bottomed drill drawn with a hoe and each should be 15-20 cm (6-8 in) wide and 5-7·5 cm (2-3 in) deep. The seeds are sown 7·5 cm (3 in) apart. It is best to place the seeds singly in three rows down the drill, although the expert can achieve the same effect by broadcasting the seed.

Alternatively, the seed may be sown more thickly in a single V-shaped drill. The first method is preferable as it gives each plant more space. The distance between rows depends on the height of the variety. As a guide, the height of the variety should equal the distance between rows, e.g. Little Marvel: height 50 cm (20 in), distance between rows: 50 cm (20 in); Gradus: height 90-120 cm (3-4 ft), distance between rows: 90-120 cm (3-4 ft).

Seed of the hardier round-seeded cultivars may be sown in November, for picking in May to June. It is debatable whether this sowing is worthwhile, especially as the round-seeded cultivars do not have the best flavour. Early in the year the first sowing should be made in February or March, providing the soil is in a fit condition. This is followed by sowings for succession at three-weekly intervals until June. For this last sowing an early variety is used. Cloches may be used to protect early sowings but must be removed as soon as the growth becomes too tall.

Cultivation

As soon as the peas are through and visible, aerate the soil and check weed growth, using a hoe. When the young plants show signs of beginning to flop over they should be given support. Use pea sticks or wire or nylon netting. It is worth noting that although netting is quick and easy to put up, it is an aggravating task to separate it from the dead haulm at the end of the season.

Although the dwarfer varieties need not be staked, it is better to do so. Both pigeons and slugs find it easier to eat the pods if they are on the ground. Be sure that the support

you use is firmly erected. There is nothing more annoying than to find the whole lot blown down in the night.

Mulching the rows with peat, strawy manure or lawn mowings helps to retain moisture. In dry weather, a good watering should be given when the flowers first appear and again when the pods are small and flat. Watering when the flowers are out may give a poor set.

Harvesting

The pods should be picked regularly as they become ready. If dried peas are required, take the whole plant and leave the pods on it until they are dry. If the weather becomes damp, the whole plant should be pulled up. Tie them in small bundles and hang them up in a dry, airy shed.

Early varieties

Feltham First may be sown in the autumn or early spring. It grows to a height of 45 cm (18 in).

Early Onward This variety is good for freezing. Sow between March and June. It grows to a height of 60 cm (2 ft).

Kelvedon Wonder This variety can be sown early or late and is less susceptible to mildew. Suitable for freezing, it grows to a height of 45-53 cm (18-21 in).

Hurst Green Shaft Resistant to mildew and suitable for freezing. It grows to a height of 60-70 cm (24-28 in).

A healthy crop of peas flowering on pea sticks. As soon as young pea plants start to flop over they should be given support by attaching them to sticks.

Maincrop varieties
Achievement Height 140 cm (4½ ft).

Lord Chancellor A reliable, heavy cropper growing to height of 90-120 cm (3-4 ft).

Note Early varieties are ready to pick eleven to thirteen weeks after sowing; maincrop, thirteen to fifteen weeks.

Pests and diseases
Pea moth The caterpillar of the pea moth is the grub to be found eating the peas in the pod. It can be controlled by spraying with gamma-HCH ten days after flowering. This spray also controls thrips and aphids. Early sowings usually escape this pest.

Mildew can be troublesome on the later varieties, especially if they have become very dry at the root. Spraying promptly with benlate when the trouble is first noticed will check the disease. Early crops should be cleared away quickly before they act as a source of infection. Good soil preparation with plenty of organic matter incorporated helps to produce a vigorous plant that is less susceptible to disease.

Foot rot may occur in heavy, wet soils. The site should not be used for peas for more than one year in succession or the infection will be carried on. The practice of rotation and good cultivation should prevent it.

Birds The only protection is netting.

Broad beans
Broad beans are one of the easiest vegetables to grow. Nevertheless, careful soil preparation is needed. There are three types: the long-pod, which is the hardiest; the broader-podded Giant Windsor; and the comparatively new dwarf types, which are well-suited for small gardens.

The ground should be dug and manured in the autumn and broken down before sowing. For autumn sowings, a light dressing of sulphate of potash can be raked in at

16 g (½ oz) per 1 m² (1 sq yd).

The earliest crop is sown in early November using a long-pod type. This should not be carried out if the soil has a tendency to lie cold and wet in winter. This sowing has the advantage of escaping severe attack from blackfly. It is ready for picking at the end of May to early June at a time when there are few other vegetables available.

This is followed by successional sowings, when the soil is in a fit condition, from late January until July, if desired. Cloches may be used to protect the sowings during the winter months.

Broad beans are usually sown in double rows, with 23 cm (9 in) between the rows and 60 cm (24 in) between each pair of rows whereas single rows should be 45 cm (18 in) apart. In both cases the seed should be 23 cm (9 in) apart. Sow four extra seeds at the end of the row. These can be used to fill any gaps where there are failures in germination.

Hoe regularly to control the weeds. In gardens exposed to the wind, use canes and stringing at about 3-m (10-ft) intervals to give some support. When the beans are in full flower, pinch out the tops of the plants to deter blackfly.

Pick regularly before the pods become tough and old.

Broad beans are usually sown in double rows with 23 cm (9 in) between the rows and 60 cm (24 in) between each pair of rows.

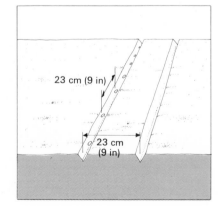

Varieties
Aquadulce Claudia or Aquadulce A white-seeded long-pod for autumn and early spring sowing, but not after the end of January. Good for freezing.

Green Longpod Suitable for early spring but not for autumn sowing.

Green Windsor Suitable for later sowings.

The Sutton A dwarf variety only 30 cm (12 in) high. Sow in autumn under cloches or for succession from February to July.

Pests and diseases
Blackfly (bean aphid) is the most serious and prolific pest. It first appears on the tips of the shoots, but soon spreads to stems, leaves, flowers and pods. A close watch must be kept for the first signs of attack. Picking out and destroying the tips of the shoots where they first attack may control them. The sight of ants trekking up the stems is usually an indication that the blackfly have arrived. Spraying with malathion or derris is a more effective control.

Foot and root rot These are diseases which cause the collapse of the young bean plants. They are more likely to occur in cold, wet conditions. The crop should be grown on a fresh site each year.

Birds The only protection is netting.

Runner beans are sown in a double row for staking. The V-shaped drills are made in a shallow trench 45 cm (18 in) wide and 5 cm (2 in) deep.

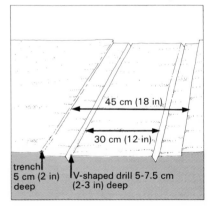

Runner beans

This is the favourite crop of most gardeners, despite the labour of special soil preparation and the erection of supports for the plants. They will produce beans over a long period and give a good return from a relatively small area. The runner bean is not hardy. The sowing must be timed to avoid damage from May frosts and the first autumn frosts will finish the crop.

Soil preparation

If the plot where the runner beans are to be grown has been well manured, this will suffice. However, it is usual to prepare a special site for runner beans during the winter. Take out a trench a spit deep and approximately 1 m (3 ft) wide and work a liberal dressing of manure or compost into the second spit. Runner beans have deep roots which need a rich soil and adequate humus to hold moisture in drought.

Seed sowing

Sow from mid-May to late June according to the likelihood of frost occurring. This will avoid frost damage to the seedlings. Dig a shallow trench 45 cm (18 in) wide and 5 cm (2 in) deep and make the seed drills in it. When watering becomes necessary later in the season, it will be concentrated at the roots.

Seed is sown in a double row for staking, 30-45 cm (12-18 in) apart and 5-7·5 cm (2-3 in) deep. If grown without stakes, they should be 60 cm (24 in) apart. The seeds should be 15 cm (6 in) apart. Some gardeners prefer to erect stakes before sowing and sow two seeds per stake.

Another method is to sow the seed in 12·5-cm (5-in) pots or boxes in a frame and plant out after hardening when the danger of frost has passed. It is questionable whether

Above right *The Sutton, a dwarf variety of broad bean.*
Right *Prizewinner runner bean showing pods and flowers, which can be very attractive.*

the time saved by making a protected sowing compensates for the check to growth by transplanting. It may be justified in cold gardens.

Cultivation

Thin out by removing alternate seedlings. This leaves one plant per stake 30 cm (12 in) apart. Hoe the plants and erect the supports as soon as the first pair of leaves has unfolded. Support may be given by strings, which are tedious to erect, nylon netting or poles. It is much easier to cross and tie the poles low down, about 1 m (1 yd) from the ground, than at shoulder level. It has the advantage that the beans above the crossbar hang outside the row and are easier to see.

Small numbers of plants may be grown in groups instead of rows, erecting a 'wigwam' of seven to nine poles tied together at the top. It is possible to grow runner beans without staking if they are dwarfed by pinching out all the shoots when they are about 45 cm (18 in) long. In this way they crop a little earlier but not for so long a period. In a wet summer the damage from slugs is considerable and the beans are usually mis-shaped from contact with the ground.

Mulch the row before the ground becomes too dry. If necessary water at the root when the first flowers begin to open. The modern opinion is that there is little advantage in spraying the flowers when they open in order to get a good set; it is the roots that should not be allowed to become too dry. Pinch out the shoots when they reach the tops of the stakes.

Harvesting

Pick regularly while the pods are young and before the seeds begin to swell. This way the pods will not be stringy and the plant will continue to crop until the frost stops them.

Varieties

Enorma; Prizewinner; Achievement; Kelvedon Marvel. Of these four varieties, Enorma and Achievement are suitable for freezing.

Sunset (Suttons) A cultivar with pale pink flowers (it is said by some that pink flowers set better in dry summers).

Dwarf Hammond Scarlet A cultivar which seems to have lost its popularity and disappeared from many catalogues. If available, it is useful for early production from cloches. It remains dwarf without any pinching out.

Pests and diseases

Blackfly Watch out for an attack and if it appears, spray promptly with malathion or derris. If the plants are in flower spray late in the evening.

Root rot If this should occur, be sure to grow the runner beans on a different site each year.

Dwarf French beans (kidney beans)

Dwarf French beans are said by some to be superior in flavour to runner beans, and they are certainly earlier.

Soil preparation

Deep digging is necessary, but the manuring need not be quite so generous as for runner beans. If required, a light dressing of a general fertiliser can be raked in before sowing.

Seed sowing and cultivation

Dwarf beans are slightly more hardy than runner beans but they should not be sown before mid-April in warm gardens and early May in exposed places. Sow the seed in drills 45 cm (18 in) apart and 5 cm (2 in) deep with the seed 12 cm (4½ in) apart. Successional sowings at three-weekly intervals may be made until July. The success of a July sowing depends very much on reasonable weather in the early autumn. Sowings for transplanting in May can be made in boxes and protected in a frame for a few weeks. Alternatively, cloches can be used to protect the rows for the first few weeks.

Thin out to 23 cm (9 in) apart. Control weeds by hoeing regularly. As the pods begin to form they will need some support or heavy rain and wind will beat them down. Twiggy stakes among the plants will be adequate.

Harvesting

Pick frequently whilst young and tender. Failure to do so will shorten the period of cropping. The cropping period is shorter than for runner beans hence the need for more than one sowing. If dried beans are required for winter use, whole plants should be retained for the purpose. None of the pods should be picked green, but left to ripen on the plant.

The plants are lifted, tied in small bundles and hung to dry in an airy shed to complete the drying off process. The weather is seldom good enough to finish drying outside.

One of several ways in which runner beans can be supported—here the canes are tied together at the cross-bar.

The beans are removed from the pods for storage.

Varieties

There is a vast choice of varieties.
The Prince is very early but of inferior flavour.
Masterpiece is early and prolific and good for freezing.
Sprite is a stringless variety which is good for freezing.

Tendergreen is a stringless variety and good for freezing.
Chevrier Vert is a dual-purpose variety which can be used either for production of green beans or for dried haricot beans.

Diseases

As with runner beans, both black-fly and foot and root rots may be a problem.

Climbing French or pole beans

These beans are similar to dwarf beans in flavour and appearance but the plants need support like runner beans. The culture is the same as for runner beans.

French dwarf beans are superior in flavour to runner beans.

Root crops

With the exception of potatoes, the root crops in this section are biennial. The roots which we eat contain stored food for the promotion of growth in the second year, when the plant will flower and produce seeds before dying. If conditions are adverse to growth in the first year the plant may bolt or run to seed and there will be no roots to harvest. Care must be taken therefore to provide the right conditions for root production.

The ideal soil for roots is a deep sandy loam. Depth is especially important for the longer roots such as parsnips. Very sandy soil, however, has a tendency to dry out in summer, which causes bolting. If fresh manure is used, its physical presence causes roots to fork and be of inferior quality. Therefore, roots need to be grown on soil that has been manured for a previous crop. This increases its moisture holding capacity and fertilisers are used to provide the necessary nourishment.

Beetroot

The soil should be dug in the autumn or winter. Before sowing it should be broken down to a fine tilth and a general fertiliser raked in at the rate of 133 g (4 oz) per 1 m² (1 sq yd).

The earliest sowings are made in the latter half of March or April, as soon as the soil is fit to work. Use a round variety for pulling young for use in the summer months. In mid-May to early June a suitable variety for storing for winter use can be sown. Make the rows 30 cm (12 in) apart and 2·5 cm (1 in) deep. It is important to sow thinly because what appears to be one knobbly seed, is in fact a cluster of three or four seeds. If the seed lies thickly in the drill the seedlings will be very overcrowded.

Thin out when the first true leaf appears so that the seedlings stand

Detroit—a particularly good variety of beetroot for storing.

5 cm (2 in) apart. Later, thin again to the final distance of 10 cm (4 in) apart. Hoe between the rows to control weeds, taking care not to cut or damage the swelling roots. Pull early sowings as soon as they are large enough to eat, which is about the size of a golf ball. Roots for storage are lifted with a fork in October. Beetroot needs very careful handling because any damage or bruising results in bleeding during cooking. For the same reason the tops should be removed by twisting not cutting, leaving about 5-10 cm (2-4 in) of the leaf stalk intact. Any roots that are damaged should be rejected and only sound ones stored.

Store them in layers in dry sand or peat, either in boxes or barrels. Put these in a frost-proof shed. Outdoors they may be stored in a clamp (see potatoes).

Varieties
Boltardy A round type for March sowing. Resistant to bolting.
Crimson Globe Another round type for sowing in April. It is also sold as Detroit New Globe.
Detroit Little Ball for late sowings. Good for storing.
Cheltenham Green Top A long variety good for storing.
Housewives Choice The cylindrical root is good for slicing.

Carrot

Carrots for use in summer straight from the garden need to be young, quick-maturing stump-rooted varieties. The long-rooted varieties are grown for winter storage.

Soil preparation and sowing

Use ground manured for a previous crop and dug in the autumn. Stony ground has the same effect on the roots as fresh manure and it should be avoided if possible. Rake down the surface to a fine tilth before sowing. If necessary, a general fertiliser should be raked in at the rate of 133 g (4 oz) per 1 m^2 (1 sq yd).

The first sowing is made in a sheltered border of sandy soil in March, although sowings can be made in early February if cloches or frames are available. Successional sowings for pulling young may be made at monthly intervals until July. Maincrop varieties for storing are sown from April. The drills should be 30 cm (12 in) apart and 2 cm ($\frac{1}{2}$-$\frac{3}{4}$ in) deep. The seed is small and sown as thinly as possible.

Cultivation

Thinning out should be avoided if possible. However, if necessary, thin out when the first true leaf appears and again later to leave the plants 2·5 cm (1 in) apart for pulling young. Maincrop carrots should stand finally 5-8 cm (2-3 in) apart. Carry out the thinning on dull days or late in the evening. Remove the thinnings, water the rows and firm the soil to deter carrot fly. The row should be hoed regularly and the soil drawn up to the rows to cover the tops of the roots to prevent them becoming green.

Harvesting and storage

Early carrots are pulled as required as soon as they are big enough to eat. The maincrop for storage is lifted with a fork in October or even later in favourable districts. The storage is as for beetroot, in peat or sand to prevent drying. Only sound carrots should be stored. If the carrots are to be left in the ground, cover the rows with rough litter to enable lifting in frosty conditions.

Varieties

Nantes for successional sowing. Good for freezing.
Early Nantes for successional sowing.
Amsterdam Forcing for early sowing under cloches or in frames.
New Red Intermediate A long type for storing.
Flak A new Dutch variety producing giant stump-rooted carrots for storage.

Pests

Carrot fly This is by far the most troublesome pest. When it is known to be prevalent, only the earliest and latest (July) sowings should be made, as these seem to escape attack. The use of pelleted seed to obviate thinning is also wise. The fly is always attracted by the scent of crushed foliage at thinning time.

Alternatively, sow the seed very thinly so that the minimum of thinning out is required. Always firm the soil after thinning out. It is possible to use a seed dressing when sowing to deter the pest.
Wireworm is only a problem on newly cultivated grassland. The seed dressing mentioned above is effective.

Parsnips

Parsnips, although not very popular, are not difficult to grow. They need deep soil, but if this is not available they can still be grown by taking a little extra trouble. Make holes with a crow bar 10-15 cm (4-6 in) apart and fill the holes with sifted soil.

The ground should have been manured for a previous crop. It is then deeply dug and left rough until

Long-rooted varieties of carrot are grown for winter storage. Only sound ones should be stored.

sowing time when it is raked down to a fine tilth.

Seed sowing and cultivation

Traditionally parsnip seed should be sown in February, but the soil is seldom fit to do so. In fact, it can safely be left until March or even later when the soil is warmer and germination quicker. Drills should be 30-45 cm (12-18 in) apart and 2·5-5 cm (1-2 in) deep according to the type of soil. As the seed is large and easy to handle, it may be space-sown, putting two or three seeds at 10-15-cm (4-6-in) intervals.

Because parsnip is slow to germinate, it is a good idea to sow radish in the drill at the same time. The radish acts as a marker so that the row can be hoed to control weeds.

When large enough to handle, thin out to stand 10-15 cm (4-6 in) apart. Hoe regularly to control weeds.

Harvesting and storage

Parsnips keep better in the ground than stored so lift them as required. If severe weather threatens, a few roots can be lifted and taken in to a frostproof place. In any case, the remaining parsnips should be lifted at the end of February and stored in sand or peat to check their growth.

Sow potatoes in February or March in drills 30-45 cm (12-18 in) apart and 2·5-5 cm (1-2 in) deep according to the type of soil. Space seeds 10-15 cm (4-6 in) apart.

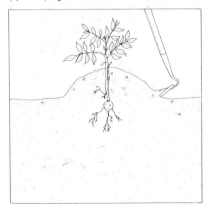

Varieties

Tender and True is long-rooted and resistant to canker.
White Gem is suitable for shallower soils because it is not so long-rooted.

Pests and diseases

Carrot fly will attack parsnips as well as carrots. (For control see carrots.)
Parsnip canker causes a black rot of the root. It is most likely to occur in acid soils. Apart from growing a resistant variety and rotating the crop to avoid re-infestation, there is no cure.

Potatoes

Not everybody has space to grow potatoes, while others only grow the first earlies which are more worthwhile. In fact there are so many troubles that can beset the potato crop and it is so easy to buy them, that this is understandable. However, there are varieties which can be grown in the garden with better flavour than many commercial ones, although they will not give the same weight of crop. It is becoming increasingly difficult to obtain the more unusual varieties and quite a search is needed to find them. The best policy is to consult a local nursery as to availability.

Ideally a seed potato should be about the size of a hen's egg—larger ones can be cut lengthwise using a sharp knife so that there are two or three good sprouts on each piece.

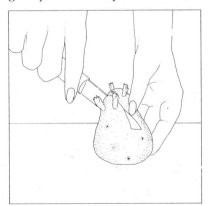

Soil preparation

Unlike the other root crops, potatoes benefit from some manure or compost dug into the ground before Christmas. Before planting, a general fertiliser should be broadcast at the rate of 50 g (1½ oz) per 1 m² (1 sq yd). If no manure was used in the preparation of the soil, double the dressing.

Planting

Buy seed potatoes and do not save them from the previous year. There are so many troubles that can be passed on with the tuber that it is best to leave the production of seed to the expert. When the seed potatoes are obtained they should be put to sprout or 'chit'. Place the tubers in trays with the eye or rose end uppermost. This is the end with most eyes and the opposite end from the remnant of stalk which is usually visible. The trays are then put in full light in an airy, frostproof place. Sturdy shoots about 2·5 cm (1 in) are required. An occasional spray with tepid water is beneficial. Keep a watch for greenfly and deal with them at once if they occur. Ideally a seed potato should be about the size of a hen's egg. Larger ones should be cut lengthwise so that there are two or three good sprouts on each. Plant in moist soil.

Potato plants are earthed up to keep the foliage upright and to prevent the potatoes from showing on the surface of the soil, where they would become green and useless to eat.

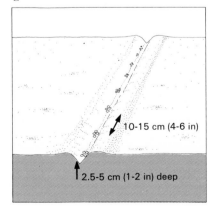

10-15 cm (4-6 in)

2.5-5 cm (1-2 in) deep

The sprouted tubers are planted in drills 10–12·5 cm (4–5 in) deep made with a large hoe or a spade. The quality of the tubers produced will be cleaner if the drill is lined and the tubers covered with fine manure, compost, peat or even lawn mowings. Early varieties are planted at the end of March, followed by the second earlies or mid-season a fortnight or so later and the maincrop at the end of April.

Planting distances are as follows:

First earlies 30 cm (12 in) apart in rows 60 cm (24 in) apart.

Mid-season 37·5 cm (15 in) apart in rows 60 cm (24 in) apart.

Maincrop 37·5 cm (15 in) apart in rows 67·5 cm (27 in) apart.

Cultivation

In the event of a frost warning, protect the young growths by drawing the soil over them with a hoe. Alternatively, cover temporarily with protective material such as bracken, straw or newspaper.

Earthing up is carried out to keep the foliage upright and to prevent the potatoes from showing on the surface of the soil where they would become green and useless. This should be done when the foliage is about 23 cm (9 in) high. First hoe the rows to kill off any weeds, then draw the soil up from either side of the foliage. A second earthing up a few weeks later will complete the job. If desired, a light dressing of general fertiliser may be given at the same time as earthing up. As a routine precaution against potato blight, the plants should be sprayed at the end of July (see pests and diseases).

Harvesting and storage

Lift early varieties as required until about mid-September. Later varieties for storing can be lifted in late September or October. Do this carefully with a fork, preferably flat-tined, and leave them for an hour or two on the surface to dry before storing. They must always be stored in the dark and in a frost-

Sprouting seed tubers in a tray.

proof place. They may be put in boxes or barrels or in a clamp out-of-doors.

A clamp is made by putting a 10-15-cm (4-6-in) layer of dry straw over the site, which should be well drained. The potatoes are heaped on the straw and covered over with another good thick layer of straw to protect them from the light. Leave them for several days to sweat before covering with soil. The ditch formed by removing the soil helps to drain away moisture from the bottom of the clamp. The covering soil should be at least 10 cm (4 in) thick and increased if severe weather is expected. A clamp should never be opened in hard, frosty weather.

Varieties
Early Pentland Javelin; Duke of York.
Maincrop Maris Peer; Pentland Crown; Desirée; Majestic. If a source of seed can be found, Catriona has a good flavour and does well on poorer soils.

Pests and diseases
These are numerous and only those most likely to occur in the home garden are mentioned here.
Wireworm can cause havoc on freshly dug grassland. Early crops are less susceptible to this pest.
Slugs are also a nuisance. They tunnel into the tubers, especially on heavy soils and in wet summers. Slug bait may be used or methaldehyde watered on the soil. Early crops suffer less damage. Crops should be lifted as soon as they are ready and not left too long in the ground for these soil pests to feed on.
Potato eelworm can be a serious pest if potatoes are grown too frequently on the same ground. Attack results in serious reduction in crop. Adherence to rotation is very important as there is no suitable chemical treatment. Some varieties are resistant and will produce a crop in infested soils; Maris Piper (maincrop) and Pentland Javelin are two such varieties.

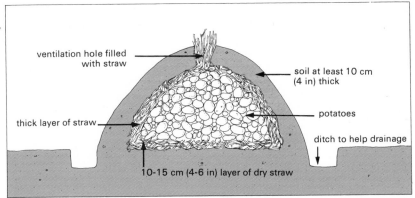

ventilation hole filled with straw

soil at least 10 cm (4 in) thick

potatoes

thick layer of straw

ditch to help drainage

10-15 cm (4-6 in) layer of dry straw

To keep potatoes outdoors they must be stored in a clamp lined with straw, well drained and with a ventilation hole in the top.

Potato blight This fungus disease first affects the foliage, appearing as brown patches. These increase and finally destroy all the foliage in a wet season. It can then spread to the tubers which will rot in store. Give preventative spray of zineb or Bordeux mixture at the end of July, followed by further sprayings at intervals of ten to fourteen days if the weather is damp or the disease appears. Infected foliage should be cut and burnt ten days before lifting.

Swede
The ground should be prepared by giving a general fertiliser at the rate of 100 g (3 oz) per 1 m² (1 sq yd) before raking down to a fine tilth. Because it can suffer from club root disease, it is important to see that the alkalinity of the soil is maintained by treating with lime as necessary.

Sow in drills 37.5 cm (15 in) apart and 2 cm (½-¾ in) deep in mid-June. Thin out when large enough to handle to about 5 cm (2 in) and continue to thin until the plants are 23 cm (9 in) apart. Lift in the autumn. Store as for beetroot and carrots.

Purple Top swede.

Pests and diseases
Turnips are prone to the same diseases as swedes. Cabbage root fly may also attack them.

Onions, leeks and shallots

These three vegetables come under the category of gross feeders, which means they require good, rich soil. Although they require elaborate soil preparation for exhibition, it is not so complicated to produce the rather smaller onions and leeks preferred by the housewife.

Onions

The grower has the choice of sowing seed in the autumn, the spring, early spring in the greenhouse or planting onion sets. The last method is preferable on soils which are not so well suited to growing onions.

Soil preparation and sowing

The ground should be well and deeply dug in the autumn, incorporating manure or compost. This is broken down to a fine tilth in the early spring as soon as it is dry enough. It is then allowed to settle thoroughly. Tread firm before planting if necessary.

Sow in mid- to late August for transplanting or thinning in spring or early March. Drills should be 2 cm ($\frac{1}{2}$–$\frac{3}{4}$ in) deep and 30 cm (12 in) apart. Sow in January in the greenhouse and harden off before planting out in March.

Transplanting

Transplant onions with a trowel taking care not to set them too deeply. The base of the bulb should be only fractionally below the surface level of the soil. Thin or plant 15 cm (6 in) apart. Plant both greenhouse-raised and autumn-sown plants in March, as soon as the soil is fit.

Onion sets

These are small, immature onions whose development has been ar-

Varieties

Purple-topped varieties are best for eating young and for storage.

Pests and diseases

Flea beetles attack the seed leaves, especially in dry weather. Watering checks them or they may be dusted with gamma-HCH at weekly intervals until the rough leaves appear.
Club root disease Liming of the soil and rotation help to check this disease.

Turnips

Turnips can be sown in succession for pulling young or for storage. Turnip tops can be used as greens.

Early sowings should be made on ground manured the year before and dug after clearing the previous crop. Rake in a general fertiliser at the rate of 100 g (3 oz) per 1 m² (1 sq yd). Later sowings should be on

Golden Ball turnip makes a good, round shape and is a variety particularly recommended for storing.

ground cleared of an earlier crop, lightly forked and a fertiliser at the same rate hoed in.

Sow in succession from early April to July using an early variety and in late July, using a suitable variety for storage. Drills should be 2 cm ($\frac{1}{2}$–$\frac{3}{4}$ in) deep and 37.5 cm (15 in) apart. For turnip tops, sow thinly in drills 23-30 cm (9-12 in) apart in late August. Thin in stages to 10 cm (4 in) apart. Hoe regularly. Lift in the autumn and store as for beetroot and carrots.

Varieties

Early Snowball Round.
White Milan Flat.
Golden Ball For storage.
Green Top For tops.

rested to enable storage through the winter. They are planted in March or early April. A drill should be taken out and the sets placed 15 cm (6 in) apart. They are then covered over leaving only the tips exposed. Manuring need not be so liberal and it will suffice to give a dressing of general fertiliser instead.

Cultivation

Thinning is carried out in two stages, the second batch being suitable for use as spring onions. Hoe regularly, taking care to draw the soil away from, rather than up to, the bulbs. This assists with ripening. If the tops are not showing signs of falling over by the middle of August they should be bent over to encourage ripening.

Harvesting and storage

A fortnight after bending over the tops or in early September the bulbs can be lifted and dried off. They should be left in the sun and protected from the rain, ideally on slatted or netting racks so that the air can get underneath them. When thoroughly dry, store them in bunches, ropes or nets in a dry, airy shed.

The best way to store onions is on a rope, twisting the stem of each onion twice round a string and pushing in each onion in rotation.

The simplest way to make an onion rope is to hang four strings from a hook and twist the stem of each onion twice round a string pushing in each onion in rotation. Those with thick necks will not keep well and should be set aside for immediate use.

Varieties

Bedfordshire Champion Spring-sown.
Solidity August-sown.
Japanese varieties These are new and only suitable for autumn sowing. They mature early and are worth watching. F1 Hybrid Express Yellow is an example.
Sturon For sets.

Pests and diseases

Onion fly The maggots burrow into the base of the bulbs. The first indication is yellowing and drooping of the leaves. Young onions may be completely killed, older ones never develop properly. Badly infected plants should be burned. A commercial deterrent may be raked in before sowing or calomel dust applied along the rows when the seedlings are 2·5 cm (1 in) high.
Eelworm produces swelling and distortion of the leaves. Infected bulbs will not be fit for storage. Lift and burn infected plants and do not use the same ground for onions or

Onions are transplanted with a trowel, taking care not to set them too deeply. The base of the bulb should be just below the surface of the soil.

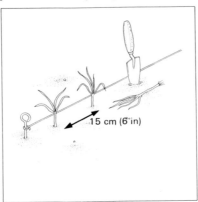

any related crops for several years.
Mildew appears as a greyish mould on the leaves which die back from the tip. Dust or spray with Bordeaux mixture or zineb at the first indication. Avoid growing onions on ground that lies wet and practise rotation.
Bolting is usually due to adverse weather or loose soil. Cut off the flower stem, lift and use at once, as they will not store.

Shallots

Soil preparation for growing shallots is the same as for onions. Plant shallots in rows 30 cm (12 in) apart as soon as the soil is dry enough, at the end of February or in early March. Either press them into the ground 15 cm (6 in) apart or take out a shallow drill, set them in it and fill it in so that the tips remain above ground.

Sometimes birds can be very troublesome, pulling the shallots out of the ground. To avoid this, start them into growth by pressing them into a box of moist peat, about 2·5 cm (1 in) apart. Keep watered for about two weeks then plant them out with a trowel when about 2·5 cm (1 in) of roots have grown to hold them in the ground. Hoe regu-

Above right Ripening onions.
Below right Shallots drying.

Onion sets are planted in March or April, 15 cm (6 in) apart in a drill. They are covered over, leaving only the tips exposed above the surface.

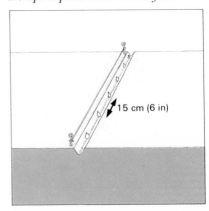

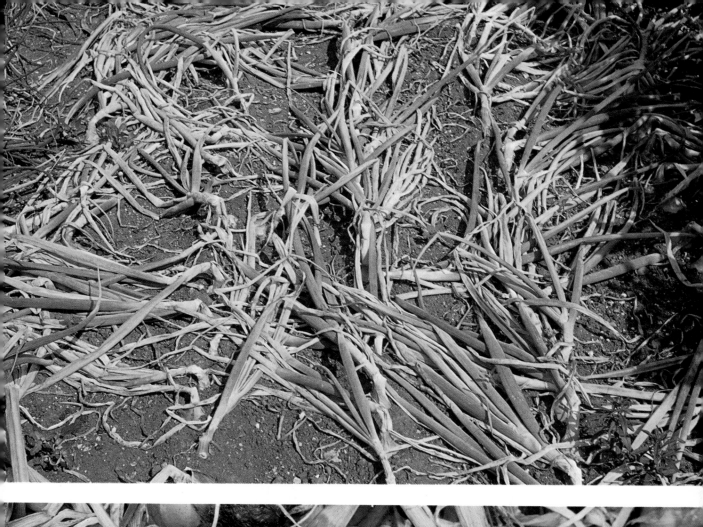

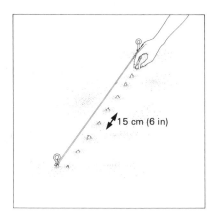

Shallots are planted by pressing them into the ground 15 cm (6 in) apart with the tips sticking up above the surface of the soil.

larly. At the end of July lift the shallots and dry them off. Hang in bunches or nets to store in a dry place.

Leeks

Leeks are not planted out until July. They can therefore follow an early crop such as broad beans, which will have been well manured. This is probably enough, but if necessary, a light dressing of manure or compost can be forked in after clearing the previous crop. Leeks do not need such rich soil as onions.

Seed is sown in late February or early March in a prepared seedbed, as for brassicas. The earlier sowing produces a larger plant which is better for transplanting.

If necessary, water the seedbed well the night before transplanting. Lift the plants, which should be about 20 cm (8 in) tall, with a fork. Lightly trim both the leaves and the roots with a sharp knife. Plant with a dibber 23 cm (9 in) apart with 37.5 cm (15 in) between the rows. The plant is simply dropped in the hole without filling it in or firming. Watering afterwards and subsequent hoeing consolidates it. An alternative method is to rake out a drill and plant as described.

Hoe regularly. If a drill has been made gradually draw up the soil and fill it in. Dig up as required.

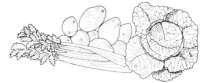

Varieties
The Lyon and Musselburgh.

Pests and diseases
There are no pests of any consequence.

Rust disease may attack the plants, possibly as a result of too rich a soil. Burn any trimmings from infected plants and do not grow again immediately on the same site.

Miscellaneous crops

The following vegetables do not fall into any of the previous categories in that they are neither brassica, legume or root crop. However, with the exception of asparagus and Jerusalem artichokes, they are included in the normal crop rotation.

Asparagus
Although regarded as a luxury crop, quite a few people like to grow asparagus. The initial preparation and planting is arduous but otherwise cultivation is not difficult. What it does need is a lot of space. Not only do the roots extend far beyond the limits of the asparagus bed itself, but the height is such that it can shade other crops if the position is not properly planned. Secondly, the asparagus shoots do not come up all at once, but here and there over a long period of time, so quite a lot of plants are needed to ensure enough for a meal. Finally, there is a three year wait from planting time until cutting begins. If it is grown it will crop for twenty years or more. It can be cut for eight to ten weeks in the year and what is not eaten fresh freezes well.

Soil preparation
Asparagus will grow on most soils providing they are not waterlogged, but it is the lighter sandy

Leeks can be sown from seed in the spring, the earlier sowing being better for transplanting.

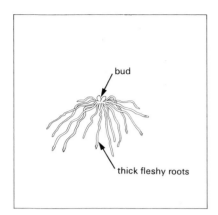

A one-year-old asparagus plant showing buds in the centre and the roots, which tend to be thick and fleshy and prone to drying out.

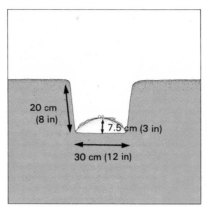

Asparagus is best planted on a mound of soil 7·5 cm (3 in) high in a trench 30 cm (12 in) wide and 20 cm (8 in) deep. Cover with soil then firm well.

soils which are most suitable. It should be deeply dug and manure liberally worked in, well in advance of planting time in March. A few weeks before planting apply hydrated lime at the rate of 66 g (2 oz) per 1 m² (1 sq yd).

Plant raising

It is possible to buy one-, two- or three-year-old plants but they have very fleshy roots which easily dry out and do not travel well. Growing one's own plants is more satisfactory because they can be lifted and planted immediately when conditions are favourable. It will mean waiting four years, from the time of sowing the seed to the time of cutting. Three-year-old plants can be cut lightly the following year.

Seed should be sown in March 1-2 cm ($\frac{1}{2}$-$\frac{3}{4}$ in) deep and 30-45 cm (12-18 in) between rows if more than one is sown. As the seed is slow to germinate and the seedlings very difficult to see, it is a good idea to sow radish in the drill to act as a marker. Thin the asparagus seedlings to 15 cm (6 in).

Planting

The following March to early April the plants may be transplanted in rows 120 cm (4 ft) apart with 45 cm (18 in) between the plants in the rows. The best way is to take out a

trench 30 cm (12 in) wide and 20 cm (8 in) deep. Along the bottom of this trench place a ridge or mound of soil 7·5 cm (3 in) high. Set the plants on this mound, cover the roots quickly and firm. Then fill the trench in. This leaves the crown of the plant covered by about 12·5 cm (5 in) of soil.

Cultivation

Weeds must be controlled at all times. Perennial weeds must not be allowed to become established. No cutting should be allowed for the first two years after planting but in the third year shoots may be cut for four to five weeks. From then on

Celery should be planted in a trench 37·5 cm (15 in) wide and 30 cm (12 in) deep, with manure or compost worked liberally into the bottom.

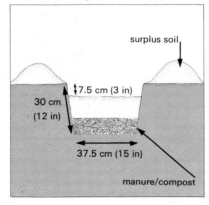

cutting can go on until the end of June each year when the 'fern' is allowed to grow to build up next year's crown.

When the foliage turns colour in the autumn, it should be cut down and removed to prevent seeding. The bed should be cleaned and the soil mounded up over the rows. If manure is available, give the bed a liberal dressing. In spring a general fertiliser should be given at the rate of 100 g (3 oz) per 1 m² (1 sq yd). The ridges are broken down when cutting finishes.

Cutting

When the shoots are about 10 cm (4 in) above the ground cutting can be carried out with a sharp knife. Slip the knife down the side of the stem and turn it to cut about 10 cm (4 in) below the soil level.

Varieties

Connover's Colossal; Martha Washington; Kidner's Pedigree.

Pests and diseases

Asparagus beetle Both beetle and larva feed on the foliage. It should be sprayed with derris or malathion. **Violet root rot** is serious and it may be necessary to make a new bed on a fresh site. When a plant becomes infected with this disease the foliage begins to yellow.

Earth up when plants are about 30-35 cm (12-15 in) high. Tie loosely just below the leaves and earth up in stages, about every 3 weeks.

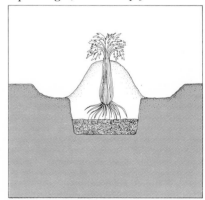

Celery

This crop requires considerable care and attention if it is to grow well. It is naturally a ditch plant and therefore needs adequate moisture. On no account will it stand waterlogging.

Light soils are much more suitable than cold, wet soils. A trench should be prepared 37·5 cm (15 in) wide and 30 cm (12 in) deep. Manure or compost is liberally worked into the bottom of the trench and the soil returned to within 7·5 cm (3 in) of the ground level.

Seed is sown in the heated greenhouse in March, pricked out in boxes and hardened off by the end of May. Plant out at the end of May or early in June 15 cm (6 in) apart in the rows. A single row in the trench is easier to earth up when the time comes. Self-blanching celery is grown on the flat and planted 23 × 23 cm (9 × 9 in). It blanches better if grown in blocks rather than rows.

Water in dry weather and never allow the plants to become dry. Keep down any weeds in the trench. Remove any suckers that form. Earthing up should begin when the plants are about 30-35 cm (12-15 in)

Golden Self-Blanching—a crisp, white variety of celery.

high. Tie loosely just below the leaves. Earth up in stages when the soil is moist at intervals of about three weeks. Take care not to let the soil drop in the heart of the plant and not to earth up above the leaves. In cold weather cover plants with bracken, straw or similar protective material.

Self-blanching celery should not be earthed up. It is not hardy and should be eaten before hard weather sets in.

Varieties
Giant White; Giant Red; Golden Self-blanching; American Green (no earthing up required).

Pests and diseases
Celery fly or leaf miner Blisters on the leaves are caused by the feeding maggot. Remove and destroy any affected leaves. If the plants are badly infected give a nitrogenous fertiliser to stimulate growth. Spray with malathion when first detected.
Slugs and snails Use slug bait or methaldehyde.
Heart rot This bacterial rot usually follows slug damage, particularly under wet conditions. It is not discovered until the celery is lifted by which time it is too late to do anything about it. Celery should not be grown on the same ground the following year.

Jerusalem artichoke
This is one vegetable that can be put in an out-of-the-way corner as it will stand fairly poor conditions. It is quite useful to grow as a screen for the bonfire and compost heap although it will only be effective as such in the summer months.

Plant the tubers in March 10-15 cm (4-6 in) deep and 37.5 cm (15 in) apart in the row. If there is more than one row, put them 75 cm (30 in) apart. Hoe regularly through the summer. In early winter cut down the tops or the wind will blow them over lifting the roots out of the ground.

Lift as required remembering to reserve some tubers for replanting in the spring. Tubers can be very misshapen so it is worth selecting the smoothest ones each time for replanting in the hope of attaining a less knobbly strain.

Pests
Slugs, chafer grubs and swift moth caterpillars may feed and hollow out the tubers. Use slug pellets or rake in an insecticide for soil pests.

Jerusalem artichoke tubers.

Marrows and courgettes

Marrows appreciate a sunny site. Three or four marrow plants are usually sufficient for one family's needs. Dig a hole for each plant about 30 × 30 cm (1 × 1 ft) and one spit deep. Place a good forkful of manure or compost in the bottom of the hole and return the soil, mounding it up so that the top is slightly above the level of the ground. This prevents water collecting round the neck of the plant causing stem rot. Planting stations should be 90 cm (3 ft) apart for bush varieties and 135 cm ($4\frac{1}{2}$ ft) for trailing varieties.

Seed sowing

For the earliest cutting, plants are sown under glass and planted out under cloches or frames. They may also be sown under glass and planted in the open when there is no further danger of frost. Outdoor sowings are made wherever the plants intend to be grown. In each case the sowing must be carefully timed to ensure that the plants are not lost by a late spring frost.

The first sowings under glass can be made in about mid-March provided the frame and cloches are large enough to accommodate the plant until the end of May. After this there should be no further danger of frost. It is probably wiser to delay making this first sowing until early April. It can then be hardened off and planted out in a frame or under cloches at the beginning of May. For planting in the open at the end of May or early June, the seed should be sown under glass at the beginning of May. Sow two seeds in a small 7·5-cm (3-in) pot and potting compost. Later the seedlings should be thinned to one in each pot. Outdoors, sow two to three seeds on each prepared site at the end of May. Later they can be singled, leaving one plant per station.

Cultivation

The earliest flowers under glass may need to be pollinated to achieve a set. The male flower, which has stamens, should be picked and the pollen rubbed on to the stigma of the female flower, which has an embryo marrow behind the petals. Sometimes, if the weather is cool in early June, these early plants are reluctant to produce female flowers. The only remedy is patience.

Hoe regularly to control weeds and water copiously in dry weather. A weekly foliar feed is particularly beneficial to marrows. In fact, if it is not possible to water the plants, the foliar feed seems to compensate for lack of water at the root. Trailing marrows are sometimes grown as a wigwam. The plants are set 75 cm ($2\frac{1}{2}$ ft) apart either in a square or a triangle. Each plant is given a sturdy stake and the stakes are tied together at the top.

Harvesting and storage

Marrows must be cut regularly to ensure continued production. Cut marrows when they are about 20 cm (8 in) long and courgettes 10 cm (4 in) long.

If the fruit of one plant is allowed to ripen towards the end of the season, these may be cut when mature and hung in a net in a dry, airy place where they will be protected from attack by frost.

Marrows appreciate a good, sunny position. Dig a hole for each plant about 30 × 30 cm (1 × 1 ft) and one spit deep, and place a forkful of manure or compost in the bottom.

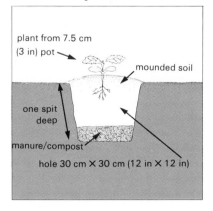

plant from 7.5 cm (3 in) pot

mounded soil

one spit deep

manure/compost

hole 30 cm × 30 cm (12 in × 12 in)

Varieties
Little Gem A trailing marrow with round fruits.
Green Bush A bush variety of courgette. Good for freezing.
Zucchini A good courgette for freezing.

Pests and diseases
Slugs and snails Marrows are susceptible to damage by slugs and snails, especially during a wet summer. Slug pellets should be used. A slate or piece of broken flower pot under each swelling fruit may help by raising the marrows off the damp ground.
Cucumber mosaic This virus can also attack marrows. The foliage becomes mottled and puckered, the fruit distorted and undersize. The plant should be removed and burned before it can infect others.

Spinach
The different types of spinach can be a little confusing. True spinach can be round-seeded or prickly-seeded. The difference is in the seed itself. Prickly-seeded varieties are a little

Right Courgettes are ready for cutting when they are 10 cm (4 in) long.
Below (Left) *Perpetual spinach;*
(centre) *New Zealand spinach;*
(right) *sea kale.*

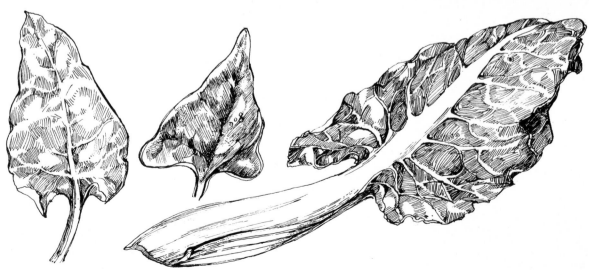

hardier and less likely to bolt. New Zealand spinach is quite different with almost fleshy leaves and a very spreading habit. It is susceptible to frost but good in dry, hot conditions. Perpetual spinach or spinach beet is good for autumn and winter supplies and is better for dry soils. Yet another type is the Swiss chard or seakale beet.

Soil preparation

A rich moisture-retentive soil is needed to ensure a good supply of succulent leaf growth. The ground should be well manured to produce these conditions. This is one vegetable crop that appreciates some shade in summer. It will fit in quite well between rows of peas.

Seed sowing

Round and prickly varieties should be sown successively for summer use from February to May. The drills should be 2 cm ($\frac{1}{2}$–$\frac{3}{4}$ in) deep and 30-35 cm (12-15 in) apart. For winter use sow in the same way in August and again in September. Perpetual spinach is sown in April or July. The drills should be 45 cm (18 in) apart. Both these sowings will run to seed in the late spring following sowing. New Zealand spinach may be sown under glass and transplanted or sown outdoors in late April or early May. The seed is very hard and will germinate better if soaked in water before sowing.

Cultivation

Thin all types in two stages. First thin to 7·5 cm (3 in) and then remove alternate plants and use them. Keep the rows hoed. To maintain sup-

Above *Long Standing Round, a variety of spinach which freezes very well. The different types of spinach can be confusing. The difference is actually in the seeds which can be round or prickly. Prickly-seeded varieties are the hardiest.*
Left *Perpetual spinach or spinach beet is good for autumn and winter supplies.*

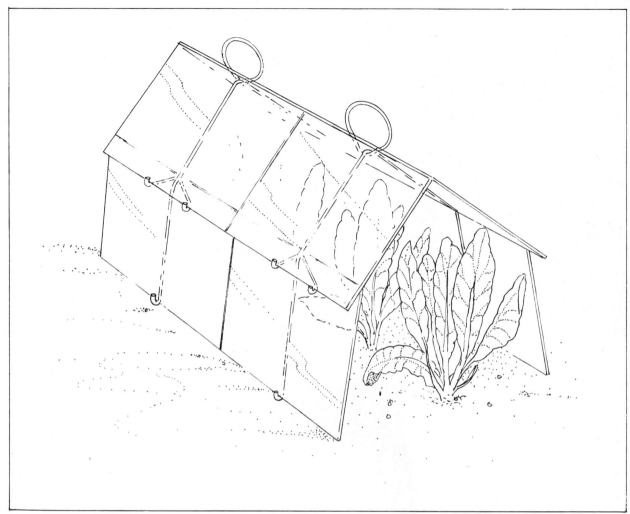

Spinach growing under cloches.

plies, water regularly in dry weather. If cloches are available to protect the rows through winter, supplies will be increased and quality improved. A feed of sulphate of ammonia or nitro-chalk at the rate of 33 g (1 oz) per 1 m² (1 sq yd) hoed in at the end of March is good for perpetual spinach and may delay bolting.

Harvesting
Start gathering the leaves when they reach usable size. With perpetual spinach, remove coarse and old leaves to encourage new growth.

Varieties
Long Standing Round; Broad-leaved Prickly; Perpetual spinach; New Zealand spinach. All these varieties freeze well.

Culinary Herbs

But first—what is a herb?

The definition of a herb

The meaning of the word herb is open to argument. The botanical definition, 'a plant whose stem is not woody and persistent', immediately excludes the evergreen bay, rosemary, sage and thyme, the herbs most frequently used in the kitchen today.

The second definition of herb, 'a plant of which the leaves are used for food, medicine, scent, flavour etc.', would both include the evergreens mentioned above and cover vegetables and lavender.

Why, for instance, is a shallot considered a vegetable while chives and garlic are commonly grouped as herbs? And why is groundsel today called a weed when it used to be infused to make one of the many herbal teas? Experience in the use of different herbs, and increased knowledge of their properties, have caused them to be divided into three groups —those of medicinal value, those for culinary use and those which are purely aromatic.

Culinary herbs

The majority of culinary herbs belong to one of only two of the extensive number of botanical families. The majority of Mediterranean aromatics belong to the *Labiatae* (labium–lip), easily recognised by their lipped flowers. Usually three of the petals form a hood, balanced by the remaining two, which join to form the lower lip. Another distinctive characteristic of this family is its quadrangular stem.

Aromatic Labiatae
Balm
Basil
Bergamot
Hyssop
Marjoram
Mint
Rosemary
Sage
Savory
Thyme

Most other culinary herbs belong to the *Umbelliferae*. They are easily distinguishable by the umbel flower head. The cow parsley is a typical example of this. *Umbella* is Latin for sunshade but its linguistic cousin, umbrella, is probably more familiar.

The Umbelliferae
Angelica
Chervil
Dill
Fennel
Lovage
Parsley
Sweet cicely

Also included among the *Umbelliferae* are certain spices such as aniseed, caraway, coriander and cumin.

History of herbs

Man has always relied on plants for food and medicine. Nomadic tribes experimented with the plants they found along their route, and knowledge of which plants were beneficial and which were poisonous was slowly built up by experience and passed on from tribe to tribe, from country to country, from century to century.

An early summary of the supposedly curative properties of plants was made by the Greek physician, Hippocrates, about 400 BC. During the first century AD another Greek, Pedacious Dioscorides, compiled a treatise covering about five hundred medicinal and culinary plants. His work, on a collection of parchment sheets, was to be copied and recopied

and was still being used as a source of reference more than a thousand years later.

In Italy, in AD 44, Pliny recorded the results and conclusions of a lifetime of observation in his still well-known *Natural History*.

Many records were lost over the next centuries, others seized and taken to Baghdad to be added to an existing collection of Arabic texts. These were translated from one language to another and eventually found their way back to Europe with the Moors, some turning up in a library in Cordoba.

Left *Sage and coriander (late 12th-century English manuscript).*
Below *Early 16th-century Flemish herbal. (Both from Bodleian Library.)*

During this time the use of herbs was kept alive in Europe by Christian monks who grew the plants in the cloisters and painstakingly copied out the various texts in their cells. It was the inaccurate copying of illustrations, without first-hand knowledge of the plant, that led to the mandrake root appearing as a little man. This fostered all kinds of superstition and folk lore about the plant.

The advent of printing made the knowledge of herbs more widely available. The first English herbal was printed in 1525 by a gentleman named Bancke, about whom very little is known. His was the first of a long line of interesting and noteworthy herbals which appeared over the next hundred years. In 1551

William Turner compiled his *New Herbal*, containing some fine woodcuts. John Gerard used a translation from a Dutch work for much of his herbal which appeared in 1597. As a result the illustrations are often incorrectly named, but the book does contain the first illustration of a potato. Gerard himself is shown holding one in the frontispiece, almost as if he had discovered the plant himself.

The next herbalist was more accurate for not only was he a practising gardener but an apothecary to James I. John Parkinson was 73 when he wrote his last work on herbs in 1640, but probably the best-known herbalist of all was Nicholas Culpeper, astrologer, eccentric and recluse, whose work is still revered.

Early uses of herbs

All the herbal books mentioned so far contained a mixture of fact and fiction, truth and superstition. However, they stimulated those who could read them to start their own herb gardens and there are records of them being planted at 'Hampton Court, Nonsuch Palace and Tibault's'. Herbs were valued by rich and poor alike for their flavour, which varied the monotonous winter diet of rabbit, pulses and dried or salt meat. Most of the livestock were slaughtered at the onset of winter because of the lack of forage, making fresh meat unobtainable for months.

The rich had used expensive spices for flavouring until they were deprived of these by an Act of 1666, prohibiting their import for some years. It was thought that the spice ships had introduced the plague and this was a measure to control it. As a result herbs became even more important and were still relied on for medicinal use.

Later, in 1673, the 'Physic' garden was laid out at Chelsea by the apothecaries, who were still very influenced by Paracelsus (1493-1541). He was a Swiss alchemist who believed that every disorder could be

cured by a plant, if only the correct one could be found.

From this time, efforts were slowly made to separate fact from fantasy in the use of herbs and the esteem in which the apothecary's shop was held reached its height in the 19th century. Since that time the advance of chemical research and the manufacture of synthetic drugs have reduced the medicinal role of herbs. It has taken nearly one hundred years for modern chemical analysis in the laboratory to vindicate much of the traditional usage of herbs.

Properties of herbs

Taste is certainly influenced by, and connected with, smell. But not every plant that has a scent has a flavour. Lavender is an aromatic plant but is not used in the kitchen. Culinary aromatics must contain other substances besides the volatile oils responsible for their flavour. The chemical formulae of some of these constituents has been established. They are mainly organic chemicals which occur in many plants but often in a higher concentration in herbs.

Inorganic elements

Sulphur occurs in alliums, garlic and onions, and is partly responsible for their characteristic taste. Medicinally, sulphur can be taken to purify the blood. Iron is found in high concentration in parsley, making it a valuable herb for those who suffer from anaemia. Other minerals and elements, such as potassium and calcium, are also present. Lovage and dill contain sodium chloride, the chemical name for common salt, which makes these herbs suitable for use as an alternative by people on a low salt diet.

Organic substances

Vitamins are probably the most important inorganic substances. They are present in all fresh green herbs but are destroyed by prolonged cooking.

Alkaloids

These are nitrogenous bases similar to amines. The best known are morphine, found in opium in the poppy, quinine and codeine. These are mostly bitter and may account in part for the bitter taste of some herbs.

Sugars

These occur as polysacharides, which means many types of sugar together, and glycosides, a term used for a compound which is part sugar and part not. Polysacharides are the main constituent of mucilage in the sap and are present in angelica, sweet cicely and lemon balm, all of which are used to sweeten fruit. Glycosides have an effect on the muscles of the body. Digitalis from foxgloves stimulates the heart muscles.

Tanins and other acids

Tanins are found in sage and peppermint and have a bitter taste when concentrated. Oxalic acid is in high concentration in sorrel.

Volatile oils

These substances need a certain degree of heat before they will vaporise. This is why the aromatics have more scent when the weather is hot, and they must be picked for drying in the early part of the day before the oil has been dispersed.

All these above mentioned substances are at their highest concentration in the plant just before flowering.

A bouquet garni of herbs tied together with string for use in cooking.

Cooking with herbs

Herbs are best used fresh and raw whenever practicable as many of the chemicals and vitamins present in them are destroyed or dispersed by heat. The thin-leaved herbs, such as pot basil and tarragon, give off their volatile oils and flavour when merely bruised. Fortunately the leaves of both these herbs are small enough to be used whole. On the other hand chive rushes, because of their impractical length, have to be cut.

Used in a hot dish, all the soft-leaved herbs, such as parsley and dill, are best added right at the end of the cooking time, or even incorporated when the cooking is over. A mixture of these soft-leaved herbs is often called *fines herbes*. Originally these were probably used fresh, but because they are now sold in a dried form, this is how they are invariably used by non-gardeners. The most common ingredients of *fines herbes* are chervil, chives, parsley leaves and tarragon.

Bouquet garni

To capture the flavour of the fresh herb at its best is one reason why herbs are added to a marinating liquid before cooking, even though they may be tough evergreens. These tougher-leaved herbs, such as bay, rosemary and sage, need heat to give off their oils and can stand cooking. Because they are tough they are removed before serving. This is made easier by tying them together with a long piece of cotton, white wool or string.

The kind of aromatics that can be used in cooking grow naturally in the south of France and are traditional ingredients of native cuisine. Hence the French expression *bouquet garni*, which is a bunch of herbs tied together to be used in the manner

Herbs make refreshing teas and tisanes.

described above. The most common ingredients are:
$\frac{1}{2}$-2 bay leaves
0-2 parsley stalks
1-2 sprigs of thyme
1 stem of majoram (optional)
1 piece of celery stem (optional)

Rosemary is not usually included in a *bouquet garni* because the tiny leaves escape into the stew. However, this herb and others can be used if cut up and put on to a 10-cm (4-in) piece of muslin which is then tied up and used as a bouquet. Dried herbs can also be used in this way.

There are no hard and fast rules about which herb must be used with which food. The choice is a matter of availability and individual taste. This means that there is always opportunity for experiment and innovation. Each person soon finds out which herb is worth cosseting and which is not worth the effort; which herb is really needed throughout the year and which can more readily be dispensed with.

Tisanes or herb teas

The leaves of many herbs can be infused with boiling water to make teas which are said to have a beneficial effect. Honey or sugar can be added to taste, if desired. A particularly popular tea was made with dill seeds. These teas or tisanes were frequently drunk until the dried and smoked camellia leaf was imported from China and India. The infusion of this leaf has since become a national habit, if not an addiction, in Britain and the herb teas have temporarily been forgotten. This is a pity, because balm tea is said to refresh without over-stimulating and is meant to revive the weary brain. Peppermint tea, with its digestive properties, might be a kinder finale to a large meal than coffee and cream.

As well as improving the flavour of food, there is a belief that herbs can purify the blood (parsley), cure rheumatism (borage), aid digestion (peppermint), improve the memory (sage), reduce blood pressure

(chives), act as a carminative (dill), or as a tranquilliser (balm). Beliefs apart, there is one certainty—not one of the leaves contains cholesterol.

Cultivation

There is no mystique about growing herbs. Most of them grow naturally in the wild, some around the Mediterranean where they survive on impoverished stony heaths, others farther north where they flourish without care or attention. The important point to remember in each case is the country of origin. Those that revel in the hot dry summers of the south need special attention when growing farther north in cold wet soil.

Mediterranean aromatics

These grow in impoverished, sometimes chalky soil, and need no additional fertilisers. They do require good drainage, full sun and shelter from the north and north east. This was one of the reasons why the traditional herb gardens of northern Europe invariably enjoyed the protection of a wattle fence when not surrounded by the cloisters of a monastery.

The evergreen aromatics, such as

Below *A compact herb garden can be made in a restricted space by placing two decorative openwork bricks on top of each other.*
Right *Parsley sown under cloches with radishes at cotyledon stage growing in alternate rows.*

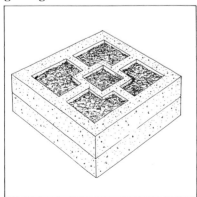

bay and rosemary, can survive the average winter but may succumb in a severe one. With this exception, cold temperatures are not so damaging as waterlogged soil. If the garden soil is not naturally sandy and well drained, it is advisable to incorporate open draining material such as rubble, shingle, gravel or sharp sand.

Raised bed

In heavy soils it may be better to make a raised bed, sited against a south-facing wall. Initially it need not be larger than 30 × 100 cm (1 × 3 ft). The edging can be made of planks of wood, already treated with preservative, held in place by wooden pegs or stiff wire pot hooks. Alternatively slanting bricks, tiles or breeze blocks can be used. The existing soil can be dug out to a spade's depth and carefully placed on a plastic sheet or 'donkey'. Some compost and drainage material can be added to this and some chalk if the soil is naturally acid. Before the soil is put back, rubble, broken crocks or stones should be laid along the base of the bed.

A plant of rosemary, tarragon, sage, hyssop, marjoram and two thymes could be planted in this area.

Because of its thinner leaves only the tarragon might need watering. If it is not possible to make a suitable bed near the house, this group of herbs takes easily and well to being grown in containers or pots.

Pots and containers

These can be any shape or size. In general they need to have up to one-third of their depth filled with drainage matter. John Innes compost No. 3 or equivalent will give sufficient nutrient for several years. To reduce the necessity of watering by cutting down the evaporation of moisture from the soil, it is advisable to dress the surface of the pots with a layer of alpine chips or shingle.

Another method is to group the pots together so that the leafy shoots shade each other and leave less bare soil. The group can stand on shingle in a circular, square or oblong plastic tray. The shingle will ensure that the pots never actually stand in water after a heavy downpour of rain or if they are over-watered.

Instead of growing each herb in a separate pot, it is more labour saving, and also more attractive, to grow three or four herbs together in a larger container. For instance a

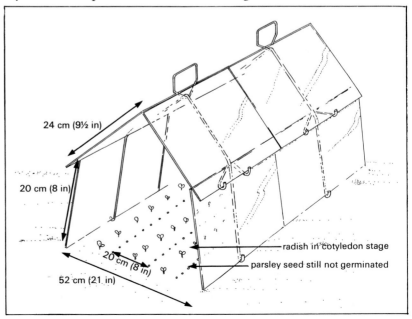

24 cm (9½ in)
20 cm (8 in)
20 cm (8 in)
52 cm (21 in)
radish in cotyledon stage
parsley seed still not germinated

Above *The herb garden at Sissing-hurst Castle in Kent.*

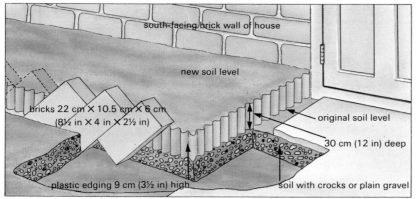

south-facing brick wall of house

new soil level

bricks 22 cm × 10.5 cm × 6 cm
(8½ in × 4 in × 2½ in)

original soil level

30 cm (12 in) deep

plastic edging 9 cm (3½ in) high

soil with crocks or plain gravel

Left *A raised bed can be made against a south-facing wall using bricks to form the edge, lined with plastic lawn edging. New soil is laid on a layer of crocks or gravel for drainage.*

A herb garden with hyssop and golden sage.

sage, a marjoram and two thymes fit into a 20-cm (9-in) pot and their roots nearly fill the available soil space. It is particularly important not to over-pot herbs. If soil is not being used and aerated by roots, it may become waterlogged and sour. In a large tub or container a tall permanent plant, such as a bay, rosemary or tarragon, could be positioned at the back, leaving the front either for a relay of chive plants or for the insertion of a pot of basil and/or summer savory. These pots can then be lifted and taken under cover before the plants are threatened by frost.

Mint and parsley
These need rich, moist soil and prefer some shade. Because of their creeping, invasive roots, mints are best planted on their own. If there is no naturally confined area, it is advisable to make one artificially. Plastic or metal lawn edging sunk below the soil will help to contain the spread of the roots. Alternatively, an old bottomless bucket or a plastic pail with holes in the base can be sunk in the ground and used for planting. As plenty of vegetative growth is needed from mints, summer feeds are helpful. A mulch of straw or leaves is always a very useful way of helping to preserve moisture in the soil and to prevent rust.

Other culinary herbs
The majority belong to the cow parsley or *Umbelliferae* family. They all thrive in a northern climate and will grow anywhere. Many of them will reseed themselves all too readily. To quote an old jingle,

> *Fennel and lovage,*
> *Balm and borage,*
> *Will always grow,*
> *No need to sow.*

Cold greenhouse
This is invaluable for prolonging the growing season and consequently the useful life of many herbs. If clumps of chives, slips of mint and tarragon are potted up in August, they will have made enough new growth by the end of September to

Herbs need to be grown near the kitchen—they can look very attractive.

carry them into the winter. Any plant that has spent the winter under cover will start into growth in spring before those outside. The tender pot basil does best in a greenhouse all the time except in very hot summers. Its seeds can be started off here as well as those of chervil, parsley and summer savory.

Methods of propagation

Chervil, dill, parsley, sweet marjoram, summer savory
These must all be sown from seed. Many of these are difficult to germinate in a cold climate. Seeds will not germinate until they are wet and the right temperature has been reached and maintained. Outside and in a greenhouse, the temperature is apt to vary in early spring. Better germination can be ensured if the seeds are kept at a constant temperature of about 16°C (60°F) indoors. Well-

damped kitchen paper can be put several layers thick at the bottom of any small covered container. Seeds are then sprinkled on this, sprayed with a mist spray and the lid tightly closed. If a larger number of seeds is wanted, a plastic sandwich box does well.

When the seeds are seen to have germinated, they can be carefully transferred to compost blocks or peat pots which should be kept at the same temperature until the cotyledons are well grown. Later the move can be made to the right-sized pot or to the garden without root disturbance.

In the open, seeds should not be sown much before May and it is best then to cover them with the lid of a propagator or a cloche. This will not only preserve the moisture, but will also prevent attack by sparrows.

Self-sown seeds
Angelica, balm, borage, fennel, lovage, sweet cicely
Self-sown seedlings of these six

herbs will occur in any soil type.
Rosemary, marjoram, thyme
These three are also self-sowing but they will only appear when the parent plant has been growing in sandy soil.

The seeds of the *Umbelliferae* do not remain viable for long. In nature they germinate almost as soon as they are ripe. This is why sowing the seeds artificially the following spring is not always successful. Whichever method is used, the resulting seedlings usually have to be thinned and in some cases may have to be transplanted.

Planting bulbs or cloves
Chives, garlic
Five or six bulbs of chives can be planted at any time of year provided the rushes have been cut down to about 4 cm (1½ in). A single clove of the garlic bulb is planted 5 cm (2 in) deep in late February or March, but this will depend on the suitability of the weather conditions. In sandy soils garlic can be planted in October.

Division of parent plant
Balm, hyssop, marjoram

The whole plant is lifted just before it begins to shoot. Two forks are inserted down the centre with their backs to each other and are then levered apart. The outer part of the plant is the more vigorous so the centre can be discarded. A little peat in the new planting hole will help the small hair roots to grow.

Plant off-shoots
Mint, tarragon, thyme

When the surface soil has been scraped away, outer pieces of root can either be pulled away from the main plant or they may have to be cut off. The best time for this is just when the plant has started to grow after the winter.

Root cuttings
Horseradish, lovage, sorrel

In early spring when shoots are just beginning to show, a slice of root can be removed and planted where desired.

Cuttings
Bay, hyssop, pot basil, pot marjoram, rosemary, winter savory

Cuttings will only root when the soil temperature is reasonably high and the plant active. Small shoots are pulled off the main stem with a 'heel'. This is a sliver of older wood containing a layer of cambium cells which will readily form new tissue. Until the roots are grown, the leaves will transpire and lose water which will not be replaced, so cuttings are usually covered to minimise this loss. The end of the cutting can be dipped in hormone rooting powder to encourage rooting. A light, peaty, sandy soil will also encourage the formation of new root hairs and roots.

Choosing a site

The most frequently used herbs need to be near the kitchen door. For this reason it is advisable to think of herbs as part of the flower garden, which is more likely to be within reach of the house, than the vegetable plot where, by association, they tend to be grown.

There is something very attractive about the idea of a herb or knot garden. However, it invariably looks better on paper than it does on the ground when planted. Certain herbs are neat and compact but many others grow to an unruly height, such as fennel, or sprawl, such as mint. Many, such as lovage, grow quite out of proportion. These naturally informal herbs are best grown where they happen to fit in with the general scheme of the garden.

A formal feature could be made around a bay tree or a sundial by using chives, parsley or pennyroyal as an edging or in a pattern, with different varieties of thyme to add colour.

The creeping thymes can be popped into gaps in a terrace or other paving, and in the sun they will give off scent when walked on or bruised. For the gardener who is not obsessed with neatness, a gravel sweep or drive is ideal for many of the Mediterranean aromatics. They revel in the dryness. This is often the only place in the garden where seedlings of rosemary and marjoram will appear.

The evergreen rosemary and bay are an asset as permanent features in any garden. Rosemary covers many hillsides in Spain and does not need any particular care except for being given a south or west aspect. The ornamental marjorams and sages, hyssop and winter savory fit in well in any dry, sunny part of the decorative garden. In heavy soil they may have to be grouped in a raised bed.

Borage, with its bright blue starry flowers, brightens the front of any flower border from August to November. Indeed it was a flowering plant much favoured by the Victorians. The self-sown seedlings which appear in May can always be repositioned during a damp spell, while still small.

Fennel is an attractive plant for the

back of a border, particularly if the bronze form is chosen. But sweet Cicely and angelica are best kept to the wild part of the garden if there is one. Although they are handsome plants, it is best to think twice before introducing them to the flower garden.

The thin greeny leaves of tarragon are unobtrusively pleasant in a flower bed from May onwards, even though there is virtually no flower. Spearmint is best on its own or in the vegetable garden but the eau de Cologne mint, with its pretty purplish-edged leaves, is an asset at the front of a sunny border. It looks attrative and has a pleasant smell.

Growing in pots

Even in a large garden there may be no soil available near the house because of existing plantings. Any kind of pot can be used, earthenware or plastic. Of the latter type, the flexible rubber kind or the thicker, softer plastic variety are preferable. Not only do they not chip so easily when picked up by the rim, but they also tend to be made in quieter colours. The pots can be arranged at different heights and, with skill, can make an attractive and useful feature. There are a number of more expensive containers which can be collected one by one.

This applies particularly to flat dwellers with only a small balcony or to those who have to grow herbs indoors. Herbs tend to become etiolated and leggy if kept inside too long. For this reason it is a good idea to have three pots of each of the selected herbs. One can be in use, one resting, sunk in the ground in a friend's garden, and another refurbishing itself there.

The kitchen is not always the best place for growing herbs. There might be a sunnier window sill in bathroom or bedroom and a reserve could be kept here. In a restricted

Left *The Old Rectory herb garden at Ightham, Kent.*
Inset *Culinary herbs growing in pots.*

75

A Table of Culinary Herbs

Herb	Height	Type of plant	Site and soil	Easiest methods of propagation
Angelica	2·5 m (8 ft)	Hardy perennial	Anywhere	Self sown seedlings
Balm	60-75 cm (over 2 ft)	Hardy perennial	Anywhere	Division of plant in early spring Self sown seedlings
Basils Dwarf or pot basil	15-30 cm (up to 1 ft)	Tender annual could be perennial under cover	Grow in pot under cover Put out in good summers only	Sow directly into peat pot or compost block. Soil warming an advantage. Take cuttings in July.
Sweet basil	up to 60 cm (2 ft)	Tender annual		Sow directly into peat pot or compost block when temperature is at least 16°C (60°F) all the time
Bay	60 cm in two yrs. (2 ft) Tree up to 10 m (40 ft)	Evergreen tree	Sun, shelter from north, north/east winds	Half-ripe short shoots taken as cuttings in July
Borage	45-60 cm (1½-2 ft)	Annual	Anywhere	Self sown seedlings
Chervil	45-60 cm (1½-2 ft)	Annual/ biennial	Partshade, rich soil, shelter	Sow in August, keep moist, protect with cloche in winter. Can be sown any other month from February onwards. Will not transplant. Self sown seedlings in sandy soil.
Chives	Varies	Handy bulb	Rich soil, moisture, sun	Divide clumps and plant 5-6 bulbs in spring, or June and July if rushes cut down to 3 cm (1½ in)

Herb	Height	Type of plant	Site and soil	Easiest methods of propagation
Dill	up to 90 cm (2-3 ft)	Tender annual	Well drained, sun	Sow matured seeds from April onwards at a temperature of 16-18°C (60-64°F) 21 days to germinate. Thin—do not transplant
Fennel	up to 1·5 m (5 ft)	Hardy perennial	Anywhere	Self sown seedlings Divide root in April
Garlic	about 60 cm (2 ft)	Bulb	Full sun, rich soil, moisture when growing	Plant single cloves 5 cm (2 in) deep February or March, 15 cm (6 in) apart
Horseradish	60 cm (2 ft)	Hardy perennial	Anywhere	Root cuttings spring or autumn
Hyssop	60-90 cm (2-3 ft)	Hardy evergreen shrublet	Sun, shelter, good drainage	Cuttings pulled off with heel in spring or after flowering
Lovage	up to 2·5 m (8 ft)	Hardy perennial	Anywhere, not too dry	Self sown seedlings Cut root as growth starts
Oregano, wild marjoram	30-70 cm (1-2½ ft)	Hardy perennial	Sun, poor, chalky soil	Divide root in spring Self sown seedlings in sandy soil
Pot marjoram	up to 60 cm (2 ft)	Hardy shrublet	Sun, good drainage	Cuttings in May or June, put under cloche Division of root in spring, or rooted layers

Continued overleaf

continued

Herb	Height	Type of plant	Site and soil	Easiest methods of propagation
Sweet marjoram	up to 30 cm (1 ft)	Half hardy annual	Sun, no frost	Sow under cover in April when at least 16°C (60°F) plant out after frost, need shade as seedlings and constant weeding
Bowles' mint	about 90 cm (3 ft)	Hardy perennials	Shade, rich moisture retentive soil	Any piece of root removed from spring onwards will form a new plant
Eau de Cologne	50 cm (20 in)			
Penny royal	10 cm (4 in)			
Peppermint	60–90 cm (2–3 ft)			
Roundleaved or applemint	60 cm (2 ft)			
Spearmint	30–45 cm (1–1½ ft)			
Parsley	20–30 cm (up to 1 ft)	Biennial	Shade, rich soil, moisture retentive Cover with cloche in winter	In sandy soil. Self sown seedlings Sow when temperature is at least 18–20°C (64–68°F). Will take 5–8 weeks to germinate. Thin and transplant. Sow again in August.
Rosemary	up to 1·5 m (5 ft)	Evergreen shrub	Sun, shelter from north, good drainage, a little lime or chalk	Cuttings in March. Put in pot under cover or any time after flowering in the open. Self sown seedlings

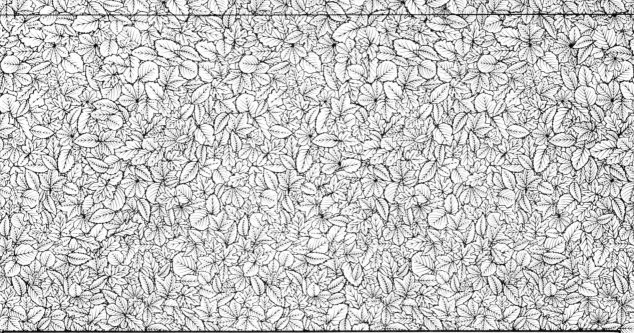

Herb	Height	Type of plant	Site and soil	Easiest methods of propagation
Sage	up to 60 cm (2 ft)	Evergreen perennial	Sun, good drainage	Cuttings in April or May Rooted stems if one plant covered with fine soil in March
Summer Savory	15–30 cm (6–12 in)	Tender annual	Sun and shelter	Sow seeds under cover in peat pot to avoid root disturbance. Plant out after frost.
Winter Savory	15–40 cm (up to 16 in)	Hardy evergreen shrublet	Sun, well drained soil, a little chalk	Cuttings or division of root
Sorrel	up to 60 cm (2 ft)	Hardy perennial	Anywhere	Division of roots
Sweet Cicely	up to 1·5 m (5 ft)	Hardy perennial	Anywhere	Self sown seedlings
Tarragon	up to 1 m (3 ft)	Perennial	Warm, sheltered site, moisture retentive soil, part shade	Pull away root runners as growth starts
Thyme	varies	Evergreen shrublet or mat	Sun, well drained soil	Layering Cuttings in April or May onwards

space it is not worth bothering with the larger herbs such as bay and rosemary, as sprigs of these from some friend's garden will last a long time in water.

Cutting and drying

The fresh leaf of any herb is tastier and infinitely more beneficial than a dried one. It is only worth the trouble of drying if sufficient cannot be guaranteed by any other method. The better the gardener, the less drying will need to be done. There is certainly no point in drying the evergreen herbs, bay, hyssop, rosemary, sage and winter savory. Thyme, although evergreen, is a much smaller plant and may not be able to provide enough sprigs for the whole winter. If this is the case, it would be worth drying some thyme during the summer when the plant is growing well and able to replace the shoots cut.

Certain herbs, basil and chives in particular, loose so much virtue when they are dried that it is probably not worth doing so. The young leaves have the maximum amount of flavour just before the plant flowers. This is the time to make the first cut for drying or freezing. This will usually be by the end of June or early July, leaving enough good growing weather for the plant to refurbish itself in time for a second harvest in September.

The best time for cutting is in the morning, after the dew has dried off but before the sun starts to evaporate the oils. Once cut, the herbs should ideally be dried as quickly as possible and as coolly as practicable. The longer the bunches or trays of leaves lie around, the more dust will they collect. If the temperature is too high the leaves will shrivel and lose some of their oils. In the sun they will lose their colour. To dry the leaves in ideal conditions there should be air, relative dark and a temperature of 27°-40°C (80°-104°F).

A bed of garden herbs with chives and sage at the flowering stage.

Thyme hanging up to dry.

The leaves or sprigs can be tied in small bunches and hung like washing from a line or they can be laid on a wire baking tray. The warm air from a fan heater will speed the process in damp, still weather.

The time required for drying depends on the humidity of the air at the time and the thickness of the leaf being dried. A leaf is ready when it can be rubbed off the stalk and crumbled. The smaller and more finely the leaf is crumbled, the more scent and flavour will be lost.

Storing

A dark, airtight, labelled container is needed. An old coffee jar is ideal for the larger leaves such as mint. Smaller containers are better for thyme and tarragon. Herbs look remarkably alike when dried, so it is important to label the jar at once. Some maintain that the shelf life of herbs is only three months, so it is also a good idea to write the date on the label.

Freezing

The freezing of herbs is still in the experimental stage. Before trying it out, it would be advisable to find out about the most recent results. It is doubtful whether frozen herbs can retain as much flavour as their fresh counterpart. The blanching process, if used for only sixty seconds, will destroy both vitamins and fragrance. The most suitable herbs for freezing are also the ones that, because of their fine flavour, are usually used raw. It is worth trying to freeze parsley and chives which do not dry well, but only if there is no possibility of keeping a fresh supply.

Herbs to be frozen are best picked in the early morning, washed under cold water, shaken dry with as little bruising as possible and put into

ing the root just as it starts to sprout in spring. This is a handsome plant and certainly merits a place in somebody else's garden.

Uses

The young stalks of leaves and flowers cut in May, before they become hard and stringy, can be candied and made into angelica for the decoration of cakes and puddings.

When cooked with rhubarb, the young leaves will help to disguise the tartness. When infused with boiling water, the leaves make a tisane similar to China tea. The seeds are also aromatic and are used in the manufacture of gin and Benedictine.

Herbs in airtight jars.

small waxed containers or plastic bags. There is little point in freezing a bouquet as is sometimes suggested, as most of these herbs are evergreen and could be used fresh. Parsley and chives can be cut up small and put straight into an ice cube with just a little water. If herbs are not blanched they should be used within two to three months.

Angelica

Angelica archangelica

This tall plant, which resembles cow parsley, was introduced into Britain to join an already existing wild form, under the mistaken belief that it could cure the plague. As its name explains, this information was vouchsafed by an angel. Ironically, the plant itself can become a plague in a small garden. It will flower after two years, self-seeding itself around to become, in time, an ineradicable weed.

The parent plant will die after four or five years. Once there are seedlings for succession, it is best not to let the plant flower. Removing the flower also encourages new green leaves to be produced over a longer period. If the flower is always removed for this reason, another plant can be made by divid-

Balm

Melissa officinalis

This herb is widely distributed from the Caucasus through the Mediterranean and up to the Alps. It probably reached Britain as a cultivated plant but has since escaped and now grows wild. It will grow anywhere. It is a hardy perennial herb about 60 cm (2 ft) high with crinkled leaves rather like those of a round-leafed mint, with which it is sometimes confused. The leaves have a distinct scent of lemon.

In a garden it will seed itself freely, sometimes too freely. Before this happens the root of the parent plant

can be divided in early spring, just as the new shoots appear. In any case it is best to split up a plant every two or three years. If left any longer, the plant will have become so dense that it will prove very difficult to uproot, particularly if it is growing in heavy clay soil.

If the tips of shoots are picked for use, this will delay the time of flowering. As with all herbs the leaves have the maximum amount of taste just before the plant flowers, and this is the time to harvest for drying or freezing.

Uses

In classical times balm was grown for its medicinal properties and also because the flowers attracted bees (*melissa* is the Greek word for a bee). Both Dioscorides and Pliny knew that balm was effective for dressing wounds and this has since been scientifically proved correct. It has also frequently been used as a calming tisane or herb tea. Five or six leaves infused in boiling water are supposed to ensure a balmy night. It can also be added to China tea or to cold drinks such as cider cup or milk. It makes an unusual mint sauce and can be used cut up in green or fruit salads.

Basil

Several species of basil grow naturally in India where it has been known from time immemorial. One species, which is sacred to the Hindus, is found growing round all the temples. Other forms are widespread there, occurring in most gardens as they were thought to be 'a defence against mosquitoes and a prophylactic in malarious districts' (Sir George Birdwood 1903). Being a native of India, basil does not grow easily in northern Europe.

It is highly esteemed in every country into which it has been introduced, as its name, *basilicus*, mean-

Left Balm, with its distinctive scent of lemon.
Right Basil, a once-sacred herb.

ing princely, implies. In France today it is still called *herbe royale*. There are two species grown in Europe, the taller sweet basil and the smaller pot or dwarf one. Away from the Mediterranean, both must be treated as delicate annuals.

Sweet basil
Ocimum basilicum

This grows to about 90 cm (3 ft) and has large leaves varying between 2-5 cm (1-2 in). There are various cultivated forms of which the purple Dark Opal is perhaps the hardiest in England. In France an even larger-leafed form is cultivated which has

lettuce-sized leaves of up to 10 cm (4 in). The cultivation is the same as for pot basil.

Pot or dwarf basil
Ocimum minimum

This is perhaps the more useful basil to grow. It takes more readily to being grown in a pot, where it can be protected under cover in all but the hottest summers. Normally it does not grow much taller than 15-30 cm (6-12 in). Constantly nipping out shoots helps to keep it compact.

Although usually green, dwarf basil can also occur in a red form. The seeds should not be sown before

April unless there is some bottom heat available. The seedlings have to be treated like tomatoes and not set out till the end of May or until danger of frost is passed. The seedlings do not like being transplanted. It is safer and less trouble to sow three or four seeds in a 10-cm (4-5-in) pot, eventually leaving just one. Alternatively, seeds can be sown in peat compost blocks and later inserted into a larger pot.

At least three pots are needed as it is such a good and useful herb. A pot of basil makes a delightful present and it is worth sowing up more pots if you have room. The plant revels in sun but will not flourish if its roots

are in permanently soggy soil. To avoid this, stand the pot on 2 cm (1 in) of moist gravel and syringe the foliage frequently.

Just before the plant flowers, all the shoots should be cut back to 5 cm (2 in). This should only be done if there is enough time left for the plant to sprout again before the winter. In this way the plants can be used through to December. The lack of sun affects basil and it is not an easy plant to keep growing on cold dark days.

Uses

This is one of the top ten herbs. The tiny leaves of pot basil sprinkled on

to sliced tomatoes in French dressing greatly enhance the flavour. The leaves can also be combined with other herbs and cooked with vegetables such as courgettes or added to them afterwards. Basil is an important ingredient of the vegetable soup *pistou*. A pot of basil on the window sill wafts an indefinable scent into the kitchen.

Bay

Laurus nobilis

The bay has long been revered, principally for its medicinal properties. Its connection with the priests and priestesses of Apollo at Delphi may have been due to the narcotic properties of the berries. They induced a trance-like state which assisted in the uttering of prophecies. The Romans later endowed the bay with symbolic importance. They used it to crown their heroes, whether poets or generals, hence its name, noble laurel.

The bay is an evergreen tree growing naturally around the Mediterranean to about 10 m (30-40 ft). It was introduced into Britain and is usually hardy in the south if given a sheltered position. An exceptionally severe winter can scorch the leaves and prove fatal. For this reason, farther north, bay is often grown in a tub or container. This can then be moved under cover whenever necessary. The other advantage of having a bay in a container is that it can be placed near the house.

As the bay is such a slow grower it is unlikely to outgrow a 12-18-in (30-45-cm) container for some years, particularly if frequently picked. If another plant is needed, half-ripe cuttings about 10-15 cm (4-6 in) can be pulled off in late June and should root in sandy peat compost. It would be difficult to think of a more welcome and perennially useful present than a well rooted cutting of bay.

Bay tree.

Uses

The purple berries that follow the yellow flowers were used in Elizabethan times. Today it is mainly the

aromatic leaves that are used for flavouring. Many bland dishes are noticeably enhanced by the addition of one or two leaves. This is why bay is the principle ingredient of the most frequently used bouquet garni.

A few leaves are always put in a moussaka; they are an essential topping to a terrine; and are invaluable when cooking ham or tongue. As the leaves are evergreen, they are available throughout the year. Although they dry easily, this is a pointless exercise as at least one bay tree grows in most villages and a spray will remain fresh in water for weeks.

Borage
Borago officinalis

The Latin word *officinalis* means that borage was originally sold for a specific, probably medicinal, purpose. The mucilage in the hollow stem was thought to reduce fever and increase the activity of the kidneys. Modern research has shown that it does in fact stimulate the adrenal gland, which may account for its Welsh name, *Llanwenlys*, or herb of gladness.

This name could equally well derive from its beautiful bright blue flowers. The five-pointed petals stand back in one plane in the form of a star and from them protrudes a beak-like steeple of black anthers. In good soil the plant can grow to 90 cm (3 ft), and the flowers, which

Borage.

can continue into November if there is no hard frost, are spectacular. There is little other blue of such intensity in the garden at that time of year. With its scratchily hairy stems and leaves, the plant is easily recognisable and will grow in poorer soil. Borage has become naturalised to Britain and occurs in the wild but it originated in southern Europe. It survives easily and is self-perpetuating. Numerous seedlings show through in May and these can be transplanted while still young during any damp spell. They will certainly need thinning out.

Uses

'The vertu of this herbe is that it wele clense the rede colour in mannys face. Also this herbe medled in wyn wyl make a man glad and merye.' This was written in the 14th century and partly based on Pliny's observations. Whether it was the borage or the wine that drove away melancholy and increased 'the joy of the minde' is an open question. However, it is true that both the flowers and the leaves of borage are used in claret and wine cups.

It can also be added to pure apple juice and added to iced tea. Some hold that it greatly improves cabbage if added while it is cooking. The blue flowers can be used as a decoration on green or fruit salads or they can also be candied or crystallised.

Chervil
Anthriscus cerefolium

This plant occurs naturally in south-eastern Europe with frequency but is only occasionally found in the wild in Britain where it has escaped from cultivation. Once established it will seed itself. Sowing seed from a packet is sometimes a matter of luck as the seed does not remain viable for long and its germination is tricky. Because of this difficulty, folk lore prescribes that the seeds can only be sown two days before the full moon. In fact it can be sown in any month from February onwards,

whatever the moon may be doing.

Seedlings cannot be transplanted without risk. It is a curious fact that it is often easier to transplant a cultivated plant than a wild one. If germination is found to be difficult in heavy soil, it is best to buy a plant in a pot, sink the pot in the ground and let the plant seed itself.

Chervil is taller than parsley but remains the most genteel of the *Umbelliferae* or cow parsley-type of herbs. In good soil it will reach 60 cm (2 ft). Only one plant should be allowed to flower and produce seeds, the other flower stems being cut off before they can set seed.

Uses

Chervil has a slight, indefinable taste. It is an ingredient of *fines herbes*. It is best used raw to preserve what little aroma it has, and in this state can be cut on to cooked vegetables or on to melted butter to make a butter sauce for poultry.

Chives

The specific name *schoinos* comes from the Latin word for a rush, which accurately describes the thin straight leaves. Although the chive is now found wild (*Allium schoenoprasum*) in different counties in Britain, it was probably introduced by the Romans. It is smaller than the Chinese chive (*Allium tuberosum*), from which it can be distinguished by the cylindrical section of its rush or leaf. Chinese chives grow twice as tall, and are usually about 45 cm (18 in), which makes some people think they are a particularly well-cultivated example of the ordinary chive.

Both chives grow naturally in damp meadows, so plenty of moisture and a moisture-retentive soil is their prime need. As they produce so many green leaves so quickly, they use up the nitrogen in the soil. They will therefore appreciate a regular dressing of compost, ammonium sulphate or general fertiliser. If the tips of the leaves begin to go yellow in mid-summer, it may either be a sign of drought or an indication of lack of food.

A foliar feed is quite beneficial at this time or, alternatively, extra fertiliser could be applied as liquid manure. The best site· for chives is near a supply of water or in half shade so that the soil does not dry out so quickly. Being neat with a decorative flower, they are often used as an edging.

Clumps of seven or eight bulbs can be planted at intervals of about 20 cm (8 in). By the end of the summer these will have made clumps which can be divided again the

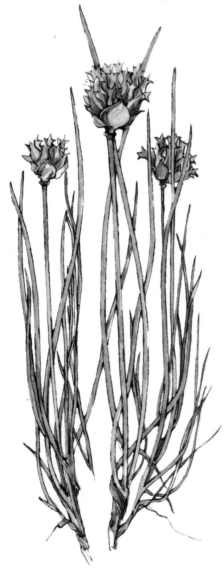

following spring. It is a good idea to have chives growing in different parts of the garden. From these, clumps can be transferred from time to time to the designated place near the kitchen door. If care is taken not to damage or disturb the roots, the leaves will not wilt.

Unless the flowers, which are rosy pink in the wild form and white in the Chinese, are needed for decorative purposes, they are best cut off so that the plant does not waste energy producing seeds.

The leaves will die down in autumn, but it is easy to have a continuous supply of chives through the winter if some clumps are potted up in mid-August. If these have been used for picking, the leaves will have been cut back to about 5 cm (2 in). The choice of pot is determined by the length of the roots and the circumference of the clump after the bulbs have been carefully teased apart a little.

Usually a shallow alpine pot or pan is ideal. Three of these can be filled with John Innes No. 3 or other equivalent compost and then sunk in the ground in a frame or brought into a cold greenhouse. The clumps of bulbs will refurbish themselves and will be ready to use by the time the outdoor chives have died down. The best idea is to use the pots in rotation.

Uses

Chives are best used raw and chopped. They are an excellent addition to cream cheese or scrambled eggs; they add spice to salads; they make an attractive garnish on cold soups; and can be sprinkled on new or old potatoes.

They lose a lot of colour if not dried carefully, so it is better to freeze small bundles in small containers. If they are not blanched, they should be used within two to three months. Chive bulbs can also be pickled like onions.

Chives, probably introduced to Britain by the Romans.

Dill
Anethum graveolens

The name dill is thought to have come from the Norse word *dilla*, to lull, as both leaves and seed have a soporific effect. The crushed seeds were an important ingredient of dill water which used to be given to crying babies. In the 18th century they were called 'meeting house seeds' and were chewed during long sermons, presumably in the pious expectation of oblivion.

The plant is a medium-sized member of the *Umbelliferae*, growing to only about 60 cm (2 ft). It has fine, thread-like leaves very similar to those of fennel. As it comes from the warmer climate of the Mediterranean, it will not survive the winter in Britain and has to be sown annually. It is a fragile plant and needs a sheltered site. The seeds will only germinate when the soil temperature is at least 16°C (60°F), probably at the end of April.

As the seedlings resent root disturbance, it is probably better to sow the seed in peat blocks or pots under cover. The seeds should germinate in fourteen to twenty-one days. Unlike lovage and angelica, the seed remains viable for years. If the seed is needed, the flowers are not cut off.

Uses

The Latin word *graveolens* means scented. The cut-up leaves are used for flavouring fish and improving bland vegetables. Both leaves and seeds are also invariably used in Europe for pickling cucumbers and gherkins.

The seed is easier to keep and store through the winter than the delicate leaf which loses its taste on drying. The seeds also have more taste and can be used in cheese instead of cumin and can be ground up into soups and sauces. The seeds were frequently drunk as a tisane or tea by infusing them in boiling water. Their popularity declined when the leaf variety came from India and China after the opening-up of new trade routes.

Fennel
Foeniculum vulgare

Fennel is a close relative of dill and is similar in appearance. For this reason they should not be planted close together as they cross pollinate and the resulting hybrid has no particular taste of its own. Fennel comes from the Mediterranean but it can stand a colder climate better than dill and has become naturalised to northern Europe, particularly near the coasts.

It is a perennial and, once established, perpetuates itself with self-sown seedlings. If this does not occur the root can be split as it starts to shoot in spring. It is an attractive plant about 1·5 m (5 ft) high and either it, or its bronze form, would look well at the back of a border, provided there is some shelter from wind. The seeds need a warm soil temperature before they will germinate so should not be sown outside before the end of April.

Uses

Fennel has always been closely associated with fish, rather than with meat, but this may simply be that it grows well naturally near the sea. There are many records of the Elizabethans using the herb with fish but whether it was because they really appreciated the taste of fennel or merely because they preferred it to that of stale fish is debatable. The aniseed taste is an acquired one. Pliny used the herb medicinally to cure more than twenty ailments.

Florence fennel, *Foeniculum dulce*, is used as a vegetable both raw and cooked, although its leaves can be used as a herb after the base of the stem has been harvested.

Fennel seeds are used in very much the same way as dill.

Garlic
Allium sativum

This bulb originated somewhere in Asia. It was much used for food as well as medicine and was distributed by nomads through the Middle East to the Mediterranean. There is a record that it was highly valued at the time the pyramids were being built. Pliny was enthusiastic about its curative properties. These can be attributed to the sulphur contained in the bulb. During the First World War tons of garlic were used very effectively as a disinfectant.

Today garlic is primarily regarded as an invaluable aid to good cuisine. Unfortunately it does not appreciate the cold damp climate north of the 65° isotherm. The ropes of enormous garlic bulbs seen in Provence can be forgotten but satisfaction can be gained by achieving a diminutive replica in this climate.

A garlic bulb consists of several cloves. These can be planted individually in rich moisture-retentive soil in March. During the growing season garlic requires both unlimited sun and sufficient moisture. When the leaves turn yellow, the single clove should have made a small collective bulb. These bulbs must be dried very carefully, out of the sun, to avoid the drying up of the essential oils. If any moisture is left the bulb will become mouldy.

Garlic

Uses

The frequency with which garlic is used in the kitchen is a matter of taste. It improves anything suitable with which it is put provided, and only provided, not too much is used at any one time. It has such a strong smell and taste that too much can absolutely ruin the desired effect. For this reason recipes often advocate crushing or pounding the clove and this can be done by using the flat blade of a knife. Less garlic is then left behind and wasted than by using a pestle and mortar.

Horseradish
Cochlearia armoracia

Many people rather sensibly do not consider this as a herb. It was not mentioned by the Romans and was probably only introduced to Britain during the Middle Ages. Since that time it has escaped from cultivation and has become naturalised or wild. The plant has large spoon-shaped leaves with wavy edges, *cochlear* meaning spoon. The white flower spikes, similar to those of any brassica, shoot up to 90 cm (3 ft), but in this country do not readily set seed. The persistence of the plant is due to the fact that any small piece of the tap root left in the ground will produce a new plant. Once growing in any area the plant is virtually ineradicable. This is another herb to grow in someone else's garden.

Uses

The roots of this coarse plant are very pungent and hot because they contain mustard oil. They were undoubtedly invaluable in Elizabethan times for completely masking the taste of bad meat. They are still used today by anyone preferring a hot peppery sensation to the natural taste of whatever it is they are eating.

Hyssop
Hyssopus officinalis

Hyssop is a neat, evergreen, spiky shrublet of about 30-45 cm (1-1½ ft), and is quite hardy. It likes the sun and prefers a sandy soil to a heavy one. Because it stands clipping, it was much used as an edging in formal gardens. There was the added advantage that bees liked the deep blue flowers in July and August. Some forms have white or pink flowers but the blue are prettier and more usual.

As the leaves have quite a strong flavour, one plant is sufficient for culinary purposes but if more are needed for decoration, cuttings are easy to take. Shoots with a heel can be pulled off either in the spring or after the plant has finished flowering. They will root in a sandy potting compost. When rooted they can replace the original plant which becomes woody after four to five years.

Uses

The chopped leaves are good with salads, meats, stews or sausages. Like sage, it helps the digestion of fat meats. In America, apricot and peach pies have a few chopped leaves included and some leaves are sometimes added to fruit salads. Herb tea made from fresh leaves is thought to cure both rheumatism and phlegmy colds. There is no need to dry hyssop as it remains evergreen throughout the year.

Lovage
Levisticum officinalis
This used to be called *Ligusticum*, which was thought to derive from Liguria in Italy where it grew in abundance. It originates from the Mediterranean area and is not a native of Britain although it does now occur infrequently in the wild. The English name probably has some connection with the fact that at one time it was hopefully used as a love potion.

This is another giant member of the *Umbelliferae* reaching 2·5 m (8 ft) on ordinary soil. Its leaves look and smell like celery. It used to be commonly grown in Elizabethan times but is not so frequently planted today, perhaps because celery is now more readily available. But where celery is not grown, lovage is still particularly useful. Over a period of up to four years, a plant will slowly increase in girth and if allowed to flower, will spread seedlings around the area. If it does not do this, a 5-cm (2-in) slice of root with a shoot can be cut off in early spring just as growth starts.

Unless lovage is wanted as a vegetable, one plant is enough. It is therefore a good idea to prevent the plant from flowering, unless of course the seeds are needed.

Uses

The leaves have a yeasty flavour and make a broth rather than a tea when infused with boiling water. Both the young stalks and the leaves are excellent in soups and stews. The stalks can be blanched and eaten raw like celery. The leaves can impart a flavour if rubbed around a salad bowl or rubbed over poultry or meat before cooking. On the continent the seeds are put in bread and cakes or put on the top of cheese flavoured biscuits. In America seeds used to be chewed, whether medicinally or for pleasure is not clear.

Marjorams
Clown: Indeed sir, she was the sweet marjoram of the salad, or rather, the herb of grace.
Lafeu: They are not salad-herbs, you knave, they are nose herbs. (All's Well That Ends Well Act IV Sc. 5)
From earlier records than this it was

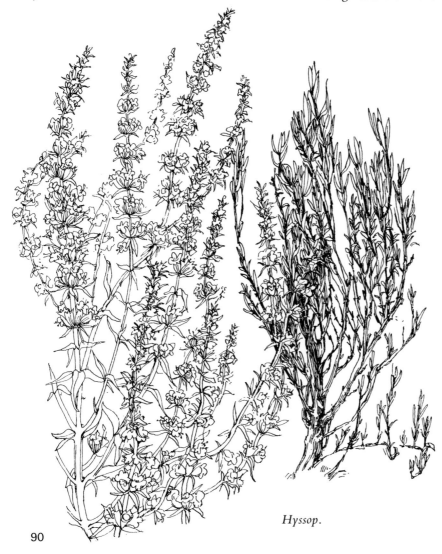

Hyssop.

90

clear that marjorams were multi-purpose herbs, sometimes used for nosegays and for scenting linen, sometimes to relieve colds or toothache, and sometimes for flavouring meat. The three forms all have magenta-pink clusters of flowers but otherwise they are quite different from each other.

The only one native to Britain is the oregano or wild marjoram and this is by far the easiest to cultivate. The sweet marjoram is more subtle in taste but as it is a native of Western Asia and North Africa, it has to be treated as a half-hardy annual in northern Europe and is more troublesome to grow.

Wild marjoram
Origanum vulgare
Being a member of the *Labiatae*, this 70-cm (2½-ft) wild flower has square stems and opposite leaves. Although it grows anywhere it prefers a chalky soil. After two years the plant can be divided in spring if more plants are wanted. The flowers are pretty but if it is much used in the kitchen it is better to cut off the flower spikes in good time. More decorative and equally good for cooking is the golden form, *Origanum vulgare aureum*. Being golden, the leaves can be scorched if the sun is too hot.

Pot marjoram
Origanum onites
This is similar to the wild form but

Marjoram.

the leaves are smaller and the plant sprawls and layers itself. Flower stems are thrown up from mounds of leaves. It came originally from the eastern Mediterranean so it needs a little more care and protection than the wild form. Cuttings can be made if required from short shoots pulled off in late July or August.

Sweet marjoram
Origanum majorana
This species is meant to be the best for culinary purposes but, as it has to be sown each year and the seeds are quite tricky to germinate and nurture through the seedling stage, it saves time and trouble to use one of the other two forms. It is sometimes called knotted marjoram as the clusters of flowers occur at intervals up the stem. It is this particular form that is used in Italy to flavour the many types of pizzas made there.

Uses
In general this herb is better used raw or dried rather than being cooked in stock or stews. The fresh leaves can be chopped on to salads, omelettes, fish or any kind of meat. The leaves are frequently incorporated into sausages and could be used in meat loaf or mince. A herb tea of mixed lemon balm and marjoram is reputed to be a relief for headaches.

Mints
Mentha
There are four mints native to Britain. There is *Mentha aquatica*, the water mint, *Mentha pulegium*, the little pennyroyal, *Mentha rotundifolia*, the round-leaved apple mint and the non-aromatic corn mint. These four have hybridised with other mints so the nomenclature of this genus is complicated and muddled.

All the mints are hardy and prefer to grow in rich, moisture-retentive soil in the shade. The better the soil the better they will grow and the more invasive their creeping underground roots will be. They will soon

smother any smaller herbs grown near them and for this reason they are either grown on their own or various methods are used to contain their roots (see Cultivation).

Of the many species and forms of mint, only those most generally used have been selected. With all of them it is the young leaves that are used and the flowering stem is pinched out in good time.

Bowles Mint
Mentha × villosa nm alopecuroides
The × signifies that this is a hybrid and the *nm* stands for nothomorph, which means a form that has become almost a species in its own right instead of being just a variety. This particular mint was used by a well known gardener E. A. Bowles (1865-1954) who maintained that the taste of this woolly-leafed mint was better than that of the traditional spearmint.

It is a rampant grower but can stand drier conditions than other mints and is not so susceptible to rust disease. It is never used commercially because the leaves wilt quickly. It grows about 90 cm (3 ft) tall but the height varies with the type of soil.

Eau de Cologne mint
Mentha × piperita nm citrata
Once anyone has possessed this purple-leafed mint they will never want to be without it. Not only is it decorative but it is easy to grow. It is only 50 cm (20 in) high and has a lovely scent. It can be used raw and chopped on salads or with a little tarragon vinegar as mint sauce. Infused it makes an unusual mint tea.

Pennyroyal
Mentha pulegium
This is the smallest of the mints. It is not easily recognised as one because of its small leaves and carpeting nature. It occurs in the wild in wet sandy places in the south of Britain but rarely in the north. It is sometimes used instead of grass as it only has to be mown twice a year. But its

chief use is as a neat edging or in a window box when herbs have to be grown indoors.

Peppermint
Mentha × piperita
This is a hybrid of our native watermint and the well-known garden spearmint. It had no name until John Ray called it peppermint around 1700. It was this and the black form that were grown commercially during the 18th century for the distillation of peppermint. This was originally more for medicinal than culinary purposes. This mint, as well as the eau de Cologne mint already mentioned and the ginger mint, can be distinguished from others by the fact that their leaves are stalked. The peppermints, whether white or black, grow to about 75 cm (2½ ft).

Roundleaved or apple mint
Mentha suaveolens
These leaves have a taste of apple but they are not considered to have as much flavour as Bowles' mint which is a hybrid of it. The leaves grow close to the stem without a stalk. There is a variegated variety called pineapple mint, which is perhaps more often used in flower arrangements than in the kitchen.

Spearmint
Mentha × spicata
This is the usual garden mint and as its name implies, it has sharply pointed leaves which are not at all hairy or felty, as are some of the other forms. If it is to be grown indoors in a pot, it needs to be kept damp all the time and would benefit

Left *Bowles mint*; centre *pennyroyal*; right *spearmint*.

from an occasional mist spray.

Some of the roots can be laid in a seed tray of peaty compost in late August and will be shooting by mid-October when the mint out in the garden has died down.

Uses

Mint sauce is traditionally used with lamb but it is a pleasant addition to other meats as well. The addition of mint to cheese is well known in Derbyshire but the leaves can also be cut up and added to cream or processed cheese. Although it is usually mentioned as a flavouring for new potatoes, mint can be added to many other vegetables and is particularly good with the pulses.

The fresh leaves are an essential ingredient of the refreshing mint julep but it is probably more often drunk as a tea. If the leaves are infused for more than five to seven minutes the taste can become bitter.

Parsley
Petroselinum crispum

This most useful and beneficial herb is unfortunately only a biennial. It has to be continually resown although it might reseed itself on warm sandy soil. In this case one plant should be left uncut to encourage flower production. Normally the flower stems are snipped off as soon as they are recognisable so that all the energy of the plant goes into making more leaves.

Parsley came originally from Caria in Turkey (whence it derives its former Latin name, *carum petroselinum*). The seeds need a relatively high soil temperature before they can be induced to germinate. This produced an old saying that a kettle of boiling water should be poured along the drill before sowing. In fact this measure was frequently used to kill unwanted weed seeds. Even at 16°C (60°F) parsley is tiresomely difficult to germinate and can take five to eight weeks. For this reason, when sowing parsley outside, it is a good idea to sow alternate rows of radish. The radish

will germinate quickly and protect the parsley not only from being scratched up by sparrows, but also from being trodden on by a forgetful gardener.

A second sowing is usually made in August in a double row that can later be protected by cloches. It is true to say that there can never be too much parsley available. If the soil is rich, one plant will need at least 20 cm (8 in). Once thinned out, the seedlings can be transplanted into pots for friends without a garden or planted as an edging in a moist, shady part of the decorative garden.

Uses

Because of its mild flavour, parsley is used in greater quantities than others herbs. It is beneficial to use it as often as possible as the plant has a high vitamin content. To preserve the vitamins, parsley is used raw whenever possible. Cut the leaves up on to ready-cooked eggs or sauce. It is a pity that parsley is still so often regarded as only an inedible garnish.

Rosemary
Rosmarinus officinalis

Rosmarinus means dew of the sea. The name was given to this evergreen shrub because it grows naturally on the coastal hills all round the Mediterranean. When the pale blue flowers are out in March the sight is unforgettable. It was frequently used in classical times for ritual as well as medicinal purposes. The Greeks believed it stimulated the brain and aided memory, which is probably how it has become an emblem of remembrance. For this last reason it was carried by all mourners at funerals in the 17th century. Because of its strong fragrance it was also carried on other occasions to disguise bad smells and it was often burnt in the sick room to purify the air.

Rosemary will grow in poor soil but must have shelter from north and east winds. It will easily grow to

1·5 m (5 ft). There is an old saying that it symbolises Christ's life on earth and will grow for thirty-three years. In this country it tends to become rather woody before that. It roots very easily from cuttings taken with a heel, in any month after it has flowered. If the surrounding soil is sandy, small seedlings may appear. Only really bad winters may damage it.

Corsican rosemary
Rosmarinus angustifolius

As its name implies, the leaves of this smaller rosemary are narrower. The flowers are a really bright blue instead of the type's washy blue-mauve. The disadvantage is that it is definitely less hardy. Really hard winters have killed the Corsican rosemaries while the others have remained unscathed.

Miss Jessup's upright

This is a fastigiate cultivar that is useful for growing in pots. It also is less hardy than the type.

Uses

Around the Mediterranean, rosemary is still used for eau de Cologne. It is also made into a tisane for medicinal purposes and can be used as a hair rinse. It is a strong herb and gives flavour to a frozen chicken if a sprig is put into the carcass before roasting. Two sprigs spiked into the plastic covering of a processed ham before cooking will also improve the flavour. The leaves are used to flavour wines and cups and some jellies but in every case the liquid is strained. Being evergreen, rosemary can be used all the year round so there is no point in drying it.

Sage
Salvia officinalis

Originally sage was used mainly as a medicinal herb, hence its name which comes from the Latin *salvare*, to save. The second name, *officinalis*, indicates its use in an apothecary's shop. It was evidently highly esteemed: 'Of all the herbes, none is of greater vertue than Sage . . . such is the vertue that if it were possible it would make man immortall' wrote Thomas Coghan in 1584. It was even valued by the Chinese who, during the 17th century, were prepared to barter their own tea with the Dutch in exchange for sage tea.

Sage grows naturally in dry sunny places in southern Europe. Its felty leaves allow it to tolerate near-drought conditions. In northern Europe it prefers protection from north winds. In a good position the plant will grow to about 60 cm (2 ft) and live for three or four years. By then it has usually become a bit woody and leggy and is best replaced. Before this happens cuttings can be taken.

If shoots are pulled off with a heel in late April or May, they can be put into a small trench lined with sand and peat. They will start to shoot when they have rooted and can then be transplanted. There is also another method of producing new plants by partially covering the parent bush with sieved soil in March. Some of the branches thus covered will send out adventitious roots which can be separated from the main plant in June.

There are three decorative sages that could be grown instead of the garden or green sage.

Sage in flower.

Golden sage *Salvia officinalis aurea*
Purple sage *Salvia officinalis purpurescens*
Tricolor *Salvia officinalis tricolor*

They are only slightly less hardy than the type. Their main requirement is good drainage.

Uses
Sage has always been used with rich meats. It contains substances which break down fats and so help their digestion. Culpeper and Gerard both maintained that sage was good for the brain and helped the memory. It was probably not for this reason but for its other properties that peasants in Italy used to eat sage sandwiches.

Chopped sage is used in Derbyshire in the local cheese and as mentioned above, sage tea, either hot or cold, was a popular drink. The fact that sage is evergreen is a great advantage as it be used instead of mint through the winter.

Savories
The fourteen species of savory come from the eastern end of the Mediterranean but only two grow in Britain. They have little thin leaves like thyme or rosemary. Pale whitish-mauve flowers grow in the axils of the leaves and the stem.

Winter savory
Satureia montana
This small 20-30-cm (9-12-in) evergreen shrublet needs a well-drained sunny spot. It will last for several years if cut back in the spring. Only one plant is needed for culinary use but if more are wanted in order to make an edging, cuttings can be taken from May onwards. If they are taken with a small heel from the main stem, they will root fairly easily in a sandy compost. It would be possible to layer side shoots if the soil were open and sandy.

Summer savory
Satureia hortensis
This savory, which is more subtle in flavour, is unfortunately only an annual in Britain and has to be sown every year. The seeds are not meant to be covered with soil so outside they should be sown under a cloche to prevent sparrows breakfasting off them. As they are slow to germinate it is best to sow them under cover, in peat pots. Later these can be sunk into the soil in June without disturbing the roots.

The plant will grow to about 30 cm (1 ft) so it needs to be planted at 15-20-cm (6-9-in) intervals. Whether the slightly more distinctive taste of this summer savory is worth all this trouble is a matter of opinion.

Uses
Savory used to be an essential ingredient of both sausages and meat pies. Today it is chopped over roast meat and ham and can be used in stews and soups. The winter savory is quite strong so only a few leaves are needed. Traditionally it is cut up over cooked broad beans but it can also be put with peas and French beans, cabbage or tomatoes.

Sorrels
Rumex acetosa
These sorrels are related to the dock family and as the name of the wild form implies, are known to have an acid taste. This is due to oxalic acid in the leaves. They like a light soil and are the only herbs to prefer a neutral to acid soil rather than an alkaline one. The seed can be sown in rows in April and the plants thinned to about 30 cm (1 ft) apart. Thereafter the plant can be propagated by dividing the root at the beginning of spring.

French sorrel
Rumex scutatus
This sorrel grows about 60 cm (2 ft) high and has broader shield shaped leaves. It is the better of the two to grow. In France it is much used in a special spring cream soup, the cream modifying the sharp acid taste. It can also be added in moderation to salads or to cooked spinach. John

Evelyn wrote in 1720 that it imparted 'so grateful a quickness to a salad that it should never be left out'.

Sweet Cicely
Myrrhis odorata

This is neither as sweet nor as retiring as its name implies. Cicely is a corruption of the Greek word *sesile* and bears no reference to any gentle maidenly characteristics. This is a giant of the *Umbelliferae* family, growing in two or three years to nearly 2 m (6 ft). In the meantime, it seeds itself everywhere with invasive abandon. It is a handsome plant to admire, if possible, from next door rather than in the confines of one's own garden.

French tarragon.

Uses

The leaves help to reduce the tartness of cooked fruit. This is useful for diabetics as the normal amount of sugar required can be almost halved. It has a taste of aniseed, which may be recognised in Chartreuse. Sweet cicely can be used to flavour any fruit drink, alcoholic or non-alcoholic.

Tarragons

Originally tarragon was given its name because it cured the bites of dragons and other poisonous creatures. It grows naturally, mainly along rivers in eastern Europe and Russia and the so-called French tarragon is probably a selected form of the wild one, improved by cultivation over the centuries.

French tarragon
Artemisia dracunculus

This is a moderately hardy perennial growing easily and splendidly to 60–80 cm (2–3 ft) in a sheltered, well-drained position with shade. It appreciates some moisture-retentive material in the soil during summer as the leaves can not withstand drought. However, the roots dislike wet conditions through the winter. For this reason, in areas of high rainfall, a raised pane of glass is often put over the roots. In other more southerly places the crown is covered with a mulch of bracken or leaves for winter protection.

The leaves are a linear shape and grow alternately from the stem. The flowers at the tip of the shoots are inconspicuous and do not even set seed. Fortunately the plant can be increased easily by pulling away pieces of root in early spring, just as the plant begins to shoot. These can replace the parent plant after three to four years.

It is a good idea to move tarragon around the garden to discover where it grows best. Its season can be prolonged if a few roots, whose shoots have been cut back, are potted up in August and taken in under cover before the first frost.

Russian tarragon
Artemisia dracunculoides

This is a taller plant growing up to 1·5 m (5 ft). Although hardier than the French form, it is a coarser edition and has not the same good flavour so is not worth growing. Sometimes it is grown by mistake.

Uses

If basil is the prince or king of herbs, tarragon is the queen. Once grown and used, no one would willingly be without it. Its flavour is best preserved by using the leaves raw whenever possible, whether on a salad, on potatoes, in tomato juice or on eggs. Tarragon vinegar is made by steeping two or three shoots in a bottle of wine vinegar and not using it for at least two weeks.

Tarragon can be cut up into melted butter or beaten into ordinary butter before spreading on biscuits. Cooked, the leaves are good in a white sauce, added to soup or put into a chicken before roasting. Too much of the cooked herb has an unpleasant taste.

Thymes

There are sixty species of this small member of the *Labiatae*, growing mainly around the Mediterranean. There are also several sub-species as thymes hybridise easily. The Romans may have introduced *Thymus vulgaris* to Britain and then at some time it made a hybrid with one of our native thymes, *Thymus pulegioides*, to give the lemon-scented thyme.

There were two other thymes native to Britain of which *Thymus serpyllum* is one. *Thymus barona* is the vernacular name given to a thyme which originated in Corsica. As well as those given here there are at least thirty decorative forms which can be used for flavouring. But *Thymus vulgaris* is the one preferred by cooks.

Garden thyme
Thymus vulgaris

This herb grows naturally on the dry, stony hills around the Mediterranean. Farther north it needs to be

Thyme amongst paving stones.

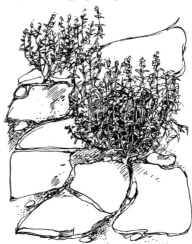

grown in a hot, well-drained situation. The tough little evergreen leaves can withstand drought. No fertiliser is necessary but additional chalk in acid soils would be appreciated.

This thyme will make an evergreen mound about 20 cm (8 in) high. The shoots are best cut back to not less than 2 cm (1 in) from the base when needed for cooking or for drying. If sheared too severely, the old wood will not regenerate new shoots. As usual, the best time to harvest for drying is before the flowers form. A second cut could be made in August as long as enough time is left for the plant to refurbish itself for the winter. The fresh sprigs are more useful through the winter than the dried leaves. When enough plants have been produced from the first, original plant there will be no need to dry thyme as the herb is evergreen.

There are two ways of propagating thyme. Cuttings can be taken in May and will root in sandy compost. Even easier is the alternative method of layering. The lower,

Another view of the beautiful herb garden at the Old Rectory, Ightham, in full flower.

longer shoots can be buried in the soil, using a stone to keep them fixed. If the surrounding soil happens to be heavy clay it is best to add a sprinkling of sandy compost as this will encourage the shoot to root. Layering can be done from the end of March onwards and the shoot can be severed from the parent plant when it has made sufficient roots. If the thyme is growing in light sandy soil it will seed itself if allowed to flower.

The life of a plant is only about four years by which time it tends to become woody and straggling and will need replacing. Thymes are perfectly hardy and are more likely to be killed by waterlogged roots than by being frozen.

Lemon scented thyme
Thymus × citriodorus
This makes a slightly less compact bush and can grow to about 30 cm (1 ft). It is also a little less hardy than the garden thyme.

Caraway thyme
Thymus herba-barona
One theory about the origin of this odd name is that it came from being used with a baron of beef. This is a low sprawler and its shoots root

easily when only slightly covered with soil. This, with other low mat-forming thymes, grows well in between stone slabs.

Wild thyme
Thymus serpyllum
There are numerous cultivars of this wild thyme all of which make splendid aromatic mats. They root as they spread, so can be increased easily.

Uses
Thyme has always had an important medicinal role. It contains thymol which is still used in toothpaste and as a disinfectant. It was also thought to contain a substance that stimulated the appetite and was recommended for inclusion in soups. It is invariably included in most bouquets. It is an excellent addition when cooking liver as it can mask the taste for those who dislike it.

Thyme is a strong herb so when cut up raw on salads, it should be used with care. In stuffing, fritters or savoury pancakes and stews, thyme is almost an essential ingredient.

A thyme tisane with honey is often used to cure a cough. Thyme has so many possible uses that it is really fortunate that it is evergreen and can be used all the year round.

Salads, Unusual Vegetables and Crops Under Glass

How to improve your salad days

Salads

Salads have always played an important part in our diet. At one time they only formed part of a meal but today they can frequently form the main dish and they can include a wide variety of ingredients.

The lettuce is probably the conventional idea of the basis of a salad and, indeed, the lettuce as a food for man has a very ancient history. There is written evidence that lettuce was served to the kings of Persia more than five hundred years before the birth of Christ and both the Greeks and the Romans valued it highly for its medicinal virtues. They grew many varieties. By the Middle Ages the lettuce as a popular salad mainstay had spread to Northern and Western Europe. Columbus is said to have introduced it into North America.

But although the lettuce reigned supreme for many centuries as the basis for salads, all sorts of grated raw vegetables are now included. Nuts are frequently used as well and tomatoes, cucumbers, radishes and spring onions—the latter providing a certain tang and relish—all go into the contemporary salad. Mustard and cress provide an excellent garnish.

Endive, corn salad, Chinese cabbage and chicory can all be used as lettuce substitutes when lettuce is not available. They can also, of course, be used with lettuce.

Lettuce

A lettuce will only grow well and be sweet in flavour if it is grown quickly in a deep moist soil. Thorough cultivation during the winter and the incorporation of humus is good preparation for spring sowing. If the soil is acid, it should be limed during the winter months. Humus can take the form of garden compost, spent hops or old mushroom bed manure. These should be used in preference to peat, which can increase the acidity of the soil.

A lettuce normally takes about

six weeks from the date of sowing to reach maturity. Slow growth combined with lack of good cultivation result in tough, bitter-tasting leaves. One of the most difficult things to achieve is continuity of succession throughout the summer months. Only a very small amount of seed should be sown at regular intervals of two to three weeks. Sowing two different types of seed at once will help the succession because each variety will mature at a different time from the other.

Webbs Wonderful lettuce.

Times for outdoor sowing are always variable as so much depends on weather and soil conditions but, hopefully, seed should be in by the end of March. Sow 1 cm ($\frac{1}{2}$ in) deep in drills of 30 cm (1 ft) apart. When the seedlings are large enough, thin them out to 22-24·5 cm (9-10 in) apart, according to variety. The thinnings can be planted out and because of the check in growth from transplanting, they will mature later

than those in the seed bed. This again will help to keep up a continuous supply. Hoe regularly, not only to keep down the weeds, but also to produce a fine surface tilth that will act as a mulch to prevent evaporation of moisture from the soil surface.

Lettuces tend to be soft in growth if given excess artificial fertiliser. They will not develop a solid heart and will be more prone to disease. Transplanting should be done in moist conditions and sulphate of

potash raked in at.60 g (2 oz) per 1 m² (1 sq yd). The last sowing of lettuce of a suitable variety can be made in late August to stand the winter and give the first outdoor cutting in spring.

Varieties

There are two types of lettuce, the cabbage or round-headed and the cos. The cabbage lettuce falls into two groups, with either smooth, soft leaves or crisp, curled leaves. The cos lettuce, which is tall and

Little Gem lettuce.

pointed and crisp in texture, is excellent in flavour but only suitable for outdoor cultivation. In between these two distinct types there are varieties which have some of the characteristics of each.

Cabbage lettuce

All the Year Round This is an old variety which is still popular. It is very reliable and easy to manage. It makes a beautiful, solid heart of

99

good flavour and is slow to bolt.

Avon Defiance A lettuce making a good heart. It is resistant to disease and stands well.

Buttercrunch This lettuce is very crisp and sweet.

Webbs Wonderful One of the most popular of all lettuces, chosen for its outstanding crispness which compensates for a certain lack of flavour. It is resistant both to disease and bolting.

Cos lettuce

Paris White A self-folding variety.

Little Gem This is an ideal lettuce for a small garden. It falls mid-way between cos and cabbage. The solid little heart has all the crispness and sweetness of the cos and it is perhaps the best-flavoured of all lettuces.

Salad Bowl This is not a hearting variety, but makes a large rosette of crisp, curled leaves which can be picked when required. This is ideal for a person living alone or a small garden.

Pests and diseases

Lettuces are not so prone to attack outdoors as they are under glass. It is only in wet summers or very humid conditions that trouble may occur.

Botrytis A grey mould which appears on the leaves. Dust with captan.

Millipedes These attack the root, causing the plant to wilt and eventually die. Treat the soil with gamma-HCH at the rate recommended by the manufacturer.

Chicory

Although chicory comes under the heading of unusual vegetables and is generally grown to force under glass, one variety must be mentioned in this section. Sugar Loaf will produce delicious hearts during the summer and fill the need left by any gap in the succession of lettuce. Seed is sown in late April in drills 2 cm (1 in) deep and rows 30 cm (1 ft) apart. For salad it is sown earlier than for forcing. This variety makes

Corn salad.

what looks like a large, domed cos lettuce. It is the heart, which has been blanched by the complete protection of the outer leaves, that makes such crisp and succulent eating with its own distinctive flavour.

Chinese cabbage

The Chinese cabbage looks like a large cos lettuce. It can be eaten as a salad or cooked as a cabbage. Its chief value for salad is during the autumn months. Seed is not sown until mid-July. Like the lettuce, it needs plenty of humus in the soil and plants should be thinned to stand 24 cm (10 in) apart in the rows.

Varieties

Nagaoka.

Corn salad

This is a green salad plant often called Lamb's lettuce. It is far more popular on the Continent than it is in Britain. It has dwindled in popularity with the increased growing of

lettuce under protected cultivation during the winter months. Nevertheless, for those who possess neither greenhouse, frame nor cloche, it makes an excellent late winter or early spring salad. A sunny position and a well-drained soil are its chief requirements. It is very hardy and will stand a severe winter without damage.

The seed is sown in mid-August in rows 24 cm (10 in) apart. Subsequent care should consist of regular hoeing. Thin out the seedlings when small to 15 cm (6 in) apart. Another sowing may be made in early September to provide a very useful salad in a late, cold spring.

Cucumber

The outdoor cucumber, better known as the ridge cucumber, is as delicious as any grown in the greenhouse, when picked young. It must have a sunny position protected

Endive.

from the wind. Good drainage is also a necessity. A small bed of half well-rotted manure and half soil can be prepared. This must be sufficiently light for surplus moisture to drain away, while there is enough humus to retain moisture which will help to swell the fruit.

The plants can be sown and grown on in the greenhouse, but as they dislike being moved, seed can be sown directly in the bed from the middle to the end of May. When the plant is growing well and has formed three to four leaves, the growing point is pinched out. This will encourage the growth of the lateral shoots which will bear the crop. Cucumbers need to grow rapidly, so they should have plenty of water during dry spells. They will also benefit from a mulch of lawn mowings or other organic material. Go over the bed regularly so that all fruits are picked whilst young and

tender. Only by regular picking will a constant supply be maintained into late summer.

Varieties
Burpee F1 Hybrid One of the new smooth-skinned hybrids:
Stockwood Ridge A prolific variety and extremely hardy.

Dandelion
The dandelion, once so esteemed for the piquancy of flavour it brought to a salad, has fallen from favour in cultivation. This is probably because of its bad reputation as a weed. Seed is sown in April and improved strains of the native dandelion can be obtained. It will grow in sun or shade and the seedlings are thinned to 15 cm (6 in) apart. By the following spring, good strong clumps will have been established. If flower pots are inverted over three or four at a time they will produce blanched leaves that will give a new and interesting flavour to a salad. It is im-

portant that the drainage holes in the pots used for blanching are stopped with a twist of paper, as any light admitted will detract from the blanching and cause bitterness. Stop picking the leaves by mid-June to enable the plants to make new growth.

Endive
It is often said that the endive possesses a better flavour than the lettuce. It is a salad plant particularly suitable for autumn and early winter use at a time of year when lettuce flavour tends to become insipid. It likes deep, moist soil, preferably enriched with decayed farmyard manure. If this is not available, garden compost or old mushroom manure can be used, whichever is most readily available. Endive runs to seed easily unless it has plenty of moisture at the root and for the same reason it does not transplant satisfactorily. The seed is sown in July in rows 37 cm (15 in) apart. The plants are thinned to 30 cm (1 ft) apart in the rows. It makes a lot of growth during late summer and therefore needs space to develop.

When the plants are fully grown, blanching can then begin. This should be done in dry weather by tying raffia round the top, pulling the outer leaves in to blanch the heart. Later in the autumn either pots or boxes can be placed over the crop or they can be lifted and brought into the greenhouse for blanching (see Crops under glass).

Variety
Batavian White.

Mustard and cress
Mustard and cress respond better to greenhouse or frame cultivation, nevertheless, they can be grown successfully outside if certain points are observed. Choose a shady site and prepare a very fine seed bed. This should be well watered and then allowed to drain before sowing. Seed is broadcast at the rate of 30 g (1 oz) per 1 m² (1 sq yd). The cress,

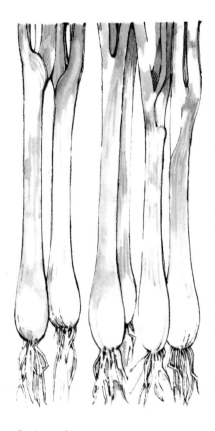

Spring onions.

which is slower to germinate, should be sown four days before the mustard. The seed is not covered, but firmed with a piece of board to prevent the crop being gritty when cut for use. Protection from birds and shading should be provided until growth has begun. It must be quick or the flavour will be too strong.

Spring onions

The spring onion plays a very important part in a salad. To have onions ready for use in April and May, sow seed in late September. Choose a sheltered situation and sow fairly thickly in drills not more than 1 cm ($\frac{1}{2}$ in) deep and 20 cm (8 in) apart. Keep the rows clear of weeds. These onions will stand the winter without thinning and start by pulling the largest roots as they develop in the spring. Another sowing can be made in March or April to give a further supply for June and July. If an exceptionally severe win-

ter is encountered, the autumn-sown onions can be protected by cloches.

Varieties
White Lisbon is a good, reliable variety.

Radish

This is an attractive salad crop, used as an hors d'oeuvre as well as a garnish. The secret of growing radishes, if they are going to be crisp, sweet and succulent, is to grow them

quickly. Slow growth results in pithy roots and hot flavour. They like a good rich soil and a sunny position in the spring. The seed is sown 1 cm ($\frac{1}{2}$ in) deep in drills 22 cm (9 in) apart. If sown thinly, the roots can then be pulled as they develop. Some protection may be needed for the seed against birds.

Although radishes are usually sown in March, it is better to be guided by the weather than a fixed date. Growth will be slower in a cold soil and one gains little by an

early sowing. They make a good catch crop since they mature quickly in twenty to thirty days, and they can be grown on ground prepared for later crops. Alternatively they can be grown between rows of peas or dwarf French beans. Later sowings should have a shadier situation.

Varieties
French Breakfast Long in shape and red and white in colour.
Scarlet Globe A radish that is scarlet in colour and has a round root.

Pests
Turnip fly Dust the ground with derris just after germination.

Winter radish
This is delicious for winter salads and not grown nearly as much as it deserves to be. There are two kinds of winter radish. The Winter Black is like a small round turnip with a black skin and crisp white flesh, but it does not acquire the hot flavour of the spring-sown radish. It is sown at the end of July or beginning of

French Breakfast radishes.

August. To be succulent and crisp it must be grown quickly. The seedlings are thinned to 15 cm (6 in) apart in the rows. They can be pulled as required up to the end of October or beginning of November. They can then be lifted and stored in sand or peat for winter use.

The second variety is China Rose. This resembles a large French Breakfast in colour and shape. The culture is the same as for the black radish.

Tomato

At one time outdoor tomatoes only had a real chance of success in a hot summer. However, in the last decade plant breeders have developed outdoor tomatoes which ripen in July, only a little later than those grown in the greenhouse. Varieties have also been raised that need neither staking nor stopping.

Soil preparation

Tomatoes need a good, deep, well-aerated soil in a sheltered position with plenty of sun. The best method is to prepare a trench during the early months of the year where the tomatoes will subsequently be planted. If only one row is to be planted, take out a trench the length of the row. Remove the soil to a depth of one spit, about 24 cm (9 in), fork the bottom of the trench and incorporate farmyard manure, spent mushroom manure or compost. If obtainable, strawy stable manure helps to aerate the soil. The top soil is then put back into the trench and

Right *Removing side shoots from a tomato plant.*

Left *Pixie—a small heavy-cropping bush tomato which can be grown easily in a pot or window box.*

Below *Planting tomatoes in a growbag with a trowel.*

in the spring a tomato fertiliser can be forked into the top spit.

Planting

Young plants raised in the greenhouse (see Crops under glass) are carefully hardened-off in a frame and planted out at the end of May or early June, depending on the weather. This varies according to the district. In the south planting out can be a week or so earlier than in the more northerly parts of the country. Plants are set out 90 cm (3 ft) apart. There is no economy in planting too closely. Plenty of light and air around the plants will keep them healthy, freer from pests and diseases and will aid ripening.

Cultivation

Water after planting. Any watering done during the life of the plant must be carefully carried out so that soil does not splash up on to the foliage. This can easily cause infection, especially with botrytis. Heavy rain can have the same effect, so

when the plants are well established, mulch with a good layer of lawn mowings or straw. Alternatively, a collar of polythene can be used. This prevents weeds from growing and surface roots need not be disturbed by cultivation. The soil will not be hardened into a pan by watering or rain, so the need for surface cultivation is again obviated.

The taller-growing varieties of tomato need staking and tying at regular intervals. Side shoots, vegetative shoots arising in the joint of leaf and main stem, are removed directly they appear, and the plants should be stopped two leaves beyond the fourth truss. In theory, the bush varieties need no staking, but they often benefit from some support in the form of brushwood. When cropped in the open, pollination is usually effectively carried out by insects, but where staked, a sharp tap on the stakes will achieve the same results.

Feeding

From the time the second truss of fruit has set, supplementary feeding may be necessary. This can be liquid farmyard manure or a proprietary brand specially produced for tomatoes. The leaves have been called the kitchens of the plant. They manufacture the food which is passed on to the growing root, shoots and developing fruit. Thus healthy foliage is necessary for a good crop.

As the first tomatoes begin to colour, their need for food gradually becomes less and the bottom pair of leaves can be removed. This allows for better circulation of air so necessary for ripening, it admits more light to the developing fruit and helps to prevent botrytis. The upper leaves can be removed in turn as the trusses of fruit colour.

Growbags

These have become a popular method of growing tomatoes, especially where space is at a premium. These bags, filled with compost, can be placed on a patio, in a yard, or even on a balcony. Usually three plants go into each bag and then the directions given with the bag are followed for watering and feeding. As all nutrients have to be supplied, it tends to be expensive but the crops are usually good and the grower has the satisfaction of enjoying a freshly picked tomato.

Varieties

Outdoor Girl This is a tall variety that needs side-shooting and staking. It is a heavy cropper of excellent flavour, bearing twelve to fourteen medium-sized tomatoes on each truss. It has a resistance to blight.

Sleaford Abundance This is an F1 hybrid and an outstanding variety in that it ripens before the middle of July in the south. A low-growing plant, it needs no staking or side shooting. It benefits from a collar of black polythene over the soil to prevent weed growth, which also keeps the fruit clean. This variety produces an abundance of small-sized fruit which will continue to ripen even in dull or wet weather.

Pixie F1 Hybrid This is a small bush tomato carrying a heavy crop of fruit. It is quick to mature and will do well in most seasons. It can be grown in a pot or window box and will appeal to gardeners with a limited amount of time and space.

Amateur Another bush variety which needs no stopping, side shooting or staking. It matures somewhat later than Pixie or Sleaford Abundance, mentioned above.

Pests and diseases

The outdoor tomato is not quite so prone to attack as that grown under glass. But it can still be threatened under adverse weather conditions or bad cultivation.

Blight A fungus disease more liable to attack plants in a warm wet summer. Dark brown spots appear on the leaves and stems. Spray with liquid copper fungicide or dust with captan three times, at fourteen day intervals, starting in early June.

Blotchy ripening This is usually due to unbalanced fertilisers.

Botrytis Brownish tissues appear on the fruit which prevent it from developing. Spray with captan.

Split fruits These can occur in outdoor tomatoes where a dry spell is followed by heavy rain.

Unusual vegetables

There are many unusual vegetables that deserve to be more widely grown. Many of them, such as celeriac, salsify, scorzonera and Hamburg parsley are in season in the winter when vegetables can be in short supply. Not only as a vegetable, but as a dish in their own right served with a sauce, they are delicious. To grow vegetables just because they are unusual does not necessarily mean they have merit. Vegetables such as courgettes, which were not widely grown at one time, have now become so popular that they have moved out of this category. Calabrese has done the same.

Vegetables imported from the Continent have introduced us to a wider range in Britain and travel abroad has also had its influence. The popularity of chicory, sweet peppers and aubergines are good examples and with recent developments in plant breeding, it has become much easier to grow many of them in the shorter season this country provides. The following are some of the more interesting vegetables worth growing.

Globe artichoke

Grown far more widely in France than in England, the globe artichoke is a culinary delicacy. A member of the thistle family, it is about 90 cm (3 ft) tall and a very handsome plant. It is grown for the succulent scales of the young flower heads which are ready for picking when half-grown and still closed. To get really fine heads the artichoke needs a deep,

rich soil, well drained and in a sunny position, sheltered from wind.

It is very averse to damp, nevertheless, it must be well manured to produce a good crop. It needs copious water in the summer months, hence the need for good drainage. It is wise to give some protection during the winter months. Straw, fallen leaves or bracken, or if none of these are available, chopped up Michaelmas daisy tops, will serve excellently. Globe artichokes should be propagated regularly as plants do not give such good heads after the fourth or fifth year.

Propagation

Initial propagation can be by seed, but once roots are established, subsequent propagation is by means of suckers. Seeds can be sown in spring in the open ground as soon as the danger of frost is over. Alternatively, and the best method where a greenhouse is available, is to sow the seed singly in 7·5-cm (3-in) pots under glass in March.

Once grown on and hardened off, they can be planted out at the end of May. The distance between clumps should be 90 cm (3 ft), but they need not necessarily be planted in a row. Where only two or three clumps are grown and space for vegetables is limited, these handsome plants can be integrated into a shrub or mixed border as long as the site has been well prepared.

If propagation is by suckers, these are removed from the parent plant in October when they are about 15–17 cm (6–7 in) long, with some roots attached. They are best potted up, kept under protection for the winter and planted out in the spring.

Pests and diseases

Artichoke leaf spot A fungus disease nearly always caused by damp. Spray with half-strength Bordeaux

Above *The globe artichoke is a great delicacy and a handsome plant.*
Below *Celeriac is a turnip-rooted celery, delicious cooked or raw.*

mixture before the flower heads begin to form.

Cockchafer The grubs of this beetle sometimes attack the roots. Treat the ground with gamma-HCH.

Celeriac

Celeriac is a turnip-rooted celery which, under good cultivation, makes large roots weighing anything from 908-1,362 g (2-3 lbs). It is very much like the stump of celery in texture. It is delicious cooked as a vegetable, as flavouring for soups and stews or grated raw in salads and growing it does not require the labour that celery involves.

The seed should be sown in early March or April (see Crops under glass). It has a high rate of germination so seed should be sown thinly and seedlings pricked out into boxes when large enough to handle. At the end of May they can be planted out in enriched, deeply cultivated ground.

Celeriac needs plenty of room for development so space the rows 45 cm (18 in) apart with 30 cm (12 in) between the plants. Planting is shallow and the root tends to rest upon the soil as it develops. When hoeing, the soil should be drawn away from the root. Remove all side shoots, allowing only the main stem to develop. During late summer, liquid manure should be given every ten days as the celeriac goes on developing through September and October.

In the south, celeriac can often be left in the ground if given some protection and lifted as required. In colder areas it is wiser to lift early in November and store in moist sand or peat in a cool, dry situation. One or two roots left in the ground will shoot in the spring and the green stems can be used for flavouring.

Varieties

Giant Prague A very hardy variety, developing big roots.

Iram The only variety that retains its whiteness when cooked.

Pests and diseases

Celery fly Eggs are laid on the leaves and the larvae cause blistering. Control with malathion.

Leaf spot A fungus disease which attacks the leaves, causing brown spots which increase rapidly causing the whole leaf to die. Control with Bordeaux mixture or liquid copper fungicide.

Chinese cabbage

This is a dual purpose vegetable. It can be cooked as cabbage, its texture being rather like that of a savoy, while the heart can be used for salad. It is best sown in mid-July to produce heads for autumn and winter use. It requires the same cultural treatment as lettuce. The seed should be sown in drills 37 cm (15 in) apart and the seedlings thinned to 24 cm (10 in) apart.

Varieties

Nagaoka FI Hybrid produces both crisp heart and leaves.

Swiss and ruby chard

This vegetable is a member of the beet family and the foliage is similar to that of the spinach beet. It has large green leaves with a thick white or red fleshy stem and mid-rib. The leaves are cooked as spinach whilst the stem is cooked like asparagus or with a sauce, so it is a good choice for a small garden.

Two sowings can be made, the first in April and the second in July, in drills 2 cm (1 in) deep and rows 30 cm (1 ft) apart. The seedlings are thinned to 24 cm (10 in) apart in the rows. A good, rich soil is necessary and it does well if grown in soil manured for a previous crop. It will benefit from an occasional watering of weak liquid manure. Stems are always pulled, never cut.

Nagaoka—a Chinese cabbage producing a crisp heart and leaves, ideal for salads and for cooking.

Varieties
Fordhook Giant and Vintage Green are among the best varieties. **Ruby Chard** is very decorative, with scarlet stems.

Chicory

Chicory is grown chiefly for forcing and is delicious both cooked and as a salad. It requires a deep soil with plenty of humus. Seed is sown in early June in rows 37 cm (15 in) apart. The young plants are thinned 22 cm (9 in) apart in the rows. These plants are deep-rooting and require plenty of moisture at all stages otherwise they tend to run to seed. The foliage dies back in late October or early November and the roots are then lifted for forcing (see Crops under glass).

Variety
Giant Witloof.

Finocchio or florentine fennel

This vegetable is gaining in popularity although the aniseed flavour can be an acquired taste. Unlike the herb fennel, it is grown for the swollen base of the stem which can be used raw in salads or cooked.

It is an annual plant needing plenty of moisture combined with a place in the sun. Seed is sown in April or May in rows 30 cm (12 in) apart, thinning seedlings to 22 cm (9 in) apart. When the fleshy stems start swelling they should have plenty of water and the soil earthed up around the base of the plant to assist in blanching.

Hamburg parsley

This is a root vegetable, white in colour and resembling a carrot in shape. Although the tops can be used in place of fresh parsley, it is grown for its root. This has a parsley flavour and can be used grated in salads or

Kohl rabi is a cross between a turnip and a cabbage and a good alternative to the maincrop turnip.

for flavouring soups and stews. It can also be cooked as a vegetable with a sauce. Like the parsnip, it needs a long period of growth. Seed is sown in March in drills 2 cm (1 in) deep, in rows 30 cm (1 ft) apart. The seedlings are then thinned to 20 cm (8 in) apart. The roots can be lifted and stored in moist sand or peat at the end of October or beginning of November. The Hamburg parsley is one of the few root vegetables where seedlings can be transplanted successfully.

Kohl rabi

The kohl rabi is a cross between a turnip and a cabbage and probably does better than the turnip on a light soil. The kohl rabi has the advantage over the turnip in that it will withstand drought and not be harmed by frost. It is, in fact, a good alternative to the maincrop turnip.

Sowings are made in late March or early April for a summer supply, in drills 1 cm (¾ in) deep with 30 cm

(1 ft) between the rows, thinning to 15 cm (6 in) apart. It is the late summer sowing, made in July to give roots for the winter, that is of most value. It can be used for soups, stews, as a vegetable or cooked and sliced cold for salads.

Variety
Early White Vienna A good variety, resistant to pests and diseases.

Sugar Pea

The sugar pea is one of those vegetables ideally suited to the small garden and the housewife with little time at her disposal. It is grown in the same way as the ordinary pea, but it only reaches some 30 cm (1 ft) in height and needs no staking. The first sowing outdoors is in March, in drills 2 cm (1½ in) deep, 45 cm (18 in) apart. Later sowings can be made for a succession. The pod is eaten whole and is delicious, providing it is picked before the peas inside begin to swell and then cooked almost

immediately. There is a tall variety called *mange-tout*, which reaches a height of 1·5 m (5 ft) and is widely grown in France but the smaller variety is much more convenient for the modern garden.

Variety
Dwarf Sweet Green.

Peppers

The capsicum, or sweet pepper, has become very popular for use in salads and cooking. Though at one time it could only be grown successfully in a greenhouse, the new F1 hybrids are far hardier and can be grown to ripen outdoors. The culture of the pepper is very much like that of the tomato. Seed is sown under glass in March at 16°C (60°F) (see Crops under glass).

Once they have been hardened off, they can be planted out in early June. The situation should be as warm and sheltered as possible. Against a south wall of a house is ideal. The border should be well prepared and compost or rotted manure dug in.

The plants are put out at 45 cm (18 in) apart. When they are about 30 cm (1 ft) high, pinch out the growing point to encourage side growths. Give a daily syringe to help flowers to set their fruits. Allow only four or five fruits per plant. They will appreciate a mulch of lawn mowings and as the fruits form, a watering with liquid manure every ten days will improve their quality. Peppers are picked green and then turn red.

Varieties
Ace An excellent early-maturing variety.
Canapé An F1 hybrid making vigorous growth. It matures early and bears well. It is a good variety to grow in a short season outdoors.
Early Bountiful A good cropper which ripens early.
Pests and diseases
Botrytis This attacks the stems, leaves and sometimes the fruit, in the form of grey spots. Use captan dust or spray.

Salsify

Salsify makes a welcome change in the winter months. It is commonly known as the vegetable oyster because of its delicate and unusual flavour. It has fleshy roots that fork very easily so it must be grown on very well-cultivated soil with no lumps or stones.

Seed is sown in April to allow for a long period of growth. The drills should be shallow, 2 cm ($\frac{3}{4}$ in) in depth with rows 30 cm (1 ft) apart. The seedlings are then thinned to 20 cm (8 in) apart in the rows. From then on hoe regularly and water in dry weather. The roots can be left in the ground during the winter to be lifted as required. Take great care not to damage the roots in any way as they bleed easily. If they are cut or broken a milky substance exudes from the stem and the distinctive flavour of the root is lost when cooked. For the same reason, never peel the roots but scrape immediately before cooking.

Variety
Sandwich Island Mammoth.

Scorzonera

The cultivation of scorzonera is the same as for salsify. The long, thin roots need only be thinned to 15 cm (6 in) apart. The roots can be lifted for use in November or, like salsify, they can be left in the ground to be used as required.

Peppers.

Sea kale

This vegetable has waned in popularity since imports of chicory have increased. It is only grown in private gardens now. The forced, tender, crisp stems can be eaten either raw or cooked, and it is a very welcome addition to the winter menu.

Initial stock can be obtained by raising plants from seed sown in March in drills 2 cm (1 in) deep, 30 cm (1 ft) apart. The seedlings are then thinned to 15 cm (6 in) apart in the rows. These plants will become forcing crowns in two years from seed. From then on propagation is by thongs or root cuttings. These are side pieces of roots cut away from the main crown when it is lifted in the autumn for forcing. These cuttings are trimmed to about 12 cm (5 in) long and stored in sand or peat for the winter to be planted out in March.

The crowns are put out 45 cm (18 in) apart with 60 cm (2 ft) between the rows. Normally only a small quantity is grown. Sea kale can be forced *in situ* by covering with fallen leaves and large pots. Alternatively, the crowns can be lifted in October, the foliage cut back and forced under glass (see Crops under glass).

Sweet corn

This crop always benefits from a really hot summer, but thanks to the work of plant breeders, varieties have been developed that enable the grower to harvest a crop within the limits of an English summer. Sweet corn, to be grown successfully, must on no account receive any checks during growth and as it is not hardy, it must have heat for successful germination.

Seed is sown singly in 7·5-cm (3-in) pots in mid-April (see Crops under glass) and planted out in its permanent position at the end of May or beginning of June. The plants should be tapped out of the pots without disturbing the ball of the roots. Alternatively, they can be sown at the same time out of doors under cloches, but the best crop is nearly always achieved from those sown in pots.

Deep cultivation with plenty of humus in the soil is necessary and the plants should be put out in a rectangular block, never as one long row. The pollen is extremely fine and easily blown away on the wind so to ensure good pollination and a full cob, the seedlings should be planted 30 cm (1 ft) apart each way. Once established, mulch with lawn mowings or compost. As they

Right Scorzonera has a long, thin root and is cultivated like salsify. Below Sweet corn is sown in pots and planted out in May or June.

grow, staking will be necessary. This is made easier by planting in a block because stakes can be put in at each corner and a tie put round to hold the crop as a whole. Cobs are ready if the liquid exuded when they are squeezed is the quality of good rich milk and not watery They should be cut early in the day and stored in the dark until ready for use.

Varieties
John Innes Hybrid is a very popular variety.
North Star does well in cooler conditions.
Early Extra Sweet is, as the name implies, an early-maturing variety of good quality. It has the disadvantage of not responding to cross-pollination, so must be grown on its own.
Aztec is an F1 hybrid, late maturing and does well in a poor summer.

Vegetable spaghetti
The vegetable spaghetti is a variety of the marrow. The seeds are sown under glass in mid-April and the plants are put out on mounds of decayed manure early in June. The culture is the same as for the marrow. When plants are established and growing well, stop each shoot to encourage laterals. The yellow-skinned marrows are cut when quite young and about 25-30 cm (9-12 in) in length. When cooked and opened, the inside flesh is like spaghetti and can be served hot or cold.

Vegetable spaghetti.

Crops under glass
Any form of protected cultivation is an asset to a garden in terms of increasing its production, whether it be a greenhouse, frame or cloche. It enables one to grow crops such as lettuce, carrots and tomatoes to maturity. It also provides a means of raising plants such as cauliflowers, cabbage, broad beans, lettuces and many others to be transplanted to open ground later in the spring, ensuring an earlier crop. One can also raise non-hardy plants such as sweet peppers, sweet corn and tomatoes, which will be hardened off and planted out when the danger of frost is over. It also provides a means of forcing and blanching.

Greenhouses
Where a greenhouse already exists, it can probably be adapted for growing crops, even if it entails using deep boxes or pots. Where a new greenhouse is going to be purchased, there are certain points to remember. The choice of site is important and should preferably be in a sheltered position getting full light and away from overhanging trees. Accessibility to the house is an advantage from the point of view of water supplies and for connecting electricity if required. The legal position regarding planning permission should be checked with the local council before any construction is begun.

There is a wide range of greenhouses on the market and considerable thought is necessary if a wise choice is going to be made. The basic framework materials are generally wood or aluminium. Wood is still the cheapest, but softwoods need regular painting so upkeep is expensive. Hardwoods such as oak, cedar and teak need only a regular brushing with linseed oil and are pleasant to the eye, they retain the heat and are easy when it comes to attaching any fitments.

Light-weight aluminium has become a very popular choice and is strong and durable. It tends to lose heat quickly and there can be a certain amount of drip through condensation. On the other hand it will not harbour pests or diseases as wood does and admits more light.

The house with glass to ground level is excellent for crops being grown to maturity, especially tomatoes. Where a greenhouse for more general use is required, such as raising plants, forcing and blanching, a span house built on a 60-75 cm (2-2½ ft) brick base with a centre path is a good choice. This allows for staging on one side, where seedlings and plants can be grown on and room for a propagator. The space under the staging allows for storage of soil and pots and sacking can be hung down in front of it to make an excellent place for blanching and forcing. The other half of the house can then be used as a border for growing crops such as early lettuce followed by tomatoes. Where a wall is available, especially facing south, a lean-to house can be erected. This will trap more heat than a free-standing building.

Heating and ventilation
Crops under glass are usually grown in what is termed a cool greenhouse. This is one which needs no artificial heat for five to six months of the year and for the remaining months enough heat to maintain a temperature of 4°-7°C (40°-45°F). The heat required is really the minimum amount necessary to overcome dampness in the atmosphere and sudden changes in temperature.

Heating can be by electricity, oil or gas, all of which can be thermostatically controlled. In a cool greenhouse there is the problem of providing the necessary heat for germinating seeds. They require a temperature of 16°-18°C (60°-65°F) in the early part of the year, and this may be supplied by the installation of a heated propagator.

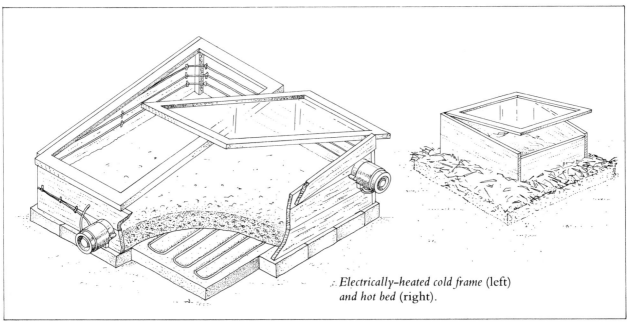

*Electrically-heated cold frame (left)
and hot bed (right).*

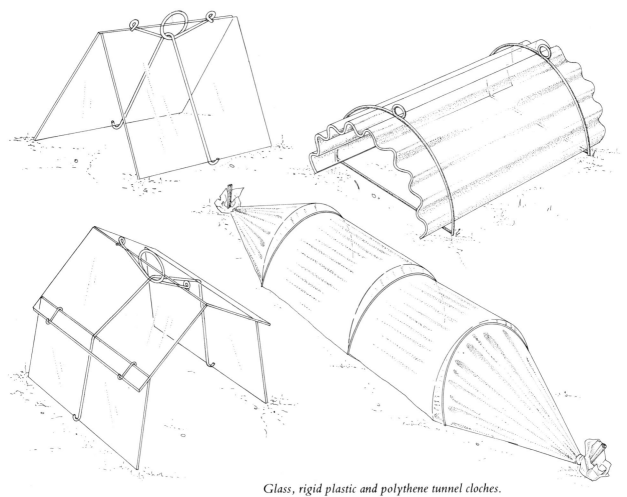

Glass, rigid plastic and polythene tunnel cloches.

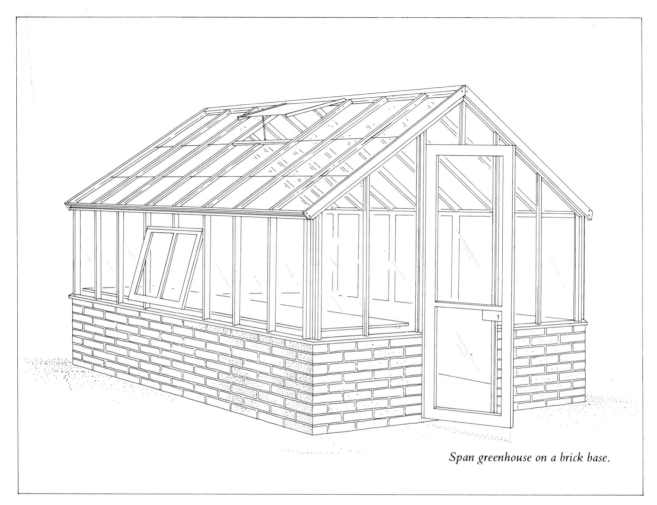

Span greenhouse on a brick base.

Frames

Frames also play an important part. They are invaluable for hardening off plants after leaving the greenhouse, before being put out in the garden. When frames are the only forms of protection available, they can produce excellent early crops, especially if they are heated. This can take the form of an electric cable, but a hot bed made of strawy stable manure is still one of the best ways of raising early crops, as most gardening experts will surely agree.

Cloches

Cloches also play an important part, not only in raising earlier crops, but in bringing existing crops into production earlier than they would otherwise have done.

The wisest plan when choosing a

greenhouse and its equipment, as well as frames, is to visit a large garden centre where different types are on show. Take advice from the expert in charge and study the relevant catalogues and literature before making a final choice.

Growing under glass

Vegetable crops grown under glass can be divided into three main groups:
1 Early vegetables and salads raised and grown to maturity under glass.
2 Vegetables grown on in the greenhouse and hardened off in a frame, to be planted at a later date in the vegetable garden.
3 Crops grown in the garden during the summer months then brought into the greenhouse to force or blanch.

Preparing the greenhouse

The greenhouse year can be said to start in September when the tomato crop is cleared and preparations are being made for winter crops such as early lettuce. The interior of the house should be thoroughly cleaned and scrubbed down with a mild disinfectant. All the glazing must then be checked to ensure panes are air-tight and that ventilators fit.

Following this, the house can be fumigated using a sulphur cone or candle. If tomatoes are grown regularly in the border, then soil sterilisation must be considered. It need not necessarily be done every year, but where the same crop is taken off annually there is every chance of the soil becoming sick.

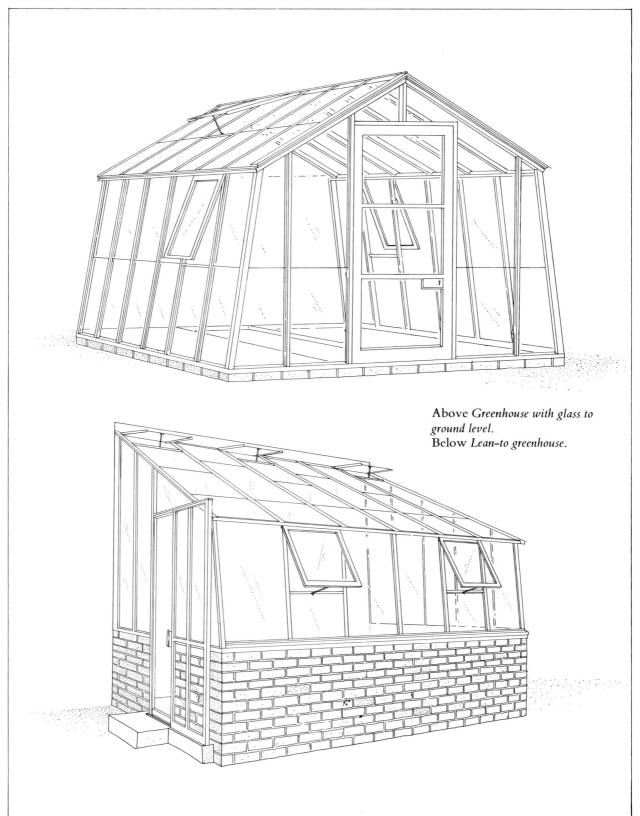

Above *Greenhouse with glass to ground level.*
Below *Lean-to greenhouse.*

If any disease has been encountered during the previous season, it can be carried over to the following year to infect the new crop. During sterilisation all plant material should be removed from the house. The simplest method for the home gardener is to use a solution of one part formalin to fifty parts of water. This is applied at the rate of 2 litres (4 gall) per 1 m² (1 sq yd).

Tomato

The tomato was originally introduced from Mexico. It was only grown for decorative purposes at first and as it belonged to the same family as the deadly nightshade, it was thought to be poisonous. Now it is the most widely grown of greenhouse crops. It has a high vitamin content and is as indispensable in cooking as it is in salads. Tomato plants have always been very prone to disease but hybrids have been bred with enough vigour to resist many of these diseases. This has made their culture much easier as they are less prone to infection. Light intensity plays a large part in producing early tomatoes. They cannot be grown with heat alone as heat is only of real value to the plant when accompanied by light.

Propagation

In the cool greenhouse, temperatures will not be high enough to plant tomatoes before early April in the south, moving on to mid-April in the Midlands and not before the end of the month in the north. There must be no sudden drops in temperature at night to check the plants unless extra heat can be supplied. To grow a particular variety entails raising one's own plants. The range of varieties that can be purchased is very limited. The seed is sown in pots or pans in John Innes seed compost or a suitable alternative. The seeds are spaced carefully and lightly covered with a little sifted soil. Water in with a fine rose and germinate in a propagator at a temperature of 18°C (65°F).

If there is no propagator to provide this temperature, it is possible to germinate seeds in the house, either in an airing cupboard or over a storage heater.

Try to grow on in a temperature of 15°C (60°F). When the seedlings have made their first pair of leaves then they can be potted up into 10-cm (4-in) pots in a suitable compost. They should then be grown on in a temperature of 12°-15°C (55°-60°F). Keep plants moist with water which is the same temperature as the greenhouse.

Planting and cultivation

Seed can also be sown in individual pots so that no potting up is necessary. Once the plants have filled the pots with roots and are 22-23 cm (8-9 in) tall, they should be planted out. The bed will have been dug and manure or compost incorporated in

Right *Ring culture tomatoes growing in the greenhouse.*
Below *Propagator.*

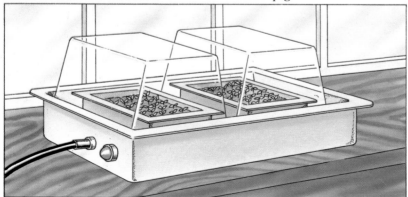

the second spit in the previous autumn. Before planting, fork it over and incorporate some peat. To prevent attack by wireworm, fork gamma-HCH dust into the top 10 cm (4 in) of soil. At the same time give a dressing of tomato base fertiliser. Allow 45-50 cm (18-20 in) between the plants. They will not need a great deal of water to begin with. When the first trusses of flowers appear they should be dusted with a rabbit's tail or a camel hair brush to pollinate them. This is normally done about the middle of the day.

Daily syringing, especially in sunny weather, is important. Evaporation of water in warm sunny conditions creates a humid atmosphere in which pollen grains can grow and effect fertilisation but they lose their activity in a dry atmosphere. Regular syringing also checks transpiration from the leaf surface as well as discouraging red spider. As the trusses set and fruit begins to appear, plenty of water will be necessary. Avoid splashing soil up on to the leaves as it can cause infection. Remove all side shoots and stand bamboo stakes by each plant and tie it to the stake with raffia.

Tomatoes produce a quantity of surface roots so give them a good mulch in June. This can be rotted manure, peat or a mixture of rotted manure and soil which will encourage root growth. A healthy root system creates a healthy vigorous plant that will bear a good crop of fruit. In July the ground can be dressed with 16-20 g ($\frac{1}{2}$-$\frac{3}{4}$ oz) per 1 m^2 (1 sq yd) of sulphate of potash which is an important fertiliser for tomatoes. This will not only aid the fruit in ripening, but also prevent greenback, where a non-resistant variety is being grown. Tomatoes like plenty of air so give them ample ventilation when the weather is warm. After the middle of May the ventilators can be left open at night unless the weather becomes particularly cold.

Stopping is carried out when the seventh truss is formed, but in a bad summer with little sunshine for ripening, it may be better to stop at the sixth truss. Defoliation starts when the trusses of fruit begin to ripen, removing the lowest pair of leaves when the first fruits start to colour. This lets light and air into the fruit and aids ripening. As the trusses continue to ripen up the plant further defoliation can take place.

Growing in pots
Tomatoes can also be grown in pots or boxes where there is no border in which to plant them.

Ring culture
Many gardeners try to grow as many crops as possible in one small greenhouse and may not be able to sacrifice a whole border to the tomato crop. If this is the case, the ring culture system can sometimes solve their problems. This method is based on a secondary root system that absorbs the water so that more concentrated feeding can be given to the plants in the pot or ring. Very heavy crops can be achieved by this method.

A bed 10 cm (4 in) deep is made of aggregate. This can be coarsish, gravelly sand, coarse ash or cinders, but must not be so close in texture that it binds down. A small area can be either bricked or boarded round to take the aggregate. A single row along the back wall of a lean-to greenhouse is a good place. The rings themselves are pots with no base. They stand on the aggregate and can be filled with the same compost used for the pots. They should be placed in position a few days before planting so that the contents can warm up.

The plants are raised in the usual way and planted one in each ring and watered. After this, watering should be avoided unless really necessary for the first ten days when the leaves will darken and the roots will be encouraged to search for water. Once the roots find their way through the ring into the aggregate

and begin forming a secondary root system, stop watering the plants themselves in the ring, but saturate the aggregate daily. When the plants are growing well and the first truss has set, feeding can begin. Pollination is carried out with a rabbit's tail or camel hair brush. Use a good proprietary brand of tomato fertiliser, following the manufacturer's instructions. The plants are staked and side shooted in the normal way.

Varieties
Moneymaker A heavy cropping, disease-resistant variety, though lacking in flavour.
Supercross F1 Hybrid This bears a heavy crop of medium-sized fruits. It is immune to leaf mould and greenback and tolerant to mosaic.
Eurocross F1 Hybrid This variety crops well and is fairly early. It is immune to greenback and leaf mould.
Alicante An old variety of good flavour.

Alicante tomato.

Ailsa Craig This is by far the best flavoured of any tomato but unfortunately prone to disease.

Pests and diseases
Blight This is a fungus disease recognisable by the dark brown spots which appear on the leaves. Use captan or benomyl spray or dust to control.
Botrytis This disease spreads rapidly in a damp cold summer or in an

over-humid atmosphere. Control by using captan or benomyl spray or dust.
Leaf mould The disease is recognised by small yellowish spots which appear on the underside of the leaves gradually turning the whole leaf brown. Spray with a systemic fungicide or benomyl in mid-June, or else only grow disease-resistant varieties.
Tomato mosaic A virus disease. Treated seed should be used.
Red spider To control, spray with liquid malathion or a systemic insecticide.
White fly This is the most difficult of any pest to control. Spray with malathion or use a greenhouse aerosol based on malathion. When white fly is serious make three applications in the first week and a weekly application in successive weeks. One application is useless if it is to be controlled effectively.

Lettuce
A first sowing of lettuce can be made in September in a half-pot. When the seedlings are large enough to handle prick them out into boxes using John Innes compost No. 1 or a suitable alternative. These may then be planted out in October for harvesting in December or January. Choose short-day varieties for growing under glass. The breeding of these varieties has proved a great advance in growing lettuces under glass.

The border should be thoroughly and deeply dug and strawy manure or compost incorporated in the bottom spit. If possible add some fresh loam or, failing this, some good garden soil.

No fertiliser need be added if the soil has been well cultivated with a plentiful addition of humus. Too much nitrogen, especially when growing lettuces under glass, leads to soft growth and lack of heart. The young lettuce plants are put in 20 cm (8 in) apart each way and should not be planted too deeply. Successful cropping depends to a

great deal on careful management. Aim to water the soil on sunny days and carry out the operation first thing in the morning when temperatures are rising, taking care to avoid wetting the plant overhead. Ventilate whenever possible, especially in sunny weather, but trap as much heat as possible by closing the ventilators early in the afternoon before temperatures begin to drop.

Another sowing may be made in October for lettuce that will turn in during February and March. If plants are being grown in frames then seedlings from an early September sowing will be planted out in the frame in October. If the frame is heated, then plenty of ventilation can be given when the weather is suitable. If grown in a cold frame, plants should be kept on the dry side and very little ventilation given. In cold, frosty weather the lights should be protected with sacking, mats or other suitable material. Grown in a cold frame, one cannot expect to cut lettuce before March. Plants may also be put out in cloches.

Short-day varieties
Kwiek An excellent variety making really good crisp hearts.
Amanda Plus A quick-growing, solid-hearted variety that will suit greenhouse, frame or cloche.
Suzan This will make a good heart with the minimum of heat.
Dandie This variety is well suited to frames and cloches and it matures quickly.
Kloek An excellent lettuce with a good tender heart.

Pests and diseases
Botrytis An attack of botrytis is recognisable by patches of grey mould appearing on the leaves which gradually rot. It is controlled by using captan or benomyl either as a dust or a spray.
Downy mildew This is most prevalent among lettuce grown in cloches or frames. An attack can be controlled by spraying with benomyl or a systemic fungicide.

Root aphid An attack can be recognised by signs of wilting. The soil should be watered with a solution of lindane.
Millipedes They attack the roots of the young plant which wilts and eventually dies. As a precaution, work gamma-HCH dust into the top 10 cm (4 in) of soil before planting.

Carrot and radish
Sowings of carrots may be made as early as January. In the greenhouse they are sown broadcast on a finely prepared seed bed. The seedlings should then be thinned to 2·5 cm (1 in) apart. These should be ready to pull by early May. If they are to be grown in a frame, prepare a really fine seed bed. Radishes and carrots can be sown broadcast together. The radishes are pulled much earlier leaving the carrots to mature.

In the early part of the year during cold weather, the frame should be closed, but take advantage of any warm sunny days for ventilation during the middle of the day. If the radishes are to be sown under cloches, put them in position where the carrots are to be sown, three weeks in advance. If a further planting of lettuce, sown in November or December, is planted out in the greenhouse in January, again a crop of radishes can be taken off. They can be sown broadcast at the same time as the lettuce are planted, but will be pulled long before the lettuce heart up.

Varieties
Carrot Amsterdam Forcing Sweetheart and Amsterdam Forcing are both excellent forcing varieties of good flavour.
Radish French Breakfast and Saxa, a good early forcing variety, scarlet and round in shape.

Mustard and cress
This very useful crop, although proverbially easy to grow, is very prone to damping off. It is better to wait until the temperature begins to rise so that the minimum does not drop below 10°C (50°F). The cress should be sown four days earlier than the mustard. Fill seed trays with a suitable compost and firm well, bringing the soil up level with the rim of the seed tray to facilitate cutting. Water with a fine rose and then allow to drain. Sow the seed fairly thickly and as evenly as possible, being sure not to cover it with soil. Press the seed down into the soil with a piece of board or a wooden firmer. Cover with glass and paper to exclude the light.

When the seeds germinate, notch up the glass at each corner but do not remove shading until the seedlings begin to elongate. At this stage the glass and paper can be removed. The aim is to draw the seedlings up quickly so that both mustard and cress are tender and mild in flavour. This crop takes about two weeks to mature and regular small sowings can be made throughout spring and early summer.

Lettuce growing under a polythene tunnel cloche.

Dwarf French beans.

Dwarf French beans

This is not only one of the easiest, but one of the most delicious vegetables to grow under glass, and does well grown in 22-25-cm (9-10-in) pots. They need a good compost, with the addition of rotted farm manure. Sow about four seeds to each pot, maintaining a temperature of 13°-16°C (55°-60°F).

In a cool greenhouse sowing has to be delayed until the end of February or early March. Once they start growing, the beans will need plenty of moisture as pots can dry out very quickly. As the beans grow, a few twigs can be put around the outside of the pot to support them. Frequent syringing is necessary as they are liable to attack by red spider.

Varieties
Masterpiece A good variety for forcing.

Pests and diseases
Blackfly If this causes trouble, dust with derris or spray with a systemic insecticide.

Aubergine

Known popularly as the egg-plant on account of the shape of its fruit, this vegetable has become very popular. Although it can be grown outdoors in a good summer, it is much more suited to being grown under glass. The seed is sown in a temperature of 12°C (55°F) in February in a propagator. If a propagator is not available then delay sowing until the sun strengthens and the weather is warmer and sow in a seed tray with a plastic cover. Using John Innes seed compost or other suitable compost, sow thinly, sifting a little fine soil to just cover the seed. Germination is quick and when the seedlings are large enough pot into

7.5-cm (3-in) pots using John Innes No. 1 or a suitable alternative. They grow fairly rapidly and within four to five weeks they will need to be potted on into 12-cm (5-in) pots. When the plants are recovered from the check of potting and have begun to make some growth, the growing point is pinched out to encourage a bushy habit.

Aubergines will grow well in big pots. Make the final potting into 21-27-cm (9-10-in) pots. They need plenty of air, water and sunlight and can be stood on the staging where they will get the maximum amount of light. They should be syringed daily to encourage the flowers to set and given a feed about every ten days to improve the size and quality of the fruit.

Lack of water will cause the skins to harden and then split in the same way as the tomato, so when grown in pots, watering must never be neglected. If large fruits are required no more than six should be allowed per plant. They are at their best when the skin has a very shiny gloss and is smooth to the touch.

Varieties
Black Prince An early variety and a good cropper.
Long Tom F1 Hybrid A very prolific variety over a long period.

Pests and diseases
The aubergine suffers from the same diseases as the tomato (see tomatoes under glass), but F1 hybrids have much greater resistance to attack.

Cucumber

Where a greenhouse is used for general purposes, especially for tomatoes in the summer months, it is difficult to grow cucumbers well. The conditions they require are quite different. Where there is only one greenhouse it may be easier to grow the cucumbers in a frame.

Propagation
If cucumbers are to be grown in a greenhouse, seed should be sown in

February or early March. Sow one seed to a 7·5-cm (3-in) pot in a temperature of 20°C (70°F). The seed should be 2·5 cm (1 in) deep and on its side. After germination grow on in a temperature of 18°-20°C (65°-70°F). When they have three or four leaves, plant on mounds of 50% soil and 50% farmyard manure or garden compost. Train the main shoot up a wire to the roof and stop side shoots at the second leaf. The sub-laterals which bear the fruit are stopped one leaf beyond the fruit. A hot humid atmosphere should be maintained by damping down the path and syringing three times a day. Ventilation should be carried out carefully, and only on warm days with plenty of sunshine.

Growing in a frame

Cucumbers can be grown in a cold frame but a much earlier crop will be harvested if it can be grown on a hot bed. Make up the hot bed towards the end of March ready for sowing the seed in early April. Allow two plants to a frame but sow four seeds, removing the two weakest seedlings. Wait until the temperature begins to drop to just below 23°C (80°F) before sowing the seed on its edge. After sowing, the frame should be kept as humid as possible until germination has taken place.

Cover the lights at night with sacking or some other material to help the frame retain its heat. This protection should be given up until the end of May when all danger of frost should be over. Stop the young shoot when it has made four leaves, then stop the laterals at the second leaf. It is the sub-laterals that will bear the cucumbers and these are then trained over the area of the frame.

Plenty of watering will be necessary to ensure a good crop but syringing should be regular to guard against red spider. Ventilate freely on warm, sunny days but be ready to shut down the light at any sign of change in temperature or wind.

Above *Aubergine*.   Below *Cucumbers*.

Growing under cloches

Barn cloches are ideal for growing cucumbers. Put the cloches in position at least a fortnight before the seeds are sown. Sow the seeds towards the end of April 120 cm (4 ft) apart. Two seeds can be put at each station, the weakest of the seedlings being subsequently removed. Training is the same as for frame cucumber.

Varieties

Butcher's A disease-resistant and very hardy variety of vigorous growth.
Rochford's Market An excellent variety for a cold frame.
Topnotch F1 Hybrid A good variety for the greenhouse.
Telegraph An old variety and a heavy cropper. It does well both in frame and greenhouse.

Melon

The melon is a climbing, tender annual. It can be grown in a greenhouse, frame or cloche. In the greenhouse the melon is usually grown on a mound of soil which can be on the staging, similar to that used for cucumbers. Seed is sown in late March, one seed to a 7·5-cm (3-in) pot in a temperature of 18°-21°C (65°-70°F).

When the young plants have five or six leaves, plant them on the mounds which will have been prepared several days beforehand, to allow the soil to warm up. When planting, ensure that the top of the ball of soil lies 1-2 cm ($\frac{1}{2}$-$\frac{3}{4}$ in) above the level of the soil.

Melons tend to suffer from stem rot disease, so make sure any moisture is drained away from the stem. Train the main stem up a cane until it is 60-75 cm (2-2$\frac{1}{2}$ ft) long, then pinch out the growing point. The laterals are then trained along wires and stopped at 45 cm (18 in). To get a good set, pollinate the flowers by hand. The female flower is recognisable by the small globular growth at the base of the flower. Pick the male flowers and remove the petals then press the pollen covered head into the female flower. This is best done in the morning in sunny weather. Allow one fruit on each lateral. When they begin to swell give them plenty of water at the same temperature as the greenhouse and a feed every ten days. The fruit is supported in nets to keep them clear of the ground.

Growing in a frame

If space in the greenhouse is a problem melons will do splendidly in a frame. Make a hot bed so that the frame is ready by the end of March. Seed can be sown in pots in a temperature of 18°-20°C (65°-70°F) early in March and transplanted, or alternatively, it can be sown direct in the bed itself at the same time when the temperature is a little below 23°C (80°F).

When the main shoot is about 60 cm (2 ft) long stop it and then allow three or, at the most, four laterals to grow. They should be trained so that they are evenly spaced over the frame and then pinched back when the flowers have appeared. The plants will need plenty of water and daily syringing always using tepid water. Give them plenty of air but do not let the temperature in the frame drop below 15°C (60°F) at night and watch the weather carefully for changes.

As the fruits begin to swell, some fertiliser should be given every ten days. Melons may also be grown under cloches but should not be planted out until later when temperatures are higher and there is less risk of cold weather.

Varieties

Sweetheart F1 Hybrid Sweet in flavour. This is a good variety for growing under frames and cloches.
Canteloupe Dutch Net An orange-fleshed variety which is also suitable for frames and cloches.

Right *A frame- or cloche-grown melon resting on a pot to ripen.*
Inset *Sweetheart—a good variety of melon for frames and cloches.*

Raising under glass

To produce an early crop the following vegetables can be raised under glass to be planted out later when conditions are suitable.

Broad beans and peas

To procure an earlier crop, both broad beans and peas can be sown in pots or boxes under glass in January. They are moved to a frame in early March and gradually hardened off to be planted out in the garden at the end of March.

Dwarf French beans

These are sown in early April as only then can a higher temperature be maintained. Sow in boxes in suitable compost. The ordinary seed tray tends to be rather shallow but wooden tomato boxes do well for this purpose. Harden off before planting out when all danger of frost is over. Gitana is a good stringless variety.

Runner beans

Slightly hardier than the dwarf French, this bean can also be sown in a deeper box to be hardened off when the danger of frost is over.

Cabbage

Seed is sown of F1 hybrids at the end of January or early in February in John Innes or other suitable compost. Prick out when large enough to handle and move to a frame at the end of March. Harden off to plant out at the end of April to be harvested in June.

Varieties

Hispi A pointed cabbage with a solid heart and quick to mature.
Minicole F1 Hybrid A round, solid heart and excellent for coleslaw.

Right *Lettuce seedlings planted in the greenhouse.*

Cauliflower

To cut good curds in June and July seed can be sown in a frame in September and over-wintered for planting out in April. Alternatively, sow in the greenhouse in February and harden off in a frame to plant out at the same time.

Varieties

Early Snowball; Snow Crown and Snow King are both F1 hybrids and mature early.

Celeriac

Celeriac needs a very long growing season. The seed is sown in early March in a temperature of 13°-15°C (55°-60°F) in a seed tray using John Innes seed or other suitable compost. It should be sown as thinly as possible as the seed has a very high rate of germination. Prick out the seedlings into a suitable potting compost. In April they can be moved to a cold frame and given plenty of air in the day time although they will need protection at night. By the end of May they can be completely hardened off before planting out.

Celery

To have a really good crop of celery the plants must be grown on without a check until they are planted out. Seed is sown in mid-March in a temperature of 12°-15°C (55°-60°F) but germination is slower than that of celeriac. When the seedlings have been pricked out they should not be overcrowded or put into too shallow a box. Let them get over the check of transplanting before moving them into the cold frame. Give them plenty of air and water well.

Plant out in early June and do not delay this because the plants may become root-bound in the box, the leaves will turn yellow and the celery will run to seed later in the season.

Courgettes

This has become one of the most popular vegetables of the age and

Above *Courgettes*.

125

has almost completely supplanted the marrow. Like the marrow, it can be sown where it is to grow but a much earlier crop is harvested by sowing under glass. The last week in April is quite soon enough because the courgette will never germinate until it has the necessary warmth. The seeds are sown singly 2·5 cm (1 in) deep on their edge in 6-8-cm (2½-3-in) pots. Once germinated the plants grow quickly and their roots will fill a 7·5-cm (3-in) pot by the time they are planted out at the end of May or beginning of June, according to the weather conditions.

Lettuce
The first sowing of lettuces for growing outside can be made in early February under glass. It is better to make small sowings than have too many of one variety. In seed trays of John Innes seed or other suitable compost they will germinate quickly and can soon be pricked out. By late March they can be hardened off to be planted out in April.

Varieties
All the Year Round is an excellent choice for an early sowing.
Winter Density is a cos variety that adapts itself well for winter or summer growing and has a very sweet flavour.

Onions
Nothing is more valuable to the housewife than a good supply of onions that will keep well. Onions benefit from being sown under glass, as weather conditions do not always allow for a good seed bed early in the year.

This crop not only demands a firm seed bed but a very fine one. Use seed boxes filled with well firmed John Innes seed or other suitable compost. Sow the seed *very* thinly in early February. Leave them in the seed box and do not prick them out. When they are growing well they can be moved to a frame

any time from the middle to the end of March. By mid-April they can be moved to their permanent positions.

An alternative method is to sow in peat blocks at the same time. The peat blocks are then planted out in April. Seed may also be sown under cloches in February, but, perhaps the best onions are those grown from an autumn sowing. Make a fine seed bed in October and sow in shallow drills 1 cm (½ in) deep under cloches. Seed may also be sown in boxes to stand the winter in a frame. The autumn-sown onions rarely get attacked by onion fly.

Varieties
Bedfordshire Champion A very consistent cropper with a mild flavour and a good keeper.
Hygro F1 Hybrid A new hybrid which produces very heavy crops with good keeping quality.

Peppers
Peppers are sown early in March in a temperature of 15°C (60°F). Sow thinly in John Innes seed compost and when the seedlings are large enough, pot up into 7·5-cm (3-in) pots. Alternatively, sow seed singly direct into the pots. They need to continue in a temperature of 13°-15°C (55°-60°F) and should be syringed regularly to keep them free of red spider.

By May they will have made sufficient growth to be potted up into 12-cm (5-in) pots. Keep moist and shaded for a day or two and when they have got over the check of potting, move to a cold frame. Leave it open on sunny days but close the light at night to begin with, giving more and more ventilation, until they are gradually hardened off. They can then be planted out the first week in June.

Sweet corn
Sweet corn can be sown either in its permanent position under cloches or in pots in the greenhouse. It is usually those grown in the green-

house that give the best crop. Seed is sown in John Innes or other suitable compost in mid-April in individual 7·5-cm (3-in) pots. This crop needs to grow on without a check if it is to be successful. The plants can be put out in May, protected by cloches, but it is better to wait until June.

Seed can also be sown under cloches in mid-April. However, as sweet corn is usually planted 30 cm (12 in) apart each way in a block, it is more difficult to plan the spacing when using cloches.

Blanching and forcing

Chicory
When chicory is lifted from the garden at the end of October or early November (see Unusual vegetables), the dead foliage is cleaned off and the roots tied into bundles and stored in a cool place in moist peat or sand. They are then ready to be forced in batches to give a succession during the winter months.

A fairly deep box can be used. Put a layer of decayed leaves into the box, then fill with soil or peat, packing the chicory roots in about 10 cm (4 in) apart with the top of the root at soil surface level. Give a thorough watering then place a layer of straw over the roots and cover the box with sacking to exclude the light. Where a little warmth is provided harvesting can commence in four to five weeks.

The space under the staging in the greenhouse provides an ideal place for forcing. Where only a small quantity is required at a time, and obviously a succession throughout the winter months is desirable, then forcing in large pots is an excellent method. Plant four to five roots in a 20-23-cm (8-9-in) pot and invert another pot over the top. The chicory is ready when about 15-20 cm (6-8 in) high and are best when cut

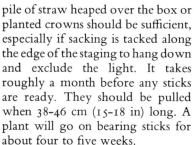

immediately before cooking. In four to five weeks the roots will produce a smaller crop after which they can be thrown away.

Endive

The earliest crop of endive to harvest is blanched *in situ* by pulling the large outer leaves in and tying with raffia or by putting boxes or pots over them. When colder weather approaches with the threat of hard frosts, they should be lifted carefully with a good ball of soil and either packed closely in a frame or in a box put under the greenhouse staging where they will give a supply for the winter.

Variety
Batavian is good for a late or winter crop.

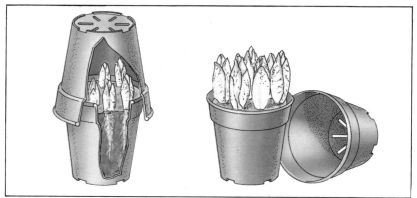

Rhubarb

The first forced rhubarb in early spring is always welcome and it can be favourably compared with any of the soft fruits. Two-year-old crowns are the best for forcing. These are lifted towards the end of December and laid on the surface of the ground to be exposed to the frost. Freezing them first makes them break into growth very quickly once they are brought in to be forced in a higher temperature. Take a good deep box containing some litter or fallen leaves and pack the rhubarb crowns in closely together in either soil or peat. Water them thoroughly and then put them under the greenhouse staging.

As an alternative, the crown can be planted in the soil of the glasshouse and covered. A really good

pile of straw heaped over the box or planted crowns should be sufficient, especially if sacking is tacked along the edge of the staging to hang down and exclude the light. It takes roughly a month before any sticks are ready. They should be pulled when 38-46 cm (15-18 in) long. A plant will go on bearing sticks for about four to five weeks.

Varieties
Royal Albert is an excellent variety for forcing and a very good colour.

Sea kale

The foliage of sea kale dies down towards the end of October and early November (see Unusual vegetables) and the plants are then lifted. Any remaining foliage is trimmed off and any side shoots, or thongs, removed. These are tied in bundles to be planted in the spring to provide the next year's crop. Force in batches, planting the crowns in a box of soil or peat or in the greenhouse soil, watering well and excluding all light. Using a deep box, allow room for a layer of straw and sacking to cover the box.

Sea kale is one of the most delicious of winter vegetables. The tender shoots are ready in about four to five weeks when they are 18 cm (7 in) long. It is better to wait a little longer for them to force in a lower temperature than to force quickly in a higher temperature. The latter will produce tough, leathery shoots.

Parsley

A supply of parsley can be maintained during the winter by making a sowing in late summer in large pots and bringing them into the greenhouse. An old-fashioned 24-cm (10-in) crock pot is ideal. Parsley

Above *Chicory.*
Below *Chicory can be forced to give a succession throughout the winter by planting four to five roots in a pot, inverting another over the top.*

127

Mint
A first supply of mint can be had early in the year by lifting roots in November or December and boxing or potting up in a little good soil and bringing it into the greenhouse.

Roots should be propagated by dividing in the spring. These divisions will make good growth during the summer for lifting in the autumn. An early supply can also be obtained by covering the roots with cloches in March.

Chives
Lift the roots in the autumn and pot into 13-cm (5-in) pots. Bring them into the greenhouse after Christmas to provide flavour for various dishes and use in salads.

Forcing strawberries
Where there is room in a greenhouse and a shelf near the light, strawberries can be forced to provide fruit in April. Runners rooted in early July are lifted at the end of August and potted into 15-18-cm (6-7-in) pots. Use John Innes No. 3 compost with the addition of some old cow manure and a sprinkling of superphosphate. They can then stand in a frame, preferably plunged in ash up to the rims, until the end of December when they can be moved into the greenhouse. Maintain a temperature of 8°-10°C (45°-50°F) at night. Give them plenty of water and on sunny days syringe the foliage.

When the strawberries flower, pollination should be carried out around midday using a rabbit's tail. As the fruit starts to colour, support the trusses on forked twigs. After gathering the fruit the plants may be replanted in the garden to fruit another year.

Varieties
Royal Sovereign This is an old variety and still the best one for forcing. It is unsurpassed in flavour, colour and size.
Red Gauntlet This is a good variety for growing under cloches.

Top *Swiss chard is one of the most delicious of all winter vegetables.*
Above *Where there is room in the greenhouse, strawberries can be forced to provide fruit in April. They can be placed on the staging where they will get plenty of light.*

requires good soil and plenty of moisture so put either peat or leaves over the drainage hole. Use John Innes compost No. 3 or a suitable alternative and add compost or a little rotten farm manure. Parsley is notoriously slow to germinate and despite several old wives' tales about this, it is the newly gathered seed that germinates most readily.

Where there is a bed of parsley in the garden let a few heads flower, collect the seed when ripe and sow immediately. It can go in a month later than the seed sown in July from a packet but germination will be quicker and it will grow to provide a good winter supply.

Top Fruit

Your harvest of good health

Characteristics of stoned fruit

No collective name covers the fruit we deal with here. Sometimes it is called top fruit and sometimes hard fruit. Again, it can be called tree fruit, although in the case of bushes this seems singularly inappropriate. Nevertheless, all the fruit that follows have two common characteristics. They are all deciduous and all of them grow in a temperate region between latitudes of 30° and 60°.

To flourish, these fruits require the following four conditions:
1 The rainfall must be at least 50-62 cm (20-25 in) per annum and not more than 100 cm (40 in).
2 The altitude must not be more than 122 m (400 ft) above sea level.
3 There should be at least one hundred frost-free days after blossom time.
4 There should be a dormancy period of at least two months with a maximum temperature of 10°C (50°F) but not falling below −40°C (−40°F) for apples, −26°C (−15°F) for peaches and −12°C (−10°F) for figs.

This means that all these types of fruit can be grown in any part of Britain, provided it is not too high and not too wet, and in any southerly part of the continent provided there is enough rain and a sufficiently cold winter.

Natural distribution

Apples are distributed right across the most northerly band of the temperate zone. For this reason, of all the types of fruit we deal with, the apple is the most easily cultivated in Britain. Wild species of pear can be found across Europe and into China and Japan, slightly south of the apple's range. The pear needs more sun than the apple and flowers just before it.

The plum is descended from the

An olive orchard from Pliny's Natural History by Nicholas Jenson, printed in Venice, 1476 (Bodleian Library).

poi nellanno. Dclxxx. Marco S
per uno asses. Ma men si marau
lato di Pompeio magno Italia m
le amaestro lauita nostra nellag
mai elfructo diquello tanto tard
no fructo anchora nel luogho do
liue. Fabiano dice che non uiuo
sose tre generationi duliuo. Orc

wild blackthorn or sloe, *Prunus spinosa* and another variety, *Prunus cerasiferus*. This is a larger tree, thought to have come from central Europe. It bears red skinned, yellow fleshed fruit and is known as the cherry plum or myrobolan in Britain. The domestic plum has been bred from a hybrid between the blue skinned sloe and the red skinned myrobolan. Damsons come from another wild plum, *Prunus instititia*, which occurs across Europe.

There are two wild species of cherry which come from the area around the Black Sea. *Prunus avium*, called the bird cherry or gean, was introduced to Britain by the Romans. The other species, *Prunus cerasus*, is a dwarf bush and is thought to be the ancestor of the culinary cherries we use today. Although the wild forms can be found all over the country, they do fruit better in warmer summers, in keeping with their southerly origin.

The quince occurs wild from Turkey to the Caucasus. It is not known precisely when the species was brought to Britain, but it was probably before Chaucer's time.

It was once thought that the peach originated in Persia, hence its Latin name, *Prunus persica*. Since no wild peaches are found there today, it is possible that the first peach in Persia grew from a stone thrown away by a member of a silk or spice caravan moving westward from China. Both peaches and apricots are still found wild there.

These two fruits flourish in a cultivated form all around the Mediterranean, growing easily in Spain, southern France, Italy and Greece. Although perfectly hardy in other respects, they flower too early in Britain, where there is a high risk of frost damage to the blossom.

Figs have the most southerly distribution of the temperate fruits, spreading into the sub-tropical zone and still found wild in parts of India. The natural habit of cropping twice, or three times, a year indicates a warm climate with a very short non-growing period as their place of origin.

Neither the walnut nor the sweet chestnut are native to Britain but they are both found throughout the Mediterranean. The hazel occurs naturally across Northern Europe.

Historical development

Peaches and figs, which are self-fertile, will breed true. It has always been possible, by selecting the best seedling from the best plant, gradually to improve a given strain. But self-sterile fruit, such as apples and cherries, rely on cross-pollination and the resulting seedling is unpredictable. As neither apple nor cherry cuttings are easy to root, an alternative method had to be found. The idea of budding and grafting is thought to have been practised before the time of Christ, by inserting a bud from a particular variety under the bark of a wild seedling. The Romans introduced many Mediterranean fruits to Britain.

Curiously there are no mediaeval pictures of wall fruit. Invasions and civil wars were not conducive to the patient tending of peach trees, but the sturdier native apple grew on undeterred.

By Tudor times it was possible for enterprising sailors and mercenaries to bring back fruit from Spain and Africa. In Kent, Henry VIII's gardener, Richard Harris, planted about one hundred acres of apples and cherries. This is held by some to be the first commercial orchard. At this time apples were used mainly for ciders and pears for perry. It was only the rich who, by building walls and later fruit houses, were able to cultivate fruit that came from the Mediterranean.

The increase in fruit varieties in the early part of the 17th century owed much to the enthusiasm of John Tradescant who worked for two or three members of the nobility before becoming gardener to Charles I in 1630. Tradescant went to Paris and saw the new dwarfing stock used by De La Quintinye for the formal gardens at Versailles, where neat geometric gardens were all the vogue. De La Quintinye had originated the wall tree or *espalier*.

Walls and fruit houses

In 1618 William Lawson, living in Yorkshire, wrote in *The New Orchard Garden* of apricots, cherries and pears grown by a wall and 'fastened to it to have the benefit of the immoderate reflex of the sun'. Later, in that century another keen gardener, John Rae, advocated a 3-m (9-ft) wall for the growing of fruit. The development and use of the wall continued and in 1731 walls were built with an arch below ground-level so that the roots could grow through into the moister shaded soil on the other side. Later on, an experiment was tried to build walls in an arc in an attempt to catch extra sun. A more practical and lasting idea was the serpentine wall based on the principle of a screen that will stand if bent, but not if straight.

The first fruit house, forerunner of the glasshouse, had stone tracery church windows around two or more sides and this again was improved later by substituting glass for the solid roof.

Development of varieties

The nineteenth century saw a very rapid increase in the varieties of good fruit available for cultivation. This was almost entirely due to the enthusiasm of individual nurserymen such as Rivers, Laxton, Cheal, Merryweather and others. By this time Mendel's genetic laws of inheritance were beginning to be more widely accepted and this resulted in some intentional cross breeding. After 1874 there was an increased market for fruit trees because of the abolition of the tax on sugar which encouraged the making of jam.

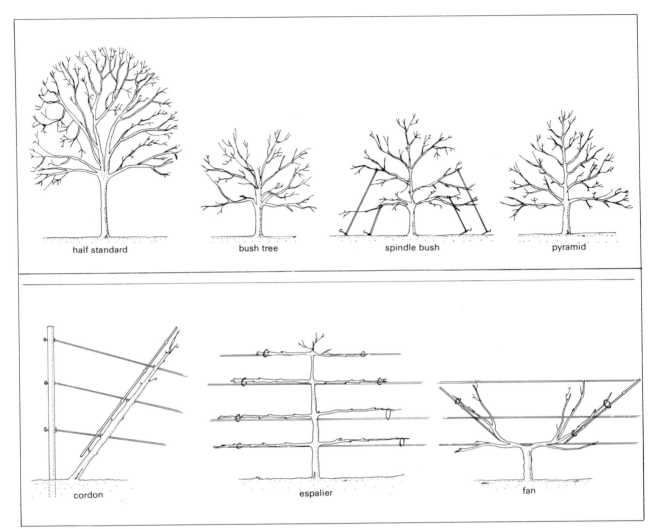

label: half standard | bush tree | spindle bush | pyramid

label: cordon | espalier | fan

Seven examples of tree shapes—there are seven examples of tree shapes which are either round or flat.

During this century the mechanics of genetics have become generally understood and the systematic, scientific and planned breeding of today's cultivars has therefore become possible. There is now world wide co-operation between research stations in America, Japan and countries in the southern hemisphere. Not only time, but skill is required to develop a good variety. The variety must also be proved to be virus free. Today, resistance to disease is of as much importance as the taste and vigour of the fruit. Since only the best varieties are marketed

it is always worth taking advantage of scientific expertise by choosing a recent introduction.

Rootstocks

A rootstock on which to graft a scion of chosen variety is essential for the reproduction of apples, pears, cherries and plums. Rootstocks influence the ultimate size of tree, the age of fruiting, crop yield and, in some cases, resistance to some pests and diseases. Figs can be propagated by cuttings, whereas quinces grow on their own roots. Dwarfing stock, available since 1600, was variable. Research started at East Malling in 1912 in an attempt to standardise the various rootstocks then in circulation. Originally the apple rootstocks

were given Roman numerals but recently these have been replaced by Arabic numbers. These are prefixed by M (Malling) or M M (Malling/Merton).

Experiments were also carried out to find suitable dwarfing rootstocks for other fruits. These were all tested for possible virus infection and are now issued with an E M L A (East Malling Long Ashton) certificate. These classified rootstocks are now famous and are widely exported.

Points to remember

1 A rich soil will need a more dwarfing rootstock.
2 A poor soil will need a more vigorous rootstock.
3 Certain rootstocks are recom-

mended for certain shapes of trees.
4 Certain rootstocks have been found to be incompatible with certain scions.
5 The more dwarf the rootstock, the more quickly the tree will come into bearing, but the smaller will be the yield.

Before embarking on fruit growing any prospective grower would benefit by visiting one of the research stations or the model fruit gardens at Wisley. The John Innes Institute, having moved from Merton to Hertford, later associated itself with the University of East Anglia in 1967 and has a large acreage at Stanfield, near East Dereham in Norfolk.

Tree shape

The large natural shape of fruit trees commonly seen in orchards fifty years ago was most attractive, whether it was upright, as in some pears, or drooping as in many apples. However, this large type of tree is rarely planted today, partly due to lack of space but mainly because of the difficulties of spraying and picking. The tendency has been to plant smaller trees which, by dwarfing, will come into bearing more quickly and, by suitable pruning, will produce larger fruit.

The ultimate yield is never as large as from the old orchard tree but each tree is easier to manage and the fruit easier to care for. The beauty of the old orchard tree may be lost but some people, especially those who prefer formal gardens, find pleasure in the neat, artificially-shaped cordon, espalier and pyramid. Recently a welcome compromise was found in Germany which was later developed in Holland and is now available in the form of a spindle bush. Artificial shapes are divided into two basic forms, round and flat.

Round shapes

Half standard This has a trunk of 1·2 m (4 ft) and is grafted on to vigorous rootstock. It is not often used today except for cooking

apples and cherries, because of its size. It grows to an ultimate spread of 8-9 m (25-30 ft) and planting distance should be the same.

Bush tree Branches are allowed to grow out into a natural goblet shape from a trunk of only 60 cm (2 ft) high. The ultimate spread may be 3-4·5 m (10-15 ft) and planting distance should be the same. The trunk needs a permanent stake as the tree can be top heavy when in fruit. This shape is used for plums, peaches and cooking apples. A dwarf or semi-dwarfing rootstock is used according to the type of soil.

Spindle bush This shape is now supplanting the bush tree. It is cone-shaped and grows from a central stem which requires a 2·5m (8-ft) pole for support. The spread will reach about 2·5 m (8 ft) and planting distance should equal this. The aim is to let the tree grow as naturally as possible. At present it is used mainly for apples and for those pears which do not have too upright a type of growth.

Pyramid This was the first free-standing dwarfed tree. It is now used commercially in hedges which

A beautiful fan-trained peach.

are kept to a reachable height. It spreads to about 90-120 cm (3-4 ft) and planting distance should be equal to this. It is easy to pick and spray, but the pruning requires application. Dwarfing, semi-dwarfing or vigorous rootstocks have all been used and one advantage of this shape is that no support is needed. Apples, pears, plums and peaches can be grown as pyramids.

Flat forms

Cordon This is a single-stem tree kept to a restricted height. The yield is never as high as from other forms but precocious fruiting is induced by close planting, combined with severe pruning which also controls the vegetative growth. The trees are planted in rows 180 cm (6 ft) apart at 75-cm (2½-ft) intervals from each other in the row.

Cordons are planted at an angle of 45°, pointing north in a north-south row, with the grafting or budding union uppermost. They are trained against wires which have to be strained between two really strong

133

posts. These should be 2 m (6 ft) high above the ground. An additional post is necessary every 3·5 m (12 ft). The bottom strand of wire should be 75 cm (2½ ft) above the soil and additional wires fixed at 60-cm (2-ft) intervals. The shoots should not be tied directly to the wire or the rubbing might form a canker. A cane is tied at an angle to the wires and the shoot is then tied to this, using very soft string or raffia.

Dwarfing or semi-dwarfing rootstock is used unless the soil is exceptionally poor. Pears could be grown against a wall in this form in the north. Apples are usually grown in the open. When these fruits are grown in containers a double or triple cordon is used.

Espalier This is another form needing support. It spreads to about 2-3 m (6-8ft) on either side of a central stem. The name comes from the Italian word *spalliera* meaning a supporting piece. One pair of laterals are grown off on either side every year, from a central trunk at intervals of 30 cm (1 ft). This way four, five or more tiers are constructed and it is a good method of utilising every bit of wall. Espaliers can also be grown like cordons in the open. A semi-vigorous rootstock is best. Apples, pears and quinces are grown in this shape.

Fan This shape spreads some 2·5-3 m (8-10 ft) on either side of the tree trunk. The preparation of the soil and the preliminary training is described later on. The shape is used against walls for plums, peaches, nectarines, apricots, figs and culinary cherries. A dwarfing rootstock is used when available.

Choosing a site

As Britain is on the northern edge of the temperate zone, the best possible conditions are needed for fruit trees. This applies particularly to those which grow naturally farther south, if they are to repay the time and money spent on them and if they are to justify their place in a small

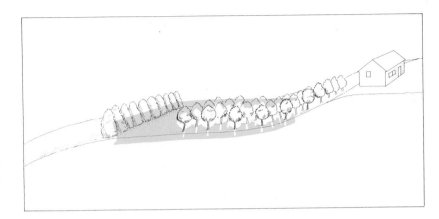

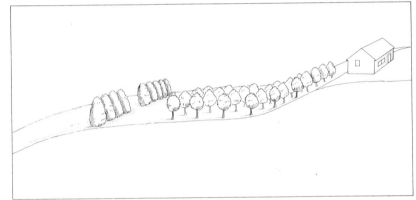

garden. They need direct sun, shelter from frost and protection from north/north-easterly winds, and protection from birds and squirrels.

Sun

The best place in the garden for a summerhouse is probably also the best place for the fruit. A southern slope is recommended so that no one tree will shadow another. For this reason, if more than one row of cordons is to be planted, the rows should run north to south. Peaches can be grown in the open in a really sunny place but figs are better against a south wall. The amount of direct sun has a pronounced influence on the flavour of fruit. Victoria plums grown against a wall have more taste than those grown in the open and early apples have less flavour than later ones.

Frost

If there happens to be an otherwise ideal southern slope, ensure that

Top Frost pockets are formed by cold air becoming trapped by a hedge or fence at the bottom of a slope. Above By creating a break in the hedge the frosty air is allowed to escape.

there is no frost pocket at the lower end. Cold air always sinks to the lowest level it can. Curiously, it cannot pass through a continuous hedge even though this appears to have plenty of small air spaces in it. To allow the cold, frosty air to escape there must be a definite break in the hedge or fence. If this cannot be done because the boundary is a wall or other houses, then the fruit should only be planted on the higher part of the slope.

Wind

Shelter from the north/north-easterly wind is strongly advised. This may already be given by other houses or trees, but failing this, a band of ornamental shrubs might have to be planted. This broken

A luscious-looking dessert cherry against a garden wall. A screen of protective netting has been erected on poles around the tree to protect the fruit from attack by birds.

shelter is better than a solid fence, which is likely to cause the wind to bounce back against it.

Protecting against birds

During the winter, bullfinches can present a major threat to a crop. Unseen, they peck the fruit buds and can devastate a whole orchard as easily as a single tree. They are particularly partial to cherries from November to February, to plums and pears up until March and apples during March and April. Experience shows that bullfinches are not conversant with the Gregorian calendar and tend to eat stolidly throughout the winter.

There are several methods of try-ing to prevent damage. The trees can be sprayed with bird repellent but this will wash off in the rain and will have to be re-applied more than once. Alternatively, Scaraweb, a plastic cobweb-like material, can be spread over smaller trees and bushes. Black cotton can be draped over and through the taller trees. To make this easier, ram the reel of cotton on to the end of a bamboo pole.

The only effective deterrent is to plant the fruit in a cage. In 1964 all the standard plum trees at Wisley were uprooted because they could not be protected and consequently bore no fruit. If there is room and money for a cage, it needs to be 2 m (7 ft) high with a mesh of not more than 2 cm ($\frac{3}{4}$ in). If all fruit grown were protected by cages, the increase in yield would be immense.

Pot-grown fruit

In very small gardens or in an established one where there is no available space, any type of fruit can be grown in a larger container. Dwarfing stock is always used and there must be a source of water nearby. Thomas Rivers was growing peaches and other fruit in pots one hundred years ago and any nursery will still provide pot-grown bushes or trees on request. The tubs or pots can be left outside for the necessary cold dormancy as long as they are protected from birds. They can be moved in to protect the blossom or later, for the ripening of the fruit.

The fruit would look as decorative on a terrace as many ornamental plants and would be a constant source of interest. A pyramid, double cordon or open bush are the best shapes to grow in this way. Start off with a pot just large enough to take the roots, then re-pot each autumn up to a maximum pot size of 30 cm (12 in). Thereafter, sufficient fertilisers and a little new soil or compost is all that is needed.

Moving the containers is sometimes a problem. This can be over-

There is no finer sight than that of ripe, juicy and succulent pears waiting to be picked. They should come away easily when lifted and twisted gently on their stems.

come by screwing four furniture castors to a crossbar of wood and standing the container on top. This way it can be rolled easily from one position to another even when full of earth. Another good hint is to treat the wood with some preservative.

What to grow?

The beginner might easily be tempted to try growing one specimen of every fruit available, but there are four good reasons for not doing this.

Except for peaches, figs, morello cherries and a few other cultivars, most fruit is self-sterile and needs another compatible pollinator. This means growing at least two specimens of any one kind of fruit.

Each type of fruit needs slightly different treatment whether for spraying, feeding or pruning. It is easier to have a group all needing the same attention at the same time.

There is quite a lot to master technically when first starting to grow fruit so it may be an advantage to concentrate on two rather than six types.

The fruit chosen must suit the site on which it is to be grown and this may not be available for certain types of fruit. Nectarines need glass protection, figs need a south wall or glass protection and peaches need a south wall or a really sunny, protected place.

With the exception of one, all sweet cherries are infertile and have to be grown in pairs. As there is no dwarfing stock available at present, quite a lot of space will be needed. Culinary cherries are self-fertile and these smaller trees can be more easily fitted in if space is at a premium.

Plums need space as there are only two semi-dwarfing rootstocks available and the tree is prone to infection if intensively pruned. Greengages and possibly a Victoria plum will have more taste when grown against a wall. Pears need more direct sun than apples for which there is a rootstock, a trained shape and a suitable cultivar to fit almost any given space. When all is considered there is great advantage in growing those types of fruit that are not available locally in commercial orchards.

Selection of cultivars

Having decided what type of fruit to grow, there are further considerations governing the choice of the actual cultivar or variety.

Quantity or quality According to needs and personal preference, a choice must be made between quantity and quality. The Cox, for example, is a splendid apple, but may not crop as heavily or as regularly as a Lambourne.

Season Most fruit have varieties that mature early or late and it takes skilled planning to have the fruit available when it is most needed.

Pollination The actual variety may be determined by available pollinators, or it may be necessary to choose a self-fertile form even though another cultivar has a better taste.

Yield The shape of the tree will determine both how early it will come into bearing and how large the ultimate crop will be.

Locality Some varieties grow better in some localities than others.

Availability New varieties well worth trying may not be available at the local nursery. The advantage of being able to collect a tree from soil similar to that in which it is to be planted, may outweigh the other advantages of choosing a new variety.

Resistance to disease Resistance to disease means far less time spent on spraying. (It is best to buy only stock with the EMLA certificate.)

Speed of fruiting How quickly a tree will bear fruit depends not only on its shape but on its age. A maiden or one-year-old tree is cheaper to buy and affords the pleasure of training but it will not bear fruit for two years or so. A two- or three-year-old tree can be bought, more expensively, already trained in any specific shape and will, generally speaking, fruit the following year.

Planting

Most fruit trees will continue to bear fruit for fifty years, and some for as many as a hundred although the useful life span is often nearer twenty-five years. Once planted, they resent root disturbance which means no additional organic material or manure can be dug in later. An hour spent preparing the planting hole will literally bear fruit for years to come. Double digging is advocated and the area of the roots below will equal the eventual spread of the branches above. The roots of a fan-trained tree against a wall will be at least 3 m (10 ft) either side of the main trunk.

Organic matter in the soil is needed by all fruit trees, but particularly by those planted in the dry soil by a wall. If manure is not available for the very bottom of the hole or trench, compost, rotted leaves or some alternative organic material should be put in. Bonemeal or other proprietary fertiliser appropriate to the particular fruit can be incorporated with the other soil as it is put back. For more efficient watering of wall fruit, vertical drainpipes can be inserted at this stage.

Stakes

Before use, stakes should be treated with preservative. A 2·5-m (8-ft) pole will need to be 60 cm (2 ft) below soil level. For holding straining wires for cordons, stakes are often set in concrete.

Feeding

The more artificially and intensively cultivated a fruit tree is to be, the more attention needs to be given to the application of fertilisers. It is quite tricky judging how to give enough food for the production of fruit and yet not so much that vegetative growth is overstimulated. Pruning maintains this balance.

The three most important elements for fruit are potassium, nitrogen and phosphorus. These are needed in different proportions according to the type of fruit, and in different amounts according to the particular soil. Certain other trace elements, those occurring in minute quantities, may also need replacing. Iron is often deficient in some chalky soils as the chalk prevents its absorption by the roots. Magnesium and manganese may also be lacking and their deficiency can be recognised by abnormal leaves. These deficiencies will probably be noticeable in other plants in the garden and are only occasionally likely to be severe.

The best time to apply fertilisers is in February, using a proprietary brand of well balanced general fertiliser at 130 g (4 oz) per 1 m² (1 sq yd). If they are applied any earlier, they could be leached out of the soil before the roots are activated by the leaves and able to take the food up. If the tree or bush looks poorly in the summer, or is bearing an unusually heavy crop, a foliar feed is beneficial.

Pruning

The naturally-shaped standard tree seen in old orchards was only pruned to remove dead, broken or crossing branches. This resulted in large crops of fruit which were often rather small and it encouraged a biennial habit, the tree having to rest a year after a particularly heavy crop. Now the aim is to obtain regularity and a constant annual crop of larger fruit. Obviously, different types of fruit and different shapes of tree require different pruning to achieve this, but there are certain general principles. On established old trees, removing with a saw or cutting back large branches is always done during the dormant period, in winter. These cuts should be painted over with protective paint.

It used to be thought that apples should not be cut in frosty weather, but A. Hellyer (*Financial Times* 1 January 1979) has never found the trees to be damaged. It is advisable to cut peaches, cherries and plums as near to leaf burst as convenient, to prevent infection by fungus. The

Above *Winter pruning—a branch growing inwards towards the centre of the tree is cut off, using secateurs. Cutting back during the dormancy period encourages more vegetative shoots, although too much pruning may encourage excessive growth.*
Left *Summer pruning—snipping back lateral shoots to four or five leaves in July encourages fruit buds to be produced. Removing the tips of shoots in summer also allows more sun to reach the ripening fruit and helps the wood ripen before the winter.*

138

snipping of thin first year shoots is usually carried out in the summer. The less pruning is done, the more quickly the tree will crop.

Principles of pruning

1 Pruning regulates the vigour of a tree. Cutting back the wood during dormancy will encourage more vegetative shoots. If this is over-done, there may be too much growth the following summer. When trying to rescue a neglected tree, the necessary pruning should be spread over two or three years.

2. The shape of a new tree can be established, or that of an older one maintained, by cutting back to a wood bud facing in the direction in which subsequent growth is desired, during the dormant period.

3 The production of fruit rather than wood buds can be induced by cut-ting back an unwanted shoot to four or five basal buds. This can be so successful in established cordon or pyramid apple trees, that there comes a time when there are too many fruit spurs and winter pruning will involve cutting some of these out. Replacement pruning for peaches and others that fruit on the preceding year's wood, consists of cutting away any wood that bore fruit the previous year and replacing it with a new basal shoot.

Summer pruning

1 The production of future fruit buds is encouraged by snipping back lateral shoots to four or five leaves in July. This is done in the hope that the sap will then go into one bud and make it a fruit bud rather than to the tip of a leaf shoot, extending this in length during the rest of the summer. When a cordon has been established a few years it can be kept in good fruiting condition by sum-mer pruning only.

2 Removing the tips of shoots in summer also lets more sun reach the ripening fruit and helps the wood to ripen before the winter.

3 Trees that are not growing well should not be summer pruned as they need as much foliage as possible to encourage the roots to spread.

4 Certain trees, such as apricots and figs, bleed and should be cut as little as possible. It is better to pinch out the young growth in the summer with the finger and thumb. Large cuts that bleed can be treated with wound sealant which helps to stem the flow of sap.

5 Other trees, such as plums and cherries, are susceptible to a fungus infection called silver leaf so the less they are cut the better. If they have to be cut, the nearer the summer the less the risk of infection.

Pests and diseases

There are numerous diseases which can infect fruit and which will kill a tree in time if not kept in check. With all these diseases part of the remedy is to cut out or remove the affected shoot. This infected ma-terial should be carefully collected and burnt at once, thus preventing the undetectable spread of spores which could cause reinfection. It is important, when appropriate, to paint any surface cut with healing bituminous paint.

Most diseases and many infesta-tions by pests can be prevented or cured by the use of sprays. Although spraying with chemicals is often dis-liked, it cannot be avoided. Ideally a spray should be used as seldom as possible, just frequently enough to keep the trees healthy and the fruit unblemished. In the future it may be possible to apply a chemical solu-tion on the soil which will be taken up by the roots, translocated to all tissues thus affording overall pro-tection throughout the season.

A pressure sprayer is the easiest way of applying chemicals and one with a long lance the most useful. These are usually available in 9-litre (2-gall) and 4·5-litre (1-gall) sizes. The smaller size is easier to carry and if there are only a few trees it would save mixing an unnecessary amount of spray. In either case, it must be carefully rinsed after each use or sediment will clog up the holes.

Spraying

1 Choose a fine, still, frost-free day. Wind will not only waste the spray but blow it over other plants. Rain soon after spraying will wash off the chemical before it has become effective.

2 Never spray when the blossom is out and bees are working.

3 Be careful not to spray too near picking time. Most sprays have printed warnings about this, al-though some new sprays are harm-less.

4 Certain varieties cannot tolerate certain sprays. For example, some cooking apples are sulphur-shy.

5 Apply the spray in the correct strength. Directions are often given for quantities larger than amateurs wish to use and mistakes can all too easily be made during a quick con-version.

6 Apply the spray at the correct time. Prevention is invariably better than an attempted cure.

Unfortunately different manu-facturers use different names for the same chemicals, which can be con-fusing. But some firms print excel-lent charts which are very helpful. It is a good idea to make an indi-vidual chart of the sprays needed, showing the exact time of applica-tion and precise strength required, and hang this up as a reminder. Spraying is a boring job and excuses to put it off are all too easy to find.

Fruit tree being treated with insecticide, using a pressure sprayer.

Equipment

By now it will have become apparent that growing fruit requires skilled attention throughout the year. It also entails an initial outlay on vital equipment. Not only is a sprayer needed, but a sharp pair of secateurs, a narrow pruning saw, possibly a pruning knife, plastic netting and, if wall fruit is grown, stakes and wire for trained trees. Large pots will be needed for pot-grown fruit.

There will also be an annual expenditure on fertilisers, sprays and possibly herbicides. The return on all this expenditure will start only after two or three years. Even then, if the man hours are costed, it may well be the most expensive fruit ever eaten. However, despite the outlay in time and money, the satisfaction of achievement is great and the therapeutic value incalculable. As William Lawson wrote more than three hundred years ago, 'the principle end of an orchard is the honest delight of one wearied with the works of his lawful calling'.

Apples

In 1975 there were over six thousand cultivars listed in the National Apple Register in Britain. This vast number is partly due to the fact that the permutations and combinations of cross fertilisation, whether intentional or haphazard, are endless. But it is also due to the genetic instability of the apple.

Shapes of scion

Choosing an apple from such a vast number of varieties is difficult enough, but on top of that there are then six possible shapes of scion from which to choose. Only a few people today have room for a standard or a half-standard. It was this lack of space which prompted the invention of the family tree where several varieties, for instance, a James Grieve, a Cox and a Spartan, could be grafted on to a dwarfed stock, at about 60 cm (2 ft). As long as the growth of these chosen var-

ieties is similar, this can be a successful way of gaining variety and saving space. The family tree can be either a standard or a bush tree.

An alternative method is to grow three or more varieties as cordons. Setting up the posts and the necessary straining wires for these cordons is sometimes a deterrent, in which case a pyramid is usually preferred.

Spindle bush

Recently the more natural spindle bush has become popular. It requires less pruning and has a higher yield which is of more use to the modern family.

It is best to start with a feathered maiden. This can be planted against

The old orchard at Hardwick Hall.

a 2·5-m (8-ft) pole, already treated with preservative, and sunk a good 45 cm (18 in) into the soil.
1 Select four laterals, 60 cm (2 ft) from the ground, as near to a diagonal cross as possible. These will form the basal framework. Tip them back by about one third to a downward pointing bud. This will encourage horizontal rather than upright growth.
2 Cut away any unwanted shoots below the chosen four.
3 Head back the leader by a half to a third of its length.
4 Cut out any upright shoots which might compete with the leader.

There are over six-thousand cultivars listed in the National Apple Register in Britain alone. Not only is there a huge variety to choose from but there are also six possible shapes as well.

First summer

Tie down the four chosen basal shoots at an angle of 30° above the horizontal, using plastic string and being careful not to tie a slip knot round the shoot. Tie the other end to a meat skewer stuck into the ground at an angle like a tent peg to secure it.

A horizontal shoot will bear fruit buds more quickly than an upright one where all the sap goes straight to the tip, promoting longer growth.

Second winter

1 Cut back the leader by about one third of its new growth or more if it is not growing strongly enough. Tip back the next layer of laterals choosing those that alternate with, and do not overshadow, the original basal four. Some of these in the second layer could be tied down the following summer.

2 Remove any shoots crowding or crossing the chosen framework. In time the basal shoots will develop a herringbone of fruiting laterals. Any laterals growing strongly upright should be cut out. In this way the maximum amount of sun will reach the fruit. Tying will not be necessary after three years. As with any other

fruit tree, a balance between fruit and vegetative growth must be maintained and this is a matter of common sense coupled with experience.

M9 is recommended as a rootstock except on very poor soils where MM106 is better. Strong growing fruit will need about 2 m (6-8 ft) between spindles, while compact types will need only 1·5 m (4-5 ft).

There is no right or wrong shape for apples. It is a matter of available space and personal taste. However, in each case there is a right and a wrong rootstock to be used. Only from a reliable nurseryman will the right rootstock be guaranteed.

Cultivation

An apple is likely to live considerably longer than the person who plants it, so well prepared soil is not only an investment for the owner but a bonus for his or her successor. The more intensively the apple is grown, the more potash it will need each year. Once it is grassed over it may also need nitrogen which is used up by the grass. Young trees are best grown without competition from weeds or unwanted grass which can be kept down by the careful use of herbicides. When using herbicides, care must be taken not to let the liquid touch the foliage.

Some experts advise hand-weeding until the tree is over two years old, but apples resent the soil being disturbed above and around their roots, so even this hand weeding has to be done with care. In areas where there are rabbits, the young trees will have to be protected with netting because young bark is as attractive to them as lettuce.

It is impossible to be specific about the amount of fertiliser needed annually. This depends not only on the type of soil but also on the type of shape chosen and the consequent amount of pruning. An average amount would be about 33 g (1 oz) per 1 m² (1 sq yd) of sulphate of potash each year, plus the same amount of ammonium sulphate and super phosphate every third year.

Thinning

In years when the crop is heavy, the fruit should be thinned in July using scissors to cut the stalk of one or two apples from each cluster. Alternatively if the stalk is held in one hand, the tiny apple can be pulled off with the other. If too many apples are left on the tree, not only will they all be undersize, but the branch will break. The tree will be exhausted and it may be prevented from cropping well the following year. There is a natural fall of immature apples called the June drop. Sometimes this natural reduction is sufficient but extra help may also be required. If large cooking apples are needed in the kitchen, it is best to thin to only one apple in the cluster.

Picking

Each variety ripens at its own time and this will vary with the year. When the apple is ready it will separate from the tree when raised from underneath by one hand. Treat apples as if they were eggs and pick them into a soft container such as a plastic trug or cardboard box. Sharp nails and wicker baskets puncture their skin all too easily and cause a blemish.

Storing

Early apples are never stored because they have a very short season and become soft and tasteless very quickly. This process can be slightly delayed by keeping them in as cold a place as possible.

The best way to store keepers is to lay them flat in a large polythene bag, loosely closing the neck and making five or six perforations in the bag. This will allow the moisture given off by the apples to evaporate, yet will prevent them from shrivelling. Again it is best to keep them in a cold place although the minimum temperature must remain just above freezing.

It is important not to store any blemished apples with the good

Apples stored flat in a large polythene bag with five or six perforations.

ones. The malic acid gradually changes as they mature and that is why there is an optimum time for eating specific varieties.

Pests and diseases

Apples are most commonly attacked by two diseases. Mildew appears as a brown stain in the tissue and gives leaves a silvery coating. Fungal canker attacks the shoots. Certain varieties are susceptible to damage by some chemicals. It is important to stress that pests and diseases can spread at an alarming rate if untreated. It is also worth stressing that prevention is better than cure.

Varieties

It is impossible to recommend any individual variety of apple. Not only do different soils alter the taste but flavour is very much a question of personal opinion. The flavour of an apple is due to a combination of acids, sugars and aromatic substances. Cookers have a higher proportion of malic acid than eaters. This ratio alters slowly after picking which is why many late-keeping cookers are excellent to eat in February and March. These late keepers have to be picked at the right time to store well without shrivelling.

Early apples are best eaten slightly unripe, straight off the tree.

The selected varieties included here have been arranged in three groups.

1 Well established varieties which

The apple is subject to a number of diseases, including (a) brown rot; (b) woolly aphid; (c) apple scab; (d) apple sawfly. With all pests and diseases it is better to kill than cure.

have stood the test of time and which have been selected to give a reasonable geographical spread.

2 New varieties raised in this century, usually by purposeful cross breeding. The parents of each cultivar are given in parentheses where known.

3 Cooking or culinary apples, though some of these are dual purpose and could be included in the first section. Preference has been given throughout to late-keeping cultivars. In September and October it is sometimes difficult to give apples away, let alone sell them. This is the time when they are cheapest to buy, so it hardly pays the private gardener to grow many early varieties. The later varieties mature from November and many can be eaten up to April. The first month given for each variety is when it starts to be at its best.

Established dessert apples

November-December Cox's Orange Pippin Mr Cox grew this apple from a pip, probably from a Ribston Pippin, in his garden at Colnbrook near Slough. The Cox does best in the southern part of the country. It is very susceptible to canker, scab and mildew, so although considered by some to be one of the best tasting apples, it is not particularly reliable or easy to grow. It is at its best in November but will keep into the new year.

February-April D'Arcy Spice This was raised at the Hall in Tolleshunt D'Arcy, Essex, in 1785 and was distributed widely from 1850. It crops lightly so has not become a

The famous Cox's Orange Pippin, grown by Cox from a pip in his garden at Colnbrook near Slough.

commercial proposition, but it is a juicy apple with a distinctive flavour. Anyone who has once grown it is loath to be without it.

October James Grieve This was discovered in Scotland and distributed in 1890. It is almost self-fertile and often used as a pollinator for Cox. It is a particularly fine, crisp apple with an excellent, slightly sharp taste and is a favourite with many. It has not become a success commercially because it bruises easily.

December–February Orleans Reinette This is partially self-fertile. It is a smallish, golden russet apple with a really good flavour. If it is picked too soon it will tend to shrivel in store.

October–January Ribston Pippin The first tree grew at Ribston Hall, Yorkshire in 1708 and it survived until 1835. A shoot from this tree lived until 1928. This has been a very popular apple but is now considered a little dry.

February–April Sturmer Pippin (Russet) This was named after a village near Haverhill, Suffolk, and was introduced about 1843. It should not be picked until November.

Twentieth century apples

December–February Crispin This was bred in Japan from Golden Delicious in 1930 and is a vigorous grower. It is an excellent cropper and is a juicy green apple.

August–September Discovery This is a better tasting apple than a Worcester Pearmain, having a more acid flavour. It is a juicier apple with a good red colour.

September–October Laxton's Fortune (Cox × Wealthy) Although it has a very pleasant and delicate pear-like flavour, it has a short season and bruises easily so it was never taken up commercially.

Top left *Bramley Seedling—probably the finest culinary apple grown.*
Left *Discovery—a juicy, red apple.*

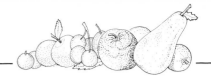

October–November Lord Lambourne (James Grieve × Worcester Pearmain) This apple was bred by Laxton in Bedfordshire. It is an extremely tasty apple with a good constitution and is a very reliable cropper. It was named after the President of the Royal Horticultural Society at the time and was awarded a First Class Certificate in 1922.

Early September Merton Ace (Early Crimson × Epicure) This one crops more heavily than Worcester Pearmain and is ready almost as early as Beauty of Bath. It has a much better flavour.

September Merton Charm (Cox × McIntosh Red) This is a crisp, juicy apple which was given an Award of Merit in 1960.

September Merton Beauty (Cox × Ellison's Orange) This was discovered in 1935 and generally released in 1962.

September–October Merton Worcester (Cox × Worcester Pearmain) This is slightly later than a Worcester but has a better flavour.

October–November Merton Prolific (Cox × Northern Greening) This was raised by Mr Crane at the John Innes Institute and, as its name implies, it is a very heavy cropper. It was awarded an Award of Merit in 1950.

December–March Merton Russet (Cox × Sturmer Pippin) This has a very good flavour but still suffers from the Cox susceptibility to mildew. Infected shoots are easily picked off from just a few trees in a private garden which makes it easier to control.

November–December Sunset This also arose from a Cox pip in 1920 and was raised in Kent. Its taste is not as good as a Cox but it is a much more easily grown form.

December–January Suntan This was given an Award of Merit in the 1970's.

December–March Tydeman's Late Orange (Laxton Superb ×

Top right *Merton Beauty*.
Right *Laxton's Fortune*.

145

Cox) This was raised by Mr Tydeman at the Malling Research Station and was released in 1949. It has a good flavour.

Cooking or culinary apples

November–February Bramley's Seedling An apple which needs no describing. It has been universally grown ever since it was first discovered in Mr Bramley's garden in 1876. This vigorous tree is self-sterile and needs other trees nearby for pollination.

November–February Blenheim Orange · This seedling was discovered in a garden in Woodstock at the gates of the palace in about 1818. It is a vigorous tree and needs other trees nearby for pollination. It is resistant to mildew. It is a dual purpose apple.

December–April Edward VII Introduced in 1910 in Worcestershire, this apple flowers late and escapes frost. It is a shy cropper but stores well. It needs a pollinator.

December–April Encore This is a heavy cropper and keeps well in store. Another advantage is that it is almost self-fertile, but it may be difficult to obtain.

September–October Grenadier The parentage of this early cooker is not known. Its foliage is damaged by sulphur sprays. It is fluffy when cooked.

December–March Lane's Prince Albert This apple was discovered by a nurseryman called Lane in Berkhampstead, Herts, who distributed it from 1857. It is best grown as a half standard or bush tree and is small enough for the private garden.

November–December Lord Derby This grows well on almost any soil and is particularly good in the north. It has the advantage of being nearly self-fertile.

December–April Monarch (Peasgood Nonsuch × Dumelows seedling) This dual purpose apple was raised in 1920 by Seabrooks at Boreham, Essex. Being rosy in colour it has never caught on as a cooker which the public always expects to be green.

December–April Newton Wonder (Dumelows seedling × Blenheim) This apple was raised at Melbourne, Derbyshire. It is late flowering so usually crops well. It is an excellent cooker and when mature, can be eaten raw. Its only disadvantage is its biennial habit. This could be curbed by thinning and not allowing it to bear too big a crop in any one year.

October–November Peasgood Nonsuch This apple was raised by a lady sowing a pip. Mrs Peasgood's seedling first fruited in 1872. It received a 1st class Royal Horticultural Society Certificate in 1874. It is a large green apple of excellent flavour.

Pears

Six varieties of pear are thought to have been introduced by the Romans and more were brought in some centuries later by the Normans. Ever since then the introduction of new varieties has tended to be from the Continent, particularly from France, as is obvious from their names. By 1665 there were four or five hundred different varieties.

Pears grow more easily farther south. They prefer a warm summer and plenty of sun. Another disadvantage in Britain is the frequency of frost in April which will damage the blossom and low temperatures which prevent pollination. For these two reasons dessert pears used, in the last century, to be grown more frequently within the protection of a walled garden than in the open. Fortunately they take very well to growing in a restricted form.

Cultivation

Sufficient moisture in summer is important for growing pears. Besides manure, plenty of other moisture-retentive organic matter should be incorporated in the soil before planting. The addition of peat helps if the soil is not already acid because pears also require iron and this is often tied up in an alkaline soil. Their third need is for nitrogen and therefore they are better not grown under grass, which will use up a proportion of the available supply.

In a sheltered, sunny area, pears can be grown very easily in the open in the form of a bush tree on quince (Angers) rootstock. The bushes will need to be 3–4 m (10–14 ft) apart. If the soil is very rich, the smaller

A pear tree—beautiful for its blossom and delicious for its fruit.

quince C rootstock can be used but this will cut down the yield. This bush tree can also be ordered as a specially budded family tree, bearing three varieties of compatible pears with balanced growth. Pears can also be grown as espaliers, cordons or pyramids. When grown in a pot, a double cordon or pyramid is recommended.

Pruning

Pears have a naturally upright form of growth, therefore the major pruning of an established bush tree tends to be the removal of crowded branches, particularly from the centre. These in turn will be replaced by younger shoots. If there are too many fruit spurs which have become crowded, and a pear makes these very readily, it may be necessary to remove them from the tree. Otherwise, the general rules for pruning pears are much the same as for apples, which are to reduce the vegetative growth.

Feeding

As mentioned above, pears tend to become short of both nitrogen and iron. An annual dressing of manure is beneficial together with a fertiliser dressing of 66 g (2 oz) of sulphate of ammonia and 33 g (1 oz) of sulphate of potash per 1 m² (1 sq yd), but failing that, ammonium sulphate can be added to the top soil in late February and an organic mulch of rotted leaves, bark or straw put down in early summer.

Picking

It is extremely difficult to pick pears at precisely the right moment. A fruit is ripe when it will come away from the tree on its stalk when lifted and slightly twisted. If the pear is picked too early it will shrivel in store and never mature properly. If picked too late it will become soft and sleepy very quickly. Birds and wasps are not bothered by these fine distinctions. To deter them, muslin bags are sometimes tied round each pear or the whole tree can be netted.

Storing pears in egg trays.

Storing

Pears usually need a little time to mature but as constant inspection is necessary, they are best kept in a single layer on a tray (an egg tray is ideal). Obviously the tray is best kept in a cool place. As varieties ripen at different times they should be stored separately and labelled.

Pests and diseases

Birds are more trouble than insects, but aphids can often be a nuisance. The over-wintering eggs are usually sprayed in early spring with a proprietary winter wash when the apples are being treated.

Fireblight is a dangerously infective disease and in Britain its appearance has to be notified, by law, to the local representative of the Ministry of Agriculture and Fisheries. The bacteria blacken the blossom and the leaves on the shoot will subsequently turn brown. However, they will not drop off and this makes the affected branches look as if they have been burnt. This bacteria can also attack other relatives of the pear such as cotoneasters, pyracantha and hawthorns, all of which are grown in the garden as decorative shrubs. Once the bushes have been inspected and the disease confirmed in the laboratory, the sad consequence is usually an order to uproot and burn the offenders.

Varieties

For practical purposes all pears can be regarded as self-sterile and in need of a pollinator. The choice of variety is complicated and the advice of a nurseryman will be useful.

September Williams' Bon Chretien This was a seedling of a French variety originally discovered by a schoolmaster called Wheeler at Aldermaston, Berkshire, in 1770. It was later propagated and distributed by a nurseryman called Williams in 1874. This variety was exported to America where the extra warmth makes it grow more easily and it comes back to us in tins as the Bartlett pear.

September–October Bristol Cross (Williams' × Conference) This cross was made at the Long Ashton research station in 1920. It was released in 1931 and was given an Award of Merit twenty years later in 1951.

September–October Merton Pride (Williams' × Glou Morceau) This was raised in 1953. It is not a heavy cropper but does produce large fruits of good flavour.

October Beurré Hardy There were a great number of pears called Beurré raised in France. This particular one comes from Boulogne and produces a medium-sized pear of pleasant taste.

October–November Conference This excellent commercial variety was yet another of the good fruit cultivars discovered by Thomas Francis Rivers (1830–1899) at his Sawbridgeworth nursery. As chairman, he was speaking at an International Fruit Conference when he introduced it, which accounts for its name. It is sad that this still widely grown pear brought little financial advantage to the nursery and today brings little tribute to the man.

November Doyenne du Comice This cultivar, raised in Angers in 1849, is acknowledged by many to be the connoisseur's pear. It is of ungainly shape but very juicy with a superb flavour.

December–January Glou Morceau This is one of the oldest pears growing in Britain and was raised by the Abbé Hardenpont at Mons. In the north it is best grown against a wall.

Plums

Plums are the most widely distributed of all the stoned fruits. They like any good moisture-retentive soil as long as it is not waterlogged. They do not do well on acid soils, but this can be improved by the addition of mortar rubble, chalk and plenty of farmyard manure or other organic matter. As plums flower in April, the blossom needs some measure of frost protection but birds pecking the buds during the winter will do even more damage than frost.

As it is difficult to protect tall trees from birds, it is better to grow smaller types of tree in the open. In the private garden, plums can be grown on the semi-dwarf St Julien rootstock. An even more dwarf stock called Pixie has been found but at the time of writing it is not yet generally available. On St Julien, a bush tree or pyramid might just fit into a cage. It is best to plant a feathered maiden which might have to be staked. Some of the lower branches can be tied down just above the horizontal and this will induce fruit rather than unwanted vegetative growth which might later have to be cut back. The bush will crop at about three or four years. A pyramid might take a little longer to come into bearing.

Before planting a plum in the open, it is best to discover whether plums already planted in the vicinity bear crops successfully or whether they are always destroyed by birds at the bud stage. An alternative is to grow plums against a wall. In the last century the Victoria plum was invariably grown against a wall. This has two advantages. Not only is the tree more easily protected

The famous Victoria plum was found in Alderton, Sussex in 1840.

Conference pear.

Glou Morceau pear—raised by the Abbé Hardenpont at Mons.

from birds, both in the winter and when the fruit is ripe, but the fruit against a wall has a better flavour. This is due to the extra amount of reflected sun. Most of the gages do better against a wall, where they are usually grown as a fan-trained tree.

Feeding
As plums need nitrogen they are not usually grown in grass. An annual mulch of farmyard manure is appreciated and ammonium sulphate is often given too. They also need extra potash annually, but phosphate only every two to three years. Care has to be taken when applying these artificial fertilisers because too much soil disturbance encourages suckers. These are best pulled up rather than cut, before they become too large.

Pruning
The less plums are cut the better because of the risk of silverleaf infection through any wound. The natural standard tree form would be the best if it were not for the birds. For all shapes of tree, any cutting is best done immediately after picking or as late in winter and as near to leaf burst as possible when the risk of infection will be less. In every case, immediate painting of the cut with a wound sealing paint is essential. Although a plum against a wall will be trained in the same way as a fan peach, as little cutting as possible should be done and it is better to reduce growth by tying branches down. The aim is to cover the available wall space with carefully positioned branches.

Thinning and picking
When the crop is heavy there will be a natural drop but even this may not be sufficient to prevent the branch from being broken by the weight of the fruit when ripe. To avoid this, artificial thinning is best carried out when the plums are the size of a nut, removing a few at a time until the plums remaining are spaced out at about 5 cm (2-3 in) apart.

When grown in a cage, it is best to leave the plums until they almost fall off before picking them. This is not practical in the open where birds and wasps attack before the fruit is really ripe. Once picked, plums keep for a week or two.

Varieties
There are five main groups of plums from which to choose. Those that are not self-fertile must have a compatible pollinator. Plums grown commercially are apt to be selected for the large size of their crop before their taste. The more unusual plums and gages crop lightly and for this reason are rarely, if ever, seen in the shops. The only way to taste a superb connoisseur's gage is to grow it privately.

Wild myrobolan
This wild plum, cultivated in fruit orchards in the last century, has been known since 1600. It makes an attractive tree of about 4-5 m (15-20 ft) and bears enormous crops of small cherry red plums in August. It tends to be biennial. The plums are excellent for jam, bottle beautifully and can even be eaten raw. Only one tree has to be planted as it is self-fertile and where space permits it is a plum well worth preserving.

Damsons
All the damsons are self-fertile, extremely easy to cultivate and best grown as small standard or bush trees. It is such a pity that so few are planted today as there is no substitute for damson jam. The fruit also bottles well and the taste improves with keeping as the stones, a nuisance though they are, add to the flavour.
Early September Merryweather Award of Merit 1907.
Mid-September Farleigh Damson Discovered in Kent in 1820.
September-October Prune Damson Shropshire Prune/Westmorland damson thought to have originated at Frogmore, Windsor in 1905.

Culinary plums
These are more often grown commercially and if there are any orchards in the locality it is probably better to be a customer there and leave the precious space in the garden for the dessert varieties.
July-August Early Rivers Distributed from 1820.
August Czar (Prince Engelbert × Early Rivers) 1871.
September Warwickshire Drooper Self-fertile.
September-October Marjorie's Seedling Another self-fertile plum discovered in Berkshire in 1912.

Gages
These are a superior type of plum. They were introduced to Britain in the 1700's by Sir William Gage. They need a warm sunny wall to grow best and they tend to crop lightly but remain a connoisseur's choice.
Early August Bryanston Gage (Greengage × Coe's Golden drop) This cross was made in Blandford, Dorset, in 1831 and the plum is a heavy cropper.
Mid-August St Ouillin's Gage Comes from Lyons and is self-fertile.
Mid-late August Early Transparent This is a self-fertile gage from the Rivers nursery.

Merryweather—an award-winning damson and one of many varieties of a fruit all too often ignored today. They bottle well and make excellent jam.

Late August Denniston's Superb Self-fertile with a good flavour.
August–September Cambridge Gage.
August–September Kirke's Gage 1831 Very good flavour.

Dessert plums

There are a great number of these and the choice is a matter of personal taste. It also depends on the soil and climate of the particular area in which they are to be grown. Not all plums are self-fertile.

Late July Early Laxton.
August–September Victoria This famous plum was found in Alderton, Sussex, in 1840. It is dual purpose.
Late September Coe's Golden Drop This was discovered in Bury St Edmunds, Suffolk, in the early 1700s. It is still a mouth-wateringly good plum.
September–October Anna Spath This plum has been grown in Hungary since 1877. It was recently introduced to Britain and is considered· to be a very promising dual purpose variety.

Pests and diseases

Aphids can be discouraged by a winter tar oil wash or equivalent.
Silverleaf, as the name implies, is a fungus which makes the leaves, usually a few at the top of a shoot, an unmistakable silvery colour. To remove the infection the shoot has to be cut well back beyond any sign of discoloration in the wood. It is very important to burn the diseased wood and leaves at once before the unseen spores reinfect the tree. This fungus can kill a tree if left untreated.

There is a simulated or false silverleaf which is caused by malnutrition. In this case there is no discoloration of the infected shoot. The cure is farmyard manure or some other nitrogenous fertiliser.
Brown rot Concentric rings of fungus tissue appear which must be removed at once. Remove the affected plums.
Bacterial canker Gum exudes

from a canker on the shoot which should be cut away and burned. This is best done immediately after fruiting or before leaf burst.

Sweet cherries

Cherries like rich, well drained, yet moisture-retentive, soil. They need rain up to fruiting time, but the fruit is spoilt if heavy rain falls late in June or July. Cherry orchards were grown in grass which grazing sheep cropped very short. In order to keep the branches sufficiently high above the ground, buds were grafted on to a previously planted wild cherry, or mazzard, at a height of about 2 m (6 ft).

Unfortunately no dwarfing stock for cherries has been found. As they are not self-fertile, two cultivars are required and this is another reason why not many cherries are grown privately as so much space is needed. The tall trees are impossible to shield from birds, both in the winter when the buds are eaten and in July when the fruit is pecked. Cherries can be successfully grown as fan trained trees against high walls.

Cultivation

One authority says that cherries need only nitrogen and a good supply of water. Another that they need sulphate of potash annually and a little phosphate every three years (see feeding plums).

Pruning

Very little pruning is needed except for initial shaping. Any cutting should be done in spring to lessen the danger of silverleaf infection.

Rootstocks

Colt semi-vigorous not yet widely available.
Malling 12/1 vigorous.

Varieties

As there are over two hundred and seventy named forms, some of which may be synonyms, it is difficult to make a selection. What is more, these types fall into thirteen

groups which are incompatible. A choice of two cultivars must be made that firstly are compatible in that they will cross-fertilise each other, and secondly which flower at the same time. The local nursery will advise on the best choice.

Mid-June Early Rivers Discovered in 1893.
Early July Roundel Good taste.
Mid-July Merton Glory Best pollinator and compatible with every group.
Late-July Merton Favourite; Stella, the first self-fertile cherry.
New variety Lambert Compact.

Pests and diseases

Apart from birds, aphids can be troublesome to cherries. A winter spray will kill the eggs. Silverleaf, bacterial canker and brown rot are the three diseases which present a threat.

Culinary cherries

These are well worth growing if they can be netted. They cook and bottle very well and can also be eaten raw although they do tend to be rather acid.

Cultivation

Unlike the sweet cherries, they are self-fertile, therefore, only one tree has to be planted. It can be free-standing but this will make it difficult to net. Usually these cherries

Morello—considered to be the finest culinary cherry for cooking and bottling.

are planted against a wall if there is no fruit cage. The wall can be a shaded one but if there happens to be a west wall available, so much the better for the cherry crop. These cherries are best grown in cultivated soil and not under grass.

Feeding
Plenty of organic material will hopefully have been dug in before planting. Against a wall, less fertiliser is required as it is important to restrict growth to the height of the wall (see plums).

Pruning
Unlike sweet cherries, but like peaches, acid cherries fruit only on the previous year's wood, therefore, the old wood needs removing from time to time. This is best done in the late spring just after the buds have broken, to cut down the risk of silverleaf infection and also because it is easier by then to see which is going to be a fruit bud.

Varieties
These varieties are all self-fertile.
Kentish Red Early.
Morello Late and thought to be the best.
Flemish Red Late.

Pests and diseases
Culinary cherries are prone to the same diseases and infections as sweet cherries including brown rot and silverleaf.

Quince
A naturally-growing quince is a very decorative, low-growing tree with an attractive bark and lovely large pinky-white blossom. Unfortunately, very few are planted today compared with the last century, when there was a quince in almost every large garden. Where space is limited, the quince tends to be at the bottom of the list when it comes to choosing what fruit to plant, particularly as it is generally only used for cooking. It has a distinctive aromatic taste and transforms stewed apple. It also makes a superb jelly. It is from the Portuguese name for a quince, *marmelo*, that the word marmalade derives.

Cultivation
Really moist soil or a position next to a pond suits the quince best, but it can be grown anywhere, even in rough grass. As long as the grass is controlled, this has the advantage of preventing the evaporation of moisture from the otherwise bare topsoil. Even in the south, the fruit is thought to appreciate shelter from north winds but the tree is perfectly hardy. Sun to ripen the fruit is far more important, which is why in the north, quinces are usually planted against a wall. A bush or tree in the open will come into bearing in four to five years.

Feeding
A dressing of potash in February, with the addition of some superphosphate every other year, is enough. An occasional mulch of farmyard manure can also be beneficial.

The quince—yet another neglected fruit which has lost popularity during this century despite its distinctive flavour.

Pruning

Quinces need little pruning except for tipping back some shoots in the early years and removing any crossing branches later. If planted against a wall, it is usually grown as an espalier and pruned accordingly.

Picking and storing

The fruit is left hanging until the end of October, after picking it needs six to eight weeks to mature. It will then keep for up to three months in a cool place. It can be laid out in a single layer in an open perforated polythene bag, but if left uncovered, its strong scent can flavour any fruit stored nearby.

Varieties

Quinces are self-fertile and cuttings root easily.

Apple-shaped quince This is better than others in the north.

Portugal Vigorous, but best in the south. Excellent for cooking.

Vranja This comes from Serbia and is recommended.

Berezki Very similar to Vranja but has a smaller crop.

Champion Bears large fruit early with a good flavour.

Havran and Tekes Good varieties from Turkey, fruit 15 cm (6 in) long.

Diseases

Leaf spot or blight attacks the leaves in the form of red spots. It appears in June and the leaves will later drop off. The remedy is to spray with Bordeaux mixture twice in June.

Peaches and nectarines

A nectarine is not a fruit in its own right, it is a peach with a smooth skin. The alternative types of skin are controlled by a pair of genes; the dominant, or stronger one produces the downy skin of a peach, and the recessive gene is responsible for the smooth-skinned form of a nectarine. Peaches, with the exception of Hale's early, are self-fertile. As they flower in early April before many

bees are working, it is best to help pollination by moving a soft brush from flower to flower during the middle of the day.

Cultivation

There are four possible ways of growing what has been called the king of fruit. It can be grown in the open sun, against a wall, in a cold house or in a pot.

Bush tree in the open

In the southern part of the country, in a really sunny spot, a peach can be grown as an open bush. This will give twice the yield of a wall tree and will be much more easily pruned. The late Justin Brooke had a successful group of trees on the open hillside near Newmarket. There is quite a lot of chalk in the soil there which suits them and the drainage was also good. Peaches are perfectly hardy and indeed must have low temperatures during their dormant period. It is the blossom that can be damaged by a severe frost. A peach tree somewhere on the lawn would be so decorative that all would not be lost if, for one year, it failed to fruit. The grass helps to release potash in the soil and also helps to protect the roots which have a large spread.

Fan-trained tree against a wall

In the north, it is advisable to grow a peach against a south wall. As the wall needs to be 3 m (10 ft) high and at least 6 m (20 ft) long, a suitable one is not encountered all that often. As the soil at the base of the wall is drier than elsewhere in the garden, extra care must be taken to incorporate as much organic material as possible in the double-dug 6 m (20 ft) trench. If the soil is at all acid, extra chalk can be added as well as bonemeal and/or potash.

If the bed is beyond the reach of a perforated hose, it is a good tip to sink two 30-cm (1-ft) lengths of land drain or plastic drain pipe vertically, at a little distance, on either side of where the main trunk is going to be. If the water is poured down these it will go straight to the roots instead of much of it being lost over the surface of the soil and then evaporating.

A peach on a wall is usually grown as a fan-trained bush. Unless a two- or three-year-old peach has been correctly trained in accordance with

A nectarine is really a peach with a smooth skin, not a fruit in its own right, and it is not so frequently grown.

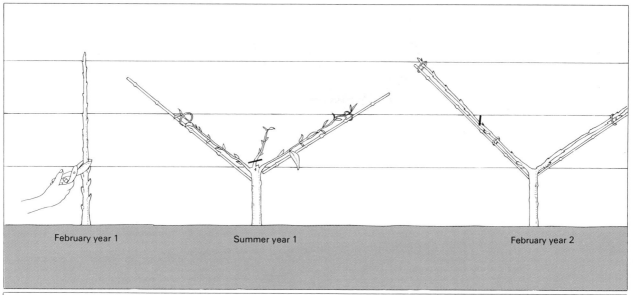

February year 1　　　　Summer year 1　　　　February year 2

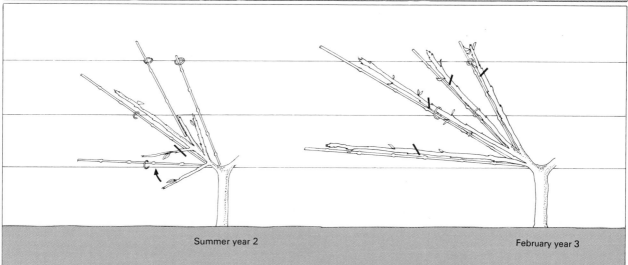

Summer year 2　　　　February year 3

the Wisley system it is worth losing
a year and planting a maiden. This
should be planted at an angle to the
wall so that the roots are at least 30
cm away, thus nearer to damper
soil. Wires will be needed every 15
cm (6 in), starting about 45 cm (18
in) from the ground. The net can
later be attached to some of the
highest staples. If it is draped over a
cross bar of wood erected in front,
the net will be kept away from the
actual shoots. Alternatively, brack-
ets can be fixed to the top of the wall
on which a 25 cm (10 in) plank is
secured, and the net hooked on.

Top *The first stages of training a
fan-trained peach begin in February
with the initial pruning, which will
cause new shoots to grow. These are
then pruned again in the summer
(centre) by cutting out all but two
shoots at right angles to each other.
The following February the two shoots
can be cut back to a good bud (right).
Above Second summer pruning allows
two shoots from the top side of each arm,
and one from the lower side, to grow
(left). Winter pruning is then carried
out as before (right).
Right Peach leaf curl.*

153

Peaches under cover

Wonderful fan-trained peaches were cultivated in the large conservatories and greenhouses of Victorian times. Plenty of ventilation is necessary during the winter as ·a cold dormancy period is essential An adequate watering system is needed in the summer and both syringing the leaves with water and extra hand pollination is necessary. Trees in a house are prone to red spider, but at least the fruits are kept away from birds, if not guaranteed protection from the occasional wasp.

Growing a peach in a pot has two advantages. It can be left out in the winter for the necessary cold dormant period and brought under cover at blossom and fruiting time for protection.

To begin with a maiden can be planted in a pot just large enough to take the roots. It can then be re-potted in alternate years and by the fifth year will need a 37-cm (15-in) pot. Fertilisers can be added easily as and when required. The maiden can be trained as an open bush which is the nearest to its natural shape.

Feeding

Peaches need nitrogen, otherwise they are apt to drop their fruit. This can be applied as a dressing of ammonium sulphate. They may also need extra potash. A peach can live for forty to sixty years if well nurtured.

Pruning

Unlike apples, peaches only have flower buds on new wood, so any shoot that has fruited is removed down to the first basal shoot unless it is wanted as framework. This basal shoot is then tied in as a replacement. Too many buds can easily develop and there is quite a skill in deciding which to rub out and which to leave. It is most important that pruning should be delayed until February, just before the end of the dormant period. If peaches are cut earlier they are liable to infection by fungus causing shoots to die.

Initial fan training

First year In February the maiden is cut back to three good buds about 60 cm (2 ft) from the ground. Other buds below this can be rubbed out now or left for a few weeks in case any of the chosen buds do not shoot.

First summer When new shoots have grown to about 30 cm (1 ft) long, select two shoots at right angles to each other and tie them at 45° to two canes. Carefully cut out any other shoot, painting the wounds with bituminous or lead paint.

Second year In mid-February, cut back the two shoots to a good bud about 30-45 cm (12-18 in) from the main trunk.

Second summer During the summer, allow two shoots from the top side of each arm and one from the lower side to grow. Tie these shoots at the desired angle and rub out any other buds not wanted. There should now be four branches on each side.

Subsequently continue similar training of shoots until the wall space is filled.

Rootstocks

St. Julian A is recommended for fan-trained trees. Brompton or plum stock can be used for peaches growing in the open but it is apt to sucker and is thought to make the peach more susceptible to silverleaf infection. For open bush trees a peach seedling is often used.

Varieties

During the nineteenth century there was a great increase in the number of good varieties. This was mainly due to interested nurserymen, Thomas Rivers, in particular. For growing in the open it is best to choose an early fruiting variety in case the summer is cold. Peaches are self-fertile.

Mid-July Duke of York
End of July Alexander
Early August Peregrine
Mid August Rochester Good for growing in the open. It ripens earlier against a wall.

Late August Royal George
Early September Bellegrade
Mid-September Dymond

Nectarines

These are best grown against a wall unless there is a site well protected from spring frosts.

Mid-July John Rivers
Early August Lord Napier
Mid-August Humboldt
Late August Elruge
Early September Pine Apple

Pests and diseases

A winter tar oil spray will kill the eggs of aphids which can be a nuisance when they hatch in the spring. On wall trees the red spider mite can turn the leaves first mottled and then a bronze colour. A malathion spray will then be necessary.

Die Back is due to a fungal infection through a cut surface. The affected shoot must be cut back beyond the point where there is any discoloration of the wood and a wound sealing paint used over the cut surface.

Peach leaf curl is another fungus which makes the leaves blister, distort and sometimes turn red before becoming brown and dropping off. All the affected leaves should be burnt immediately. This infection can be prevented by spraying twice at fourteen-day intervals in February with Bordeaux mixture, a copper spray or a 3% sulphur of lime. If any affected leaves appear during the summer, another spray can be given after the fruit is picked, but before the leaves drop.

Apricots

This appears to be one of the fruits the Romans missed and failed to bring to Britain. Henry VIII remedied the situation by sending his gardener across to Europe to bring some back. The Italian name at that time was *abricocco* which might account for the fact that right up until this century the fruit was often called an abricock.

At first they were grown against

walls and later on in glasshouses. Many believe, however, that the lack of moisture when grown under cover is detrimental to the fruit and apricots grown in the open are tastier and more juicy. Wherever they are grown, they flower in mid-March before insects are about in sufficient number to effect proper pollination. This has to be assisted artificially by hand, using a thin camel hair or soft paint brush.

Cultivation
Whether grown in the open, against a wall or under glass, apricots like a well drained and slightly alkaline soil with a high potash content. They dislike drying out in summer so plenty of organic material needs to be incorporated before planting. An annual mulch is beneficial whichever of the growing methods is used.

Bush apricot in the open
The late Justin Brooke grew an orchard on a south-facing slope at Clopton Hall, Wickhambrook, Suffolk. The trees were planted 4·5 m (15 ft) apart and were grassed down to conserve the moisture on the chalky, well drained site. Pruning was done by tipping back the shoots in May and the bush grown as an open goblet. A frost-free site is essential because there is no method of protecting the blossom.

Fan-type tree against a wall
The blossom can be protected by evergreen branches or else by double netting, provided this hangs in front of the tree and does not actually touch it. Because of the risk of die back, it might be advisable to plant an already-trained two- to three-year-old tree rather than a maiden. The soil by a wall will need constant watering in a dry summer and an organic mulch of some kind to preserve moisture is essential. As well as hand pollination, the trees may need spraying with water just beforehand if the air is very dry, to keep the stigma of the flower slightly damp to aid fertilisation.

Pot-grown apricot
An open bush shape is best planted in a 25-cm (10-in) pot. A pot-grown apricot can be left out during the cold winter for dormancy which it likes and then brought in under cover just before the buds colour. After this it can be put outside, either on a terrace or sunk in the earth to lessen the inevitable necessity of watering. It could again be brought in to hasten ripening or to protect the fruit if necessary. Each year some of the top soil should be replaced by compost and some fertiliser added. If the bush begins to look poorly after some years, an additional feed of liquid manure or a spray of foliar feed can easily be given during the summer.

Under glass
This may be the only way of growing apricots in the north but it has several disadvantages.

Above *Moorpark—a strong, vigorous apricot which crops very well.*
Below *Open bush-shaped apricots can be grown successfully in pots.*

1 The apricot needs a cold dormancy period with good ventilation and this may not suit other plants in the house.

2 Because little pruning is advocated, a wall of at least 2·5 m (8 ft) is needed.

3 A permanent hose or other supply of water is essential throughout the growing period.

4 The foliage may need syringing frequently to discourage infestation of red spider mite.

5 The soil will need renewing and bringing in farmyard manure each year is quite a task.

6 Special care has to be taken to effect pollination.

7 At the end of it all, the fruit may be woody and fibrous.

Feeding

Besides a mulch of manure, 100 g (4 oz) of bonemeal per 1 m² (1 sq yd) and 25 g (1 oz) of potash are needed in February of each year.

Pruning

An apricot is more like a plum than a peach and makes fruit spurs readily on older wood as well as on the preceding year's growth. However, as it is prone to die back, the less cutting carried out after shaping the better. Wherever possible, shoots should be tied down into position. When cutting is essential it is best carried out in spring on younger trees or just after fruiting. Pinching out the tips of shoots by hand when they are about 10 cm (4 in) long in early summer is often sufficient.

Thinning

This is best done as soon as the fruit is about 1 cm ($\frac{1}{2}$ in) long, however, it should not be too thorough as there will be a natural drop a little later on.

Early August varieties

Ouillons Early Excellent flavour.
Hemskerke Hardier than Moorpark. Delicious flavour and crops well.
New Large Early

Alfred New variety
Farmingdale New variety
Late August varieties
Breda Hardy, fine quality and flavour.
Moorpark Strong, vigorous grower and crops well.
Peach Less prone to die back.

Pests and diseases

Red spider mite could be a nuisance against a wall and if so spray with malathion. Syringing the tree with water up to the time the fruit begins to change colour helps to discourage the mite.

Die back is due to a fungal infection and shoots and branches can die back in a couple of weeks. The cause is still a subject for debate. The only treatment is to cut the affected branch or shoot right off, painting the wound immediately.

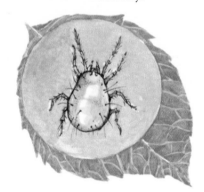

Red spider mite is a particular nuisance to wall-trained fruit trees.

Figs

The fig is definitely happier growing around the Mediterranean where it will set two crops of fruit in a year, one in June and another in the autumn. It can be induced to do this in Britain only if planted in a glasshouse. Against a south wall, one crop will ripen but the second will be frosted before it can ripen and will drop off.

The fruit buds occur at the nodes, so long inter-nodes have to be avoided. This can be done by discouraging vegetative growth by growing the figs in poor soil and restricting the roots. It is often sug-

gested that the fig should be planted in a hollow 100 cm (3-4 ft) square cube of concrete which has been sunk into the ground. This is more easily advised than achieved. An alternative is to plant the fig in a stout 30 cm (12 in) pot or plastic pail with some holes in the base. Any roots growing through will have to be cut off later. Other roots will burst out over the top and can be pruned back more easily.

Plenty of drainage material is needed at the bottom of the container. As the fig needs constant water during the summer, it will save labour if a short length of hose can be laid to the tree and left there permanently. The other end can be attached to the tap as required. Figs can stand only 10°C (50°F) so often they are protected with sacking or fir branches during the winter.

Pruning a fan-trained wall fig

Winter pruning is done as late as possible, usually in March to avoid frost damage. The aim is to have two hands of branches growing from a point 45 cm (18 in) above soil level. The initial training is as for a fan-trained peach, but after that less cutting is done and the training can be less precise. In early June the tips of shoots are nipped out to five leaves. As the second crop of figs will never mature out of doors, these embryo fruits can be rubbed off in late August to encourage the formation of the even tinier figs that will hopefully over-winter safely ready for the next season.

Pruning a pot-grown fig

There are several advantages in growing a fig in a 30-cm (12-in) pot. It can be protected under cover in the winter, put out in the summer and sunk if desired, to save on watering. It can then be brought in again after the first crop has matured to ripen off the second crop. If heat is used and the fig remains under cover then three crops might be obtained. If grown inside, the regular supply

of water is even more important. In a pot, an open bush shape should be achieved with as little drastic cutting as possible.

Feeding
If a little bonemeal is incorporated when the fig is planted, mulches and organic material later will be more important than extra fertiliser.

A fig trained against a wall.

Picking
When a fig is ripe it will hang down. It can be attacked by both birds and wasps.

Varieties
The Adriatic fig will develop without being pollinated and it does not matter that the fruit will have no seeds in it.
Brown Turkey Good both indoors and on a wall.

Brunswick Good both indoors and on a wall.
Bourjassotte Grise Very richly flavoured. Best grown in a greenhouse.

Diseases
Figs can be infected by a fungal disease known descriptively as coral spot. The affected wood must be cut out quickly and burned before the infection can spread.

Hazelnut

The native hazel bush is one of fifteen species found across Europe and in North Africa. The cultivated cob is thought by some to have been a species introduced from Turkey in 1665. This would explain the Latin name *avellana*, which could be a corruption of a place called Abellano. There is, however, an alternative theory that the hazel comes from Avellino, a region in the south of Italy, near Naples.

The hazel hybridises easily so there is confusion as to whether the many different forms are true species or not. The cultivated nut is round and called a cob, but there is another nut which has a much longer husk, called a filbert.

Large acreages of nuts used to be grown commercially in Kent. They were manured heavily each year and then skilled nutters kept the open bushes to a height of 1·5 m (5-6 ft). Although the nut is known to be nutritious, many of the nutteries have been grubbed out during this century. In a garden where only two or three bushes can be grown, it is usually the diet of the ubiquitous grey squirrel that is improved.

Cultivation

Hazels grow in any soil except very acid ones. They like protection from north winds and need a sunny place to ripen the nuts. The male catkins are out in February and rely on the wind to pollinate the tiny red-styled female flowers. These are born on older wood and are therefore conveniently lower down. Hazels are grown as an open bush of about five or six branches on a main stem of about 45 cm (18 in). New plants can be produced by layering a two-year-old branch in the atumn, and separating it when rooted the following year. Any unwanted suckers from the base are removed.

Feeding

Hazels like plenty of organic manure and need to grow in cultivated soil. They also like potash each year.

Pruning

It is best to delay this until after the catkins have shed their pollen. The main branches of a newly planted bush are cut back, always to an outward facing bud. Thereafter side shoots are shortened. Some of these are brutted in early August, that is, broken by hand and left hanging. This enables more sun to get to the nuts and checks the vegetative growth.

Picking and storing

In an ideal world where there are no grey squirrels, nuts are left until they start to fall. The husks become mildewed easily so they must be very well dried before storing. If ripe enough, they are best removed. The nuts can then be stored in an open polythene bag laid flat. This makes it easy to see if any mildew or mould has appeared.

Varieties

Duke of Edinburgh Excellent flavour, crops well.
Pearson's Prolific
Cosford Sweet Large nut, raised in Suffolk.
Kentish Cob Needs one of the above as a pollinator.

Pests

Nut weevil The grub eats the kernel of the nut and then leaves

The rich, brown fruit of the hazel tree are often known as cobnuts.

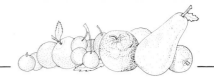

through a neat round hole. It then stays in the soil until the following spring when it will become an adult and start the cycle all over again. By cultivating the soil, it encourages birds to find the larvae. Trees badly infected can be sprayed with derris in early June.

Nut sawfly The caterpillar eats the leaves and can also be sprayed if the infection is bad.

Big bud mite or gall mite attacks the buds and makes them abortive. Infected buds can be picked off. A spray of lime sulphur in early May will act as a preventative.

Walnut

This tree is not a native of Britain. It had probably been introduced by the tenth century, as its colloquial name derives from an early English word, *wealh*, meaning foreign. The tree grows naturally in the warmer parts of the temperate area and that is why, over here, the young shoots are so often killed by frost. It is a very handsome tree of up to 23 m (75 ft) and is well worth planting for its looks, quite apart from its nuts. It likes good soil and appreciates a little extra chalk. It needs a frost-free or protected site. Young trees do not take as easily to transplanting as other fruit and will need watering in the first years if they are dry.

Some trees crop better than others but it is not possible to reproduce them by seed. The seedlings, like

Nut weevil and damaged kernel (not shown to scale).

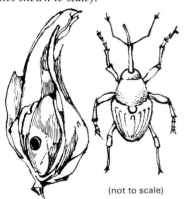

(not to scale)

children, may or may not be as good as the parents and it takes fifteen to twenty years for a tree to crop. It is not possible to graft or bud either as the spring is too cold for these methods to be successful. Grafted trees are imported from France and if these are on dwarfing stock they will fruit in ten years.

Walnuts ready for picking.

Pruning

When they are young, the tips of side shoots can be nipped out with finger and thumb. It is best not to cut a walnut with secateurs or a knife as it bleeds easily.

Picking

For pickling, the nuts are picked in June before the inner case has become hard. Nuts ripen best in a hot

has barely begun, so it is yet another contender for the sheltered spot in the garden. Unfortunately one tree can produce both sweet edible almonds and bitter, unusable ones. Which type predominates seems to be a matter of chance. The blossom is always beautiful, if the buds have not been previously eaten by bullfinches. An almond can be grown as a bush as well as a half standard, if preferred.

Varieties
Ferraduel Late flowering from France.
Ferragues Distributed from 1973.
Marcona Introduced in 1961 from Spain.

Diseases
Being a close relative of the peach, the almond is also subject to infection by the fungus which causes leaf curl. Prevention is better than cure and the tree can be sprayed twice in February (see peach diseases).

summer and can be picked by the second week in September if the squirrels and rooks have not already done this for you. The outer green skin, the juice of which stains badly, has to be completely removed. Any bits left on the shell will go mouldy. The nuts can then be stored flat in an open polythene bag. They used to be stored in layers of sand or salt in an earthenware crock.

Varieties
Northdown Claw; Malling 92, 162 and 202; Franquette (French); Meylanaise (French).

Chestnut
This tree, at about 25 m (60-100 ft) tall, is one of ten chestnut species growing naturally in the southern part of the temperate band. It is widely distributed throughout the country where there is no lime or chalk in the soil. This sweet chestnut belongs to quite a different family from the horse chestnut, which has a single nut, or conker, in a smooth case. The sweet or Spanish chestnut has a spiny case usually enclosing two nuts. If preferred, the chestnut can be coppiced and kept low. In this form it can make an attractive boundary hedge as it also suckers readily to fill in any gaps. The attractive yellow catkins do not appear until July.

Picking and storing
The principles are the same as for other nuts. The peeled nuts are not eaten raw as a rule but are first roasted and are more frequently used in a purée for stuffing. Crystallised in sugar, the French *marron glacé* is a great delicacy, if something of an acquired taste.

Varieties
Marron de Lyons; Paragon.

Almond
In Britain, this Mediterranean tree flowers early in March when spring

Left *The sweet chestnut—not to be confused with the horse chestnut.*

Below *The sweet or Spanish chestnut is delicious roasted, puréed for stuffing or crystallised in sugar.*

Soft Fruits

It's cheaper to grow than to buy

Soft fruit in the garden

Soft fruit includes the black and red currants, gooseberries, raspberries, strawberries, rhubarb, loganberries, blackberries and hybrids, as well as blueberries and cranberries.

Due to the costs of production, picking and marketing, soft fruit has become expensive. The only reasonably cheap way of buying it is to pick it direct from the field, which is only practicable for those who live near a fruitgrowing area. Growing one's own is the obvious answer, but how to plan a small garden to provide the best growing conditions for the greatest number of plants can often present problems

Plan 2 Planting where space is restricted. The centre of the garden is left open for lawn or vegetables.

for the modern amateur gardener.

Very few gardens attached to a family house provide an ideal situation for growing all types of fruit. Most houses have a medium-sized back garden and possibly a small front one, but few prospective fruit-growers are lucky enough to have a house surrounded by garden on all sides unless they are fortunate enough to live in a manor house.

During the first half of this century a private garden was often large enough to accommodate flowers, fruit and vegetables, and in some cases an orchard as well. However, since the last war both urban and rural houses have been built with smaller and smaller gardens. As a result, some ingenuity and careful planning is required to grow flowers, fruit and vegetables in these confined spaces. But it can nevertheless be done.

Planning the garden

Plan 1 shows the more conventional arrangement for planting fruit enclosed within a fruit cage. Plan 2 gives ideas for planting where space is restricted and leaves the centre of the garden open for lawn or vegetables. Since black currants like a warm situation they are planted in the border, backed by a south-facing fence. Behind them are loganberries and red currants, the latter trained as cordons. Both these are acid fruits and they need the sun if they are to be reasonably sweet. Nylon netting fastened to the top of the fence to cover the currant bushes will give protection from birds. The netting can be held in position by stones along the edge of the path.

Plan 2 shows gooseberries trained as standards. This method has been used by disabled people so that they can sit in a wheelchair and either

prune or pick from the chair. When they are planted as a row along a path, these bushes make an interesting feature since they resemble miniature trees. They can be underplanted with alpine strawberries.

Raspberries are also fitted into the plan in an unusual way. If two rows are planted out in the conventional way, they will need 1·5 m (5 ft) between the rows, which is a lot of space. In Scandinavia, raspberries are often grown as a boundary hedge and in plan 2 use is made of a narrow border at the end of the garden. The canes are planted 45 cm (18 in) apart to fill the border. Pruning is carried out each year in the normal way but no staking is given. Weeds are suppressed by heavy mulching because cultivation between the canes is difficult. When raspberries are grown in a deep, moist, soil, this method has given excellent results.

The north-facing wall or fence provides a situation for blackberries. In their natural state the best fruit is always found on the shady side of the hedge. Blackberries and some of the hybrid berries—which are also decorative—can be used as boundary hedges or as a division. Real savings in space can be made by

training on a post and wire fence parallel to the garden path.

Great advances have been made in the last twenty years in producing new varieties of fruit. As a result, growers whose gardens are low-lying or in a frost pocket can now use varieties which are either frost-resistant or late to flower and mature, so escaping the danger of frost. In the cold, northern garden blackberries and gooseberries do well, while blackcurrants prefer the warmer climate of the south. However, given good cultivation, most gardens can grow a selection of some of the small fruits.

Black currant

Quite apart from its delicious flavour, the black currant is one of the most valuable of the soft fruits, since it contains more vitamin C than any other fruit.

Fruit protected from birds by a functional wire mesh cage in the gardens at Wisley.

Below *Standard gooseberry.*

Plan 1 This is the conventional arrangement for planting fruit enclosed for protection in a fruit cage.

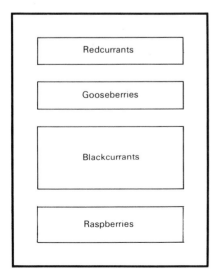

Redcurrants

Gooseberries

Blackcurrants

Raspberries

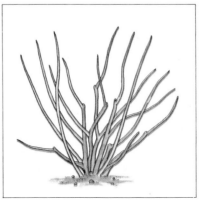

Above *Ripe Amos black currants.*
Far left *A black currant bush before
undergoing autumn pruning.*
Left *A black currant bush after the
autumn pruning has removed the old
fruiting wood, leaving a young growth
to take its place.*

To flourish it requires a warm situation, although recently new varieties have been introduced which are more tolerant of frost. A warm, sheltered position is important for growing black currants since they are pollinated by insects who only become active when it is warm. Unless they are on the wing to carry out fertilisation, the set of the fruit will be poor.

In an exposed garden, protection should be given against the prevailing wind. Hedges make an excellent barrier. They act as a filter to the wind but may take up a lot of valuable garden space. A first-class and inexpensive wind break is a hedge of ivy. Using chestnut palings for support, plant the ivy 45 cm (18 in) apart choosing either the large-leafed variety, *Hedera colchica*, on its own or mixed with the Irish ivy, *Hedera hibernica*. This will quickly fan out to cover the fencing although the space taken up is negligible. Maintenance is easy and the long shoots need only be snipped off with secateurs. Interwoven fencing makes an attractive alternative to a hedge and this can be used for training cordon fruit or blackberries.

The black currant has a long life and although it will grow in a wide range of soils, light soils must be made retentive by a good application of farmyard manure, garden compost or spent mushroom manure. The black currant is a moisture-loving plant and, provided it is well drained, it will always do better on heavier soils. Cultivation should be deep, incorporating manure into the bottom spit. Because the black currant is a long-lasting crop, the soil should first be thoroughly cleansed of all perennial weeds such as couch and bindweed.

When plants are bought they should always be officially certified stock. There are two main threats to the black currant, one is a pest called big bud and the other a virus called reversion, both of which will be discussed later. Both can be avoided if healthy certified stock are used.

Planting

Bushes are bought at two years old and planting can take place at any time during the dormant season, if the soil is in good condition and not sticky or frostbound. On a heavy clay soil it is probably better to wait until spring before planting.

Dig a hole big enough to allow the roots to be spread and then work some moist peat in around the root system. Remember that when a plant is moved, the tiny delicate hairs on the root are destroyed. These hairs are its means of taking in food and moisture and they will quickly re-establish themselves if they are given a medium of moist peat in which to do so. No plant will make good top growth until it has established a sound root system, so careful planting is absolutely essential. When the soil is filled in around the roots, sprinkle in a handful of bonemeal. The basal buds should be just below soil level and the soil should be well firmed down.

In the spring all shoots are cut back to within 7 cm (3 in) of the base. This is to encourage young growth to develop into strong shoots that will produce fruit the following year. The black currant produces its best fruit on the wood made in the previous season. This wood can always be recognised by its colour. The old wood is dark, whereas the new wood is light brown.

Pruning

Although pruning can be carried out any time during the autumn, it is best done as soon after picking the fruit as possible. This allows the young wood, which will bear the following year's fruit, to ripen. The old fruiting wood is cut out leaving a young growth to take its place. As the bush gets older, so the old wood can be cut out from the centre of the bush. Always endeavour to keep an open, well-balanced shape admitting plenty of light and air. This not only aids ripening of the fruit, but avoids a congested centre to the bush which will create a humid atmosphere, encouraging both pests and diseases to flourish.

Propagation

Black currants are propagated by hard wood cuttings taken in October and November of well-ripened shoots of the current year's growth about 25 cm (10 in) in length. Make a clean cut immediately beneath a bud at the base of the shoot, then make a slanting cut above the top bud. In the case of black currants, all the buds are left on the shoot because they will grow out to form a vigorous bush. A slit trench is then dug and if the soil is of a heavy nature, such as clay, then a little sand or ash can be sprinkled along the base of the trench. Choose a cool situation without too much sun. Insert the cuttings to a depth of 15 cm (6 in), 15 cm (6 in) apart. Replace the soil and firm the cuttings in. Little further attention is then needed.

In March it is wise to firm along the row since heavy frosts during the winter may have lifted the soil and loosened the cuttings. During the summer they should be watered if necessary and hoed regularly to keep them free from weeds. Where only a small number of plants or replacements are needed, they can be put in with a dibber or a trowel but, as in the case of those planted in a trench, it is essential that the base of the cutting is really firm and in close contact with the soil.

In the following October the cuttings can be transferred to their permanent quarters and should be planted 150 cm (5 ft) apart each way. After planting, the plants should be cut down to soil level. This encourages production of sufficient growth to bear a good crop in the second year after planting.

Black currants need plenty of nitrogen if they are to produce an abundance of growth and although organic manures are said to be the most beneficial, 66 g (2 oz) per 1 m^2 (1 sq yd) of sulphate of ammonia given at the end of March will encourage growth. Cultivation should be shallow near the bushes since the rooting system is close to the surface. Plenty of mulching is required during the summer. This can consist of compost, spent mushroom-bed manure, rotted farmyard manure or lawn mowings, all of which will also help to keep down weed growth. Dryness at the root will result in tough stems and small seedy fruits.

If the black currant bushes in your garden have been neglected for some time, decide how much young growth capable of bearing fruit exists. If there is some, then cut out all the old wood and crossing branches and cut back to any young shoots. Some fruit can then be harvested, but it may take at least two years to get the bush back into full production. The alternative method is to cut the whole bush back to within 7.5-9.5 cm (3-4 in) of the base, giving a liberal dressing of rotted manure in the autumn with an application of sulphate of ammonia in the spring. This will encourage strong new growths to produce fruit the following year. However, if the bushes are infected with big bud or reversion it is better to dig them up and burn them and to plant fresh certified stock.

Varieties
By planting early, mid-season and late varieties black currants can be picked over a fairly long season.

Early season
Boskoop Giant This produces very good quality berries on long trusses. A warm and sheltered situation is required since flowering is early and frost and cold winds must be avoided.

Mendip Cross A good early variety for cold climates, since it tolerates both wind and frost.

Wellington XXX A very good variety that does well in moist soils. It makes plenty of growth but does need extra nitrogen. The fruit, which is rather thick-skinned, is excellent for freezing. This variety blooms just a little later than Mendip Cross, so that it often avoids frost.

Mid-season
Seabrook's Black A compact, upright bush, it is a good choice for the smaller garden. Because it flowers late, it usually escapes the frost and the fruit has the advantage of maturing close on the heels of the early varieties. It is an excellent jam-making variety and very rarely succumbs to attack by big bud.

Late
Amos Black Compact in habit and non-spreading, this is another useful variety for the smaller garden. It blooms very late in the season and is therefore ideal for gardens situated in frost pockets.

Laleham Beauty This currant will crop heavily and consistently on most types of soil and since they have thick skins they freeze well.

Pests and diseases
Gallmite is the most destructive of pests. It is better known as big bud and can be recognised by the large swollen buds formed in the spring by the gallmites gathered inside. Attack by big bud results in loss of crop. Any affected shoot should be removed and burned. If a number of shoots are affected, dig up and burn the whole bush. If the bush is only lightly affected it should be sprayed with one part of lime sulphur in a hundred of water as soon as the blossom trusses appear in the bud.

Reversion This is a virus disease which alters the habit of growth. The leaves start showing symptoms in June. They become longer and narrower with smoother foliage and there is a reduction in the number of leaf veins. Immature fruit drops off and the bush becomes practically infertile. To prevent the spread of infection, bushes should be dug up and burned since no remedy is known. The only safeguard is to buy clean, healthy, certified stock at the outset. If bushes have to be burned through an attack by the virus, replant on another site if possible.

Black currant propagation—making a clean cut immediately beneath a bud at the base of the shoot.

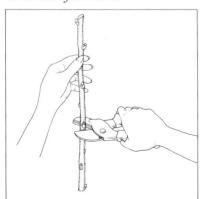

Black currant propagation—firm the cuttings into a slit trench to a depth of 15 cm (6 in), 15 cm (6 in) apart.

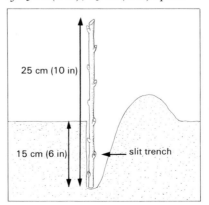

Black currant propagation—once established, the bush is cut back to soil level.

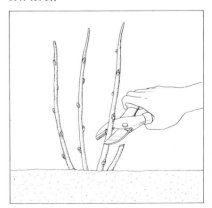

Inset *Attack by gallmite can be recognised by swollen buds in spring.* Right *Boskoop Giant black currant.*

Red currant

The red currant does not have such a wide range of uses as other soft fruits and is chiefly grown for making jelly to serve with lamb. Nevertheless, the fruit can be used in conjunction with other soft fruits, such as gooseberries and raspberries, and because of its high pectin content it is useful in helping to set strawberry jam. A small planting can provide adequate fruit for these purposes since the red currant fruits on the spurs and carries a large quantity of fruit in a small area.

The bushes should be spaced 150 cm (5 ft) apart each way when planting, although red currants may also be grown very successfully as cordons. Grown in this way, they can be either double or single or, alternatively, espaliers. These are ideal on a south-facing wall or fence.

Red currants are rather an acid fruit, especially if grown in the shade. They need all the sun they can possibly get if they are to be reasonably sweet when ripe. They are one of the glossiest and most brilliant of fruits, especially when the trusses are really large, making them a certain target for birds. Unfortunately, red currants always seem to ripen just when the second brood of blackbirds are fledged, making protection vital. If they are not grown in a fruit cage, then they can be covered with netting held down firmly in position. If planted as cordons, then netting draped over them from the top of the fence is an ideal arrangement. When plants or fruits are going to be grown against a fence, the best plan is to train them up three strands of galvanised wire stretched and secured along the length of the fence. The first wire should be 45-60 cm (18 in-2 ft) from the ground and the others spaced at 45-cm (18-in) intervals.

Red currants can be grown as single cordons, planted 45 cm (18 in) apart or as double cordons, 90 cm (3 ft) apart. They are grown on a leg, that is to say a short stem. Young bushes are planted any time during

the dormant season into soil well enriched with humus and thoroughly cleared of any perennial weeds, the worst of which are couch, ground elder and bindweed. This will be well worth while.

Pruning

Red currants do not make the strong vigorous growth of black currants, so a newly planted young bush has each young shoot cut back to about half its length, always cutting to an outward-facing bud. Red currants fruit on the short spurs made on the old wood, so subsequent pruning consists of shortening the leading shoots to 135 cm (4 ft 6 in) and the laterals to within 5 cm (2 in) of the base to form fruiting spurs. It may be necessary to cut out some of the

Laxton's No. 1—an early variety of red currant, particularly popular for its excellent crop.

older branches to allow them to be replaced by young growth as the bushes get older.

Propagation

As with the black currant, take cuttings of well-ripened wood of current year's growth. Red currant cuttings should be at least 30 cm (12 in) in length and all the buds should be removed except the top three or four. Doing this will make the bushes grow on a short stem or leg. If rooted cuttings are to be grown on and trained as cordons, then grow on the leader shoot until it has reached the required height, cutting

Late Red—red currants fruit on the spurs and carry a large quantity of fruit in a small area.

back all the side shoots to within 7 cm (2½-3 in) of the main stem. In subsequent years, cut back the laterals to about 3-4 cm (1-1½ in). Summer pruning can be carried out in June by cutting the laterals back to four or five leaves.

Varieties
Laxtons No. 1 An early variety bearing an excellent crop.
Rivers Late Red A later-fruiting kind than Laxtons No. 1.

Pests and diseases
Greenfly These sometimes attack the young leaves and shoots. The

leaves are punctured by the fly, so allowing disease to enter. Spraying can be done when the bushes are completely dormant with tar oil, and when aphids appear in spring or early summer, with a systemic insecticide or malathion.

Red currant bush before pruning the leading shoots and laterals to form fruiting spurs (left).
Red currant bush after pruning the leading shoots by 135 cm (4 ft 6 in) and the laterals to within 5 cm (2 in) of the base (right).

Currant clearwing moth This attacks the young shoots causing them to shrivel up and die. They should be sprayed with a tar oil wash when bushes are fully dormant.

Coral spot This is a wound parasite, entering through dead tissues and gradually becoming parasitic. It will attack young, damaged shoots and can also enter after insect damage. Any cuts should be made crosswise as cleanly as possible and then painted.

Gooseberry sawfly This will occasionally attack the red currant and can be controlled by spraying either with malathion or derris when the leaves unfold.

Above *Gooseberry sawfly. This troublesome little pest can be controlled by spraying. Use either malathion or derris when the leaves unfold.*

Below *Currant clearwing moth larvae.*

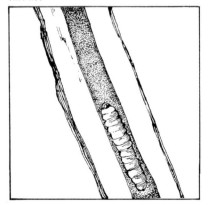

Gooseberry

A native of the British Isles, the gooseberry, is one of the most easily grown of all soft fruits. It tolerates widely varying weather and soil conditions and is not troubled by frost. The fruit is rarely attacked by birds and can be harvested over a long period. The gooseberry likes cool conditions which enables the fruit to mature slowly, giving it an excellent flavour. Gooseberries are invaluable for summer sweets and puddings, jams, jellies, chutney and vinegars. They also bottle well and when deep frozen, are hardly distinguishable from freshly gathered fruit. At their best, ripe gooseberries can equal any other dessert fruit and in districts where strawberries are difficult to grow they provide a delicious alternative.

The gooseberry does well in most soils and most situations. It tolerates both wind and frost but always responds to good cultivation and the incorporation of some sort of humus to hold the moisture. Lack of moisture at the roots will result in undersized, seedy, hardskinned fruit and the gooseberry is particularly vulnerable in this respect.

Planting

As with most deciduous plants, planting can be carried out any time

Left *Careless—a white gooseberry with an excellent flavour, it crops well on any type of soil and freezes well.* Below *Pruning a cup-shaped gooseberry bush, keeping the centre open.*

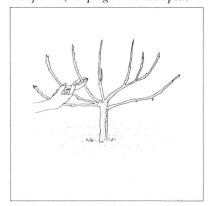

during the dormant season—that is, from November until March, provided the soil is in the right condition. Any broken roots should be trimmed and the remainder spread out evenly over the base of the hole. Moist peat and a little fine soil is worked in around the roots, which should not be deeper than 15 cm (6 in) below the surface leaving 22 cm (6-9 in) of clear stem above the ground. The plants are then firmed in well.

Pruning

Gooseberries fruit on the old as well as the new wood. Like the red currant, they bear fruit at the base of the short spurs which may be of wood from one to ten years old. The best quality fruit is produced on the young, vigorous wood of the previous year's growth. It is therefore necessary to practise two systems of pruning. Pruning should be sufficiently hard to produce plenty of new growth. Lateral growths on old wood should be cut back to about 7 cm (3 in) to encourage fruiting spurs.

Always maintain a cup-shaped bush, keeping the centre of each reasonably open. The main branches should be no less than 22 cm (8-9 in) from each other when they open out and produce fruit. Cut back all crossing shoots. Very strong growths should be cut right out since spurs from these rarely form fruit buds. As the bush ages, replace the old wood with healthy young shoots since this will help to prolong its productive life.

Give a good dressing of some form of organic manure in the autumn and 19 g (1/3 oz) of sulphate of potash in the spring. If there is a lack of potash, the leaves will have a brown, scorched appearance. If this occurs, a dressing at the same rate can be given immediately.

On young bushes, it is best to pick all the fruit when it is young and green. Even if they are intended for dessert, by removing the fruit, the energy of the plant will be directed

171

into building up a strong bush for the following year's fruiting.

Propagation

This is done by hard-wooded cuttings 30 cm (12-15 in) in length. Select strong, well-ripened shoots of current year's growth. All buds and spines should be removed except the top four. The cuttings are inserted in the same way as for black currants.

Varieties

For cooking, most varieties are picked whilst green. However, when they are allowed to ripen for dessert, they can be either red, yellow, green or white.

Lancashire Lad (red) A very old variety raised in 1829. It is good for cooking as well as dessert and resistant to mildew. It makes a large bush and is not therefore suitable for the smaller garden.

Bedford (red) A neat bush ripening early with excellently flavoured berries.

Warrington (red) Late maturing, it has very firm berries and is a good choice for freezing.

Leveller (yellow) This is another old variety, unequalled as a dessert. It crops heavily but needs generous feeding.

New Gem (yellow) Upright in growth, it is a good all-round variety for all cooking purposes.

Howard's Lancer (green) This is susceptible to American gooseberry mildew but, if kept in check, it bears a good crop on almost any type of soil. The fruit serves all purposes and makes a very fine dessert.

Drill (green) Chosen because it makes a neat, compact bush.

Careless (white) A variety with a reputation for cropping well on any type of soil. Its excellent flavour is retained both in bottling and freezing.

Keepsake (white) A good all-round variety, cropping well on most soils.

Pests and diseases

Gooseberry sawfly This is the

An unpruned gooseberry bush—the best fruit will be borne on the new wood but old wood will fruit as well.

A cup-shaped gooseberry bush after pruning back lateral growths on old wood and crossing shoots.

172

most familiar pest liable to attack the gooseberry. The leaves fall off the bush very quickly and the caterpillars are easily seen. The adult fly lays its eggs on the underside of the leaves and within a week the caterpillars hatch out and start eating the foliage. Although the fruit may not be damaged, the loss of leaves will deprive the bush of its vigour and the following year's crop will be badly affected. To control this pest, spray with malathion or derris when the leaves unfold and then repeat as soon as the fruit has set.

Magpie moth The caterpillars of this moth also cause damage to the foliage. A light attack can be controlled by hand-picking, otherwise spray with tar oil emulsion during the dormant season or with derris when in leaf.

American gooseberry mildew This is by far the most serious disease affecting gooseberries and can completely destroy the crop. Control it by spraying with benomyl, a systemic fungicide, karathane or lime sulphur. (Do not use on yellow fruit varieties.) If the mildew gets completely out of hand, it can be sprayed with common washing soda, 4·5 g (1 lb) in 50 litres (10 gall) of water to wash it off.

Left Gooseberries can be grown successfully as cordons against wires strained between well-secured posts.

Red Spider The gooseberry is most likely to be attacked by red spider when grown against a wall or fence as a cordon. Spray with systemic insecticide or liquid malathion.

Raspberry

The raspberry is found wild in Britain and most European countries. It is a deciduous shrub with a creeping perennial rootstock and a biennial stem, producing shoots one year which bear fruit the following season and then die. The soil should preferably be rich, moist and retentive. In their natural habitat raspberries enjoy woodland conditions where the roots are always shaded.

Avoid extremes of soil such as heavy clay or light gravel, unless it has been ameliorated before planting. Although they like the sun, raspberries will still do well in partial shade and once planted, they should last for ten to twelve years. In common with other fruit crops, the ground should be deeply dug and manure or other humus material dug in at the outset. If one row is being planted across the garden, then a trench can be dug on the line of the row. Take the soil out to the depth of a spade. Fork the second spit and dig in the manure or compost, then replace the top soil.

Planting

Raspberry cane planting should be done as early as possible after the leaves fall when the soil is warm and the plants will commence rooting at once. If planting cannot be carried out at this point, it can be done at any time during the dormant season, provided the soil is in a friable condition for planting. Work a little moist peat around the roots to help them get started and firm very well since the crown has a tendency to rise.

The rootstock should be covered with at least 7 cm (3 in) of soil and never less than it was before transplanting. Canes are usually planted 45 cm (18 in) apart with 150 cm (5 ft) between the rows if more than

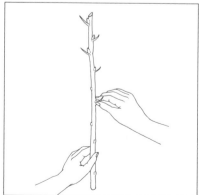

Gooseberry propagation—removing all buds and spines except the top four from a well-ripened shoot.

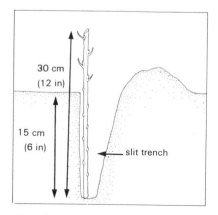

30 cm (12 in)

15 cm (6 in)

slit trench

Gooseberry propagation—the prepared shoot is planted in the same way as for black currants.

one row is planted. Two good terminal posts need to be driven into the ground at the end of each row and three wires stretched from post to post. The lowest wire should be 60 cm (2 ft) from the ground and the top one 135 cm (4 ft 6 in). If a long row is planted then more lighter-weight stakes can be driven in 270 cm (9 ft) apart.

Another way to save space is to grow raspberries as a hedge. Alter-

Left Glen Cova—an excellent variety for growing in the north. It flowers late, avoiding the risk of frost damage, and freezes extremely well.
Below Raspberry cane support.

natively, they can be grown in a triangle with a central pole driven in and the canes planted 45 cm (18 in) apart round the three sides. Each side should be 120 cm (4 ft) and tied in to the centre stake. A third method is to train them up wires on a fence. After planting, cut the canes down to within 22 cm (9 in) of the ground.

Cultivation
The young canes will fruit the second year after planting and should be strong and vigorous enough to bear a good crop. In March they can be given a dressing of sulphate of potash at 35 g (1 oz) per 1 m² (1 sq

yd). The ground should be kept free of weeds. This is not always easy and once the suckers start to grow it becomes more difficult to keep them clear. Take great care when cultivating close to the canes because the roots are very near the surface.

If the ground is clear in May a good mulch may be given. This can take various forms. Well-rotted farmyard manure, if obtainable, is the best. It contains nutriment as well as mulching properties but garden compost, spent hops or spent mushroom manure, are all satisfactory. Failing all else, a really good mulch of lawn mowings will conserve the moisture in the soil which

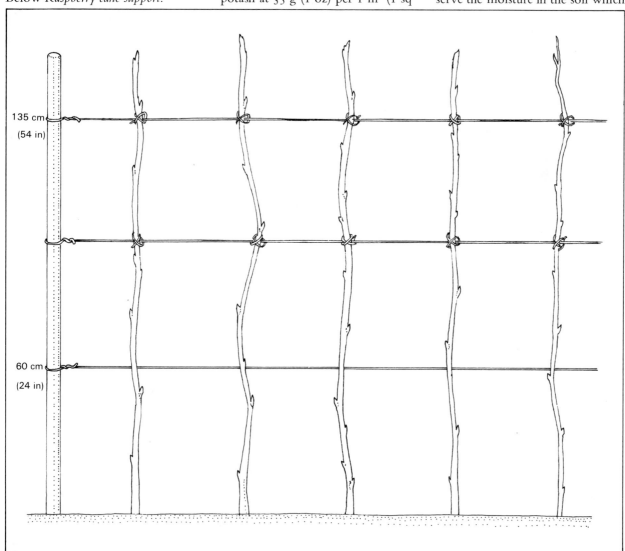

135 cm (54 in)

60 cm (24 in)

is what the raspberry needs most if it is to produce a good crop.

Pruning

Pruning is best carried out immediately after the fruit is picked, when the old fruiting canes are cut out and the new young canes are tied in to the wire. Remove any weak canes and only tie in eight to ten canes to each root. This will depend to a certain extent on the vigour of the variety. In the spring, remove the tip of the young canes at the height at which they begin to bend so that growth will be directed to the lower buds. This will also enable them to support the crop. Suckers which arise at some distance from the row should be lifted, as these cannot be tied in and will only weaken the main root. In the autumn the bed should be forked over and all rubbish and dead leaves removed from around the base of the canes.

Propagation

Suckers are produced freely from the creeping roots of most varieties. Those issuing at a distance from the rootstock are best for propagation. They lift with plenty of root fibres and basal buds for pushing stout shoots the following season. Lifted and carefully planted in autumn, these suckers will produce good canes the first year to fruit the following year.

Autumn-fruiting raspberries

Autumn-fruiting raspberries can be grown on canes of current year's growth. The canes produced during the summer, which would not normally carry fruit until the following year, in some varieties, will bear fruit at the tips of the new canes the same year.

Early varieties

Lloyd George One of the oldest varieties, although not one of the best for flavour, it is a very heavy cropper and still popular. It is vulnerable to frost. The virus-free strain from New Zealand should be grown and it will also fruit a second time in late summer and autumn.

Malling Promise Possibly the earliest of all raspberries to ripen, it is very vigorous, with upright canes which are easy to tie in. It will tolerate a certain amount of frost, has the advantage of being a very heavy cropper and is excellent for both freezing and bottling.

Royal Scot A good, vigorous variety and a splendid one to grow in the north of the country. It continues to bear its berries over a long period which is an advantage to the small grower if there is insufficient room to grow a selection of varieties for all seasons.

Malling Exploit This matures slightly later than Malling Promise. Another hardy variety which will do well in the north.

Malling Enterprise This has a delicious flavour for dessert purposes. Since it does not make strong new canes readily, it needs plenty of feeding, preferably with organic manure to supply nitrogen.

Glen Clova A good variety for the north, this is a late flowerer, so escaping frosts. Freezes well.

Late-season varieties

Norfolk Giant An old but very vigorous variety and a good cropper that withstands frost and disease. It is a good all-round raspberry for bottling, freezing and jam-making.

Malling Admiral Another of the excellent Malling varieties derived from Malling Promise with the same qualities. A heavy cropper, the fruit is particularly good for freezing.

Autumn-fruiting varieties

November Abundance The latest fruiting variety, often continuing into November.

September Bridges the gap between the latest summer-fruiting varieties. Not suitable for northern gardens.

Malling Promise—an excellent, heavy-cropping raspberry.

Pests and diseases

Raspberry moth A pest known at caterpillar stage as the red grub. It occurs mainly in the south and eastern parts of the country, causing considerable damage by burrowing into the flowering shoots. Damage can be detected if the canes are examined towards the end of April or early May. Many of the young shoots, particularly those towards the tops of the canes, will have withered and died because the inside of each shoot has been eaten away.

Moths appear at the end of May or in early June and lay eggs in the flowers. In about a week the young caterpillars are hatched out and burrow into the fruit receptacle on which they feed. They do little damage at this stage but when the fruit begins to ripen, they leave and find a place to make a cocoon. This is usually a crack in a stake where they can spend the winter. The following April they crawl up the stems and attack the young shoots. It is important to clear round the base of the canes in the autumn, removing any loose bark from the stakes where they might shelter during the winter. To control them, spray the soil around the canes with tar oil emulsion in the dormant season.

Raspberry weevil This lives in and feeds on the flower, entering the bud when it is very small. It is extremely difficult to detect since the damage is done inside the bud before the flower opens and the essential organs of the flower are eaten away. It is

controlled by spraying with derris in May and early June.

Raspberry beetle This also bores into the flower bud in May and lays its eggs. When they hatch out, the maggots feed on the fruit which fails to swell. They can be sprayed or dusted with derris ten days after full bloom, repeating the spraying ten days later. Alternatively one can spray with malathion.

Aphid The aphid not only attacks and damages young shoots, but provides an entrance for virus disease through the punctured leaves, resulting in stunted growth. The canes can be sprayed with tar oil emulsion in winter and then with derris before the fruit sets.

Cane spot This affects the leaves and canes, causing purplish spots to appear. Anything affected should be burned, otherwise it will spread until the canes eventually die. Control by spraying with Bordeaux mixture when buds on the canes are 1 cm ($\frac{1}{2}$ in) long and then give a second spraying just before blossoming.

Mosaic This is a virus disease which causes curling of the leaves and yellow discoloration. It is often caused following damage done by aphids. Since there is no known control, it is essential to prevent aphids. Any infected canes should be dug up and burned immediately an attack is discovered. There is a virus-free strain of the Lloyd George variety and Malling Promise and Norfolk Giant are also resistant.

Strawberries

Strawberries are undoubtedly one of the most delicious of all soft fruits used for dessert and, apart from rhubarb, give the quickest return. They can be grown profitably on a variety of soils ranging from a light sand to a heavy clay, but a good heavy loam with a warm aspect suits them best.

The strawberry is very susceptible to frost. A south-west aspect is ideal, sheltering the bed from the morning sun. If the frost disperses before the sun reaches the plants then damage may be avoided. Fortunately, thanks to the breeding of new varieties, a grower living in a frost-prone area can choose a later-flowering variety to avoid frost damage.

Preferably, the soil should be on the acid side. Strawberries do not do so well on limestone soils and plenty of humus or peat should be added to counteract the alkalinity. Drainage is the first consideration because crowns will tend to rot on a badly drained soil. Really deep cultivation is essential. Small motor cultivators are labour saving but they often create a hard pan of soil at the depth of their blades. This prevents the circulation of air and moisture in the soil. The advantage of digging by hand is that every fork or spadeful can be turned over and any pieces of root of perennial weeds can be carefully picked out. The strawberry bed should last about four years and must be thoroughly clean at the outset. Once the plants send out runners it is very difficult to keep the crop free from weeds. Cultivate the ground well in advance of planting allowing the soil time to settle. The young plants can then go into a really firm bed.

Planting and cultivation

Strawberries may be planted either in the autumn or the spring. If planted out in September or October, they will become well established before the winter frosts set in and will bear a crop the following year. If planted out in the spring, however, the energy should be directed into forming a strong plant and flowering trusses should be removed. September is sometimes considered too early for planting as runners may not be sufficiently well rooted. But it is quite possible, with careful attention, to get good runners by that date from home-grown stock.

Rooted runners, or maiden plants as they are called, should be purchased from a reliable source and be

Royal Sovereign—a beautiful looking strawberry with a superb flavour.

of certified stock, as the strawberry is very vulnerable to disease. The plants are put out 37 cm (15 in) apart in rows lying 75 cm (30 in) apart. Unless it rains, plants should be well watered-in and hoed regularly to keep down weeds, which grow very quickly. During the autumn give a top dressing of garden compost or rotted manure.

After planting, the root system will develop very rapidly compared with the crown throughout the late autumn and winter. When growth begins again in the spring, roots only develop gradually compared with the crown which starts to grow vigorously from mid-April onwards. The main root system is developed in late summer and autumn. The bulk of new roots in established plants are produced from the base of new crowns which develop from mid-summer onwards. If any runners have been planted in the autumn, look over the bed and replace any plants lost during the winter. Tread round and firm any that have been loosened or lifted by frost. Cultivate between the rows then dress with sulphate of ammonia using 25 g (1 oz) per 1 m² (1 sq yd).

Harvesting

At the end of April or early in May, the plants will send up flowering trusses and a mulch of peat can be worked in round the crowns and under the leaves. Towards the end of May the first small fruits will appear. Once they begin to swell it is not long before the first ripe berry is ready to be picked. Some protection is needed to keep them clean. Straw is excellent, tucked under the trusses, lifting them and exposing them to more sunlight and air. Straw also has its drawbacks since it harbours pests as well as introducing weeds. Strips of black polythene 26-27 cm (10-11 in) wide or plastic mats, can also be used.

If the weather is dry the plants may need to be watered as the fruit begins to swell. Once it begins to ripen it must be picked over daily,

into two baskets. The small, unripe or damaged fruit can be put aside for jam-making and the good quality ones kept for dessert.

Propagation

Even before the plants have finished fruiting they will start sending out runners. When selecting runners for propagation, only choose ones from plants throwing the best trusses and only take one plant from each runner. These will root easily when pegged down into the soil between the rows.

To grow really good plants, fill the required number of 7.5-cm (3-in) pots with John Innes No. 1 compost or a suitable alternative. Sink into the soil up to the rim. Peg down the runner and water thoroughly. When the runners are well rooted they can be separated from the plant. Lift the pots out of the ground and tap the young plants out for planting in the bed without any root disturbance. The earliest runners rooted can be used to pot on for forced strawberries in greenhouse or frame in early spring.

The life of a strawberry bed is usually three to four years. Rather than renew the whole bed at one time, it is better to propagate enough

runners each year and as two rows come up for renewal, so two rows of young plants can be planted up.

Protection from birds is vital. Nothing attracts blackbirds more than a ripe strawberry. If they cannot be protected by a fruit cage, they can be covered with nylon netting. This can be laid over a small-sized bed and held down by stones. These can be removed easily and the net thrown back for picking.

Growing in barrels

There are other methods of growing strawberries specially designed for those who have no room for a bed. The most popular by far is to grow them in tubs or barrels. They can be any size and a variety makes a more effective display. The whole barrel can be used and holes drilled in the sides through which to insert plants. Alternatively they can be planted in a half-barrel. The barrels themselves need to be treated with a wood preservative if they are to last and the iron bands should be painted.

Place the barrels in position before filling them with soil. They will be far too heavy to shift once they are full. Make sure there are two or three good drainage holes in the bottom of each and cover every hole

Left Netting is the most effective way of protecting the strawberry bed from attack, particularly by blackbirds.

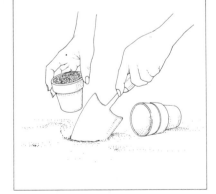

Strawberry propagation—7·5-cm (3-in) pots are filled with John Innes No. 1, then sunk to the rim in soil.

Strawberry propagation—runners will root easily when pegged down into the pots and watered.

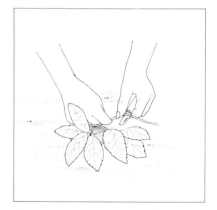

Strawberry propagation—when runners are well-rooted they can be separated from the parent plant.

with either a piece of broken pot or zinc gauze. Over this lay a 5-cm (2-in) layer of drainage material consisting of coarse gravel, washed cinders, broken pot crocks or small broken brick.

Something to retain the moisture is important. A layer of peat can be used, although a piece of rotted turf placed grass-side downwards is ideal. The fibrous loam is an excellent medium for retaining moisture. The barrel is then filled with John Innes No. 3 or any other suitable compost. Add compost or farmyard manure to the John Innes. Half-fill the barrel and allow it to settle then firm well before filling completely. Add a handful of bonemeal to the top layer of soil.

Plant much closer in a barrel than in the garden, about 20 cm (8 in) apart each way. According to weather conditions, watering will have to be watched carefully during the spring. Watering occasionally with liquid manure will help to produce good quality dessert fruit and build up strong plants for the following year.

Strawberries can also be grown in large flower pots, preferably of clay. By growing a small quantity this way they can be moved to shelter from frost then back to the sunniest position to ripen. Always remember that they will dry out easily and frequent watering and feeding during late spring and summer is essential.

Varieties

Cambridge Brilliant A good early variety, compact in shape and ideal for barrel planting.

Cambridge Premier Another early variety which makes a compact plant. It does well under cloches or in tubs. Resistant to mildew.

Cambridge Regent Very hardy and resistant to frost. This is one of the earliest strawberries to ripen. It does well in most soils but is not suitable for growing under cloches because it develops mildew.

Cambridge Favourite A good early variety suited to many dif-

ferent conditions. It does better than most varieties on a light soil and is resistant to botrytis, mildew and frost.

Red Gauntlet A very reliable mid-season variety. It crops well in most soils and is a compact grower, making it good for cloches, pots or tubs.

Royal Sovereign This mid-season variety excels in flavour and appearance. The Malling 48 strain is the best. It has a glossy surface and does well in places with high rainfall.

Cambridge Late Pine A variety which crops well in most soils and ripens late.

Talisman A late, heavy cropper. Resistant to red core.

Autumn-fruiting varieties

Plant out at the end of March under barn cloches. Runners are formed and with the parent plant, produce fruit in late autumn. Remove all bloom until the end of June, cover with cloches again in mid-September except on sunny days.

San Rivale is a recommended autumn variety.

Alpine strawberries

The delicious Alpine strawberry can be grown instead of the perpetual strawberry. It can be planted in many places where the strawberry would be difficult to grow successfully. Seed is sown under glass at the end of March or early in April. The seedlings are then pricked out and hardened off to be planted out in May. They are decorative plants and as they do not object to a certain amount of shade they can be planted under standard gooseberries (see plan 2) or integrated in the flower garden as ground cover among shrubs.

There are several varieties, but Baron Solemacher has the largest berries and is one of the best. They should not be picked until they are fully ripe otherwise they will be hard.

Strawberries can be grown very successfully in barrels and look very decorative on a patio.

Pests and diseases

Strawberry tortrix moth The damage is done by the caterpillar eating into the foliage in May and June. The moths that appear in June and July should be sprayed with derris.

Strawberry blossom weevil The insects appear when the blossoms are about to open. They lay their eggs in the flower buds, drilling holes in the stems and sucking the juice out of the leaf stems and shoots. An adult weevil spends the winter in rubbish, so clear and burn any dead leaves in the autumn. Apply garden spray just before the flowers open.

Eelworms One species of eelworm causes cauliflower disease. The stems become swollen and the buds crowd together, giving the appearance of a cauliflower. The other species causes decay of the root and crown. Dig up and burn affected plants or dust the ground with gamma-HCH.

Strawberry mildew This fungus develops on the underside of the leaf, later attacking both young and old fruit causing them to decay. Use benomyl or systemic fungicide.

Botrytis This appears on the leaves as a white powdery dust. Control with systemic fungicide or captan.

Red Core A fungus disease which attacks the root at the centre or crown of the plant. The roots turn red and the plants die back. This disease rarely occurs on well-drained soil. If an attack is discovered the plants should be destroyed, clean stock purchased and planted on a fresh site.

Rhubarb

A vegetable by definition, rhubarb is generally used as a soft fruit. It is not only popular in puddings and desserts, but bottles and freezes well, makes good jam and chutney and excellent wine. It comes at a time of year when soft fruit of any kind is more than welcome. The first sticks from forced rhubarb can be pulled at the end of January, followed by those brought on early in the garden, covered with boxes or pots.

Rhubarb does not take up much space in the garden if odd corners can be utilised but it must not be relegated to unsuitable situations on the assumption that it will grow easily anywhere without attention.

To produce a good crop of plump, juicy fruit there must be a correct amount of moisture-retaining humus and the deep cultivation that makes for even distribution of plant food and moisture. Compost, manure, shoddy or other forms of humus dug in deep helps to hold the necessary moisture and the ground should be thoroughly cleared of all perennial weeds. Rhubarb is an easy crop and will go on producing for many years. It is not affected by frost, pests or diseases but it can be killed off by over-pulling.

Planting and cultivation

Rhubarb is planted as a root or 'thong'. These are pieces of root each with one bud or eye. They are planted any time during the dormant season, between the middle of October and the end of February. A mild autumn is ideal for getting the plants established before the winter.

Space them 90 cm (3 ft) apart in a row or the same distance from other plants. The foliage is very large and allowance must be made for the size it will grow to in three or four years time. Plant very firmly, just covering the bud. Rhubarb needs plenty of nitrogen so give a small handful of bone meal to each plant. This is slow acting and will be released over a period of time. No sticks should be pulled at all the first year and not too many the second year, even if the crop is plentiful.

By the time the clumps are four years old they will have reached a good size. Divisions can now be made or pieces of root detached with one good bud and planted out to provide new stock or roots to grow on for forcing. In the autumn, when the leaves have died down, remove all rubbish and give a good dressing of rotted manure or spent mushroom manure. Any seed heads that appear should be removed. In very dry weather watering may be necessary, otherwise the sticks will become thin and stringy.

Growing from seed

Rhubarb can also be raised from seed. Sow in the spring in drills 2 cm ($\frac{1}{4}$ in) deep, 30 cm (1 ft) apart. The seed should be sown very thinly. They are large enough to be placed by hand about 15 cm (5-6 in) apart, allowing them to grow without further disturbance until they are planted out in their permanent positions. Growing from seed can be useful when a certain variety is not available in plant form.

Varieties

Hawkes Champagne A deep red early variety and one of the earliest for forcing.
Royal Albert A very popular early variety that forces well, is a good colour and excellent for freezing.
Canada Red A good mid-season variety for outdoor forcing with a long season.
The Sutton A late variety and one of the best of all. It does not run to seed easily and produces good-coloured sticks over a long period.

Loganberry

The loganberry was introduced from the United States in 1900. It has a long fruit like the raspberry but retains its core and is not such a good dessert fruit. It is invaluable for stewing, jam-making and bottling and because of its firmness, freezes extremely well. The fruit is very

Above left *The Sutton rhubarb*. Below left *Timperley Early rhubarb*.
Below *Among its many other uses, rhubarb bottles extremely well.*

juicy with a touch of acidity that makes it refreshing. It should never be picked until fully ripe.

The loganberry has a perennial root stock throwing up new canes every year to bear fruit the following year. It is a very vigorous grower and needs a good depth of soil, although it is not as demanding as the raspberry. As long as it has a good top dressing of manure or garden compost, it will grow on most soils from heavy clay to chalk. Loganberries do not do well on badly drained soil or in an area of high rainfall and a very hard winter can cause the canes to die back. If these are not properly ripened they will not produce a good crop the following year.

Loganberries can be trained against either a garden fence or a wall. They love the sun so a south-facing one is ideal. Alternatively, they can be trained against wires strained between posts similar to those used for growing raspberries. The distance usually allowed between plants is 1·5 m (5 ft). The fibrous surface rooting system should be spread carefully when planting and fine soil and peat worked in round the roots. Planting can be carried out any time during the dormant season.

After planting, the loganberries are cut to within 7 cm (3 in) of the ground. This encourages the growth of strong young canes which will bear fruit the following year. This plant needs nitrogen to support its vigorous growth, and so, as well as plenty of organic manure, it can be given a dressing of sulphate of ammonia at 100 gm (3 oz) per 1 m² (1 sq yd) in the spring.

Pruning

The old canes should be removed as soon as they have finished fruiting and the young, brittle, ones which will have been tied in temporarily can now be tied in permanently. Choose only the strongest canes and cut the weaker ones out. Some will grow to about 3·3-4·5 m (12-15 ft),

but it is better to cut them back to a convenient length.

Propagation

Although the loganberry is like the raspberry in some respects, it does not throw up suckers and the method of propagation is by tip-rooting. A shoot is bent over and the tip covered with 5-7·5 cm (2-3 in) of good soil. This is done in July. By the spring, new roots and a basal bud will have formed which can be severed from the parent and planted out.

Pests and diseases

Raspberry beetle This attacks the loganberry in the same way as the raspberry. The control is the same. Spray with derris ten days after full bloom and repeat the spraying ten days later or use malathion.

Greenfly This can also be trouble-some and the canes are best sprayed with tar oil wash in winter or derris before the fruit sets.

Right *The loganberry was introduced from the United States in 1900 and closely resembles the raspberry.*
Below *Loganberry fruit.*

Blackberry

The blackberry is native to all parts of the British Isles. It is very hardy and can be grown at altitudes of up to 300 m (1,000 ft) above sea level. It does well in sun or shade and because the berries are smooth and glossy, rain water runs off them leaving it untroubled by wet weather. Under good cultivation the blackberry comes up to the standard of the best dessert fruits and freezes well.

One advantage of growing this berried fruit in a small garden is that it will not encroach on valuable vegetable space. Blackberries can be put to practical use in forming a dividing hedge or windbreak to shelter other plants. Some varieties can also be used for decorative purposes to enhance a wall or fence. They have a long life and will be productive for as long as thirty years if properly looked after.

Cultivation

In common with all fruits, it is the initial cultivation that counts. It must be thorough and deep with plenty of humus because blackberries like moisture. They should be planted out, 2 m (6 ft) apart, but not too deep, in suitable weather from November to March. Spread out the roots carefully just below the surface and work in moist peat around them. Firm in well.

In April cut back the growths to within 8 cm (3 in) of the base of the plant and then give them a good mulching in early summer. During this period strong shoots will be sent up. Tie in the two strongest, then cut them back to 10-150 cm (4-5 ft). In July the side shoots can be cut back to the third or fourth leaf. Each year the fruiting canes and any weak or spindly canes should be cut out after the crop is picked and the new wood tied in for the next year's crop.

Oregon Thornless blackberry.

Propagation

The tips of the current season's growth are layered in July and buried 8-10 cm (3-4 in) deep. In five to six weeks time they will have formed bushy roots. These rooted tips are then detached from the parent plant and planted out 45 cm (18 in) apart each way. They can then be left until they are ready to be moved to their permanent positions in a year's time.

Varieties

Merton Early This is an early-ripening blackberry with a beautiful flavour. It is of smaller habit than some, so canes can be planted 1.5 m (4 ft 5 in) apart making it ideal for small gardens. This variety will come true from seed.

Merton Thornless This is a mid-season variety and picking is easier

because it has no thorns. It has an excellent flavour and is a good cropper.

Oregon Thornless This has a parsley-like leaf. It can be used decoratively as well as for its fruit.

Himalayan Giant The heaviest fruiting of all the blackberries. A very vigorous grower requiring plenty of space.

Parsley-leafed blackberry This is a British species raised from a chance seedling. It is valuable both as an ornamental climber and for its large and tasty fruit.

Pests and diseases

Cane spot Purple spots appear on canes and foliage, which dies back. The plants should be sprayed with Bordeaux mixture, first when the buds on the canes are 2 cm ($\frac{1}{2}$ in) long and then again just before blossoming.

Raspberry beetle This occasionally attacks the blackberry and can be sprayed with malathion or derris ten days after full bloom and then again ten days later.

Hybrid berries

There are several hybrid berries which produce very pleasant fruit at a time when soft fruit is scarce.

Veitch berry This is a hybrid of the raspberry and blackberry. The fruit is a ripe mulberry colour and about twice the size of a raspberry. It has the flavour of both its parents and is self-fertile. The fruit is in season mid-way between the raspberry and blackberry crop.

Wine berry This is a very vigorous berry. The shoots have red hairs and the undersides of the leaves are grey, making it a good choice for decorative purposes. The fruit, which ripens towards the end of August, has a delicious wine-like flavour.

Young berry A heavy-cropping hybrid with large blue-black berries maturing in June and July.

Blueberries

Blueberries are a native fruit and they are common on peat soils and

moorland. They are extremely hardy and can be grown in areas where the soil is very acid. The blueberry makes a shrub 120 cm (4 ft) tall and bears small blue berries with a distinctive bloom rather like that of the sloe. They can be eaten fresh or used for tarts or preserving. They will grow in a neutral soil providing it can be top-dressed with plenty of peat. This fruit can easily be grown in the decorative part of the garden. It makes an attractive shrub with sprays of small bell-like flowers.

Blueberries, a native fruit of Britain, are extremely hardy and can be grown in areas where the soil is very acid.

Planting and cultivation

Plant in March, fairly deeply to encourage sucker-like growths. Two varieties should be planted together to ensure fertilisation. If fed regu-

Left *Raspberry beetle.*
Below *Cane spot appears as purple spots on canes and foliage. To control spray with Bordeaux mixture.*

larly with a complete fertiliser, they will go on cropping for twenty years at least. They start fruiting from mid-August onwards but should never be picked before they are fully ripe, otherwise they will lack flavour.

Propagation
Propagation is carried out by cutting semi-ripe wood about 15 cm (6 in) long in August. This can be put in a trench in a shady place outside, but will root more quickly in a mixture of equal parts peat and sand and rooted in a cold frame. The alternative method of propagation is to pull away suckers with a piece of root which can be planted immediately in a permanent position. Seed can also be sown when ripe in October.

Varieties
Pioneer; Rubel; Early Blue; Pemberton.

Cranberries
The cranberry is a very hardy, low-growing plant needing an acid soil. Its natural habitat is marshy bogland and it will grow particularly well in wet peaty gardens. The sharp tasting crimson berries ripen in September and October. They make a fairly dense mat and can be used in conjunction with peat-loving shrubs as ground-cover. They like plenty of moisture and peat should be worked round the base of the plant. Shoots will then layer into this to provide new plants. Plant in the autumn.

Medlar
The medlar is a tree rarely grown these days. It is a small tree about 6 m (20 ft) high originating from Persia and South-eastern Europe. It has round, hard, brown fruit and a calyx similar to a pomegranate. It grows well on most soils and likes a sheltered garden or orchard.

To prune a newly planted tree, cut back the main shoots to about one third of their length. This will produce wood growth to build up

Above left *Mulberrys are rarely planted today although old trees still survive in some gardens, where they can be both decorative and useful.*
Above *The medlar is another tree rarely grown in the modern garden.*
Below left *Cranberries—probably most popular as jelly with turkey.*

a good tree. Once established, pruning can be lighter and aimed at keeping a good shape and encouraging production of fruit buds. All weak shoots and crossing branches should be removed. In the summer, lateral shoots are stopped at five to six leaves, then in winter, back to two to three buds.

The fruit should not be gathered until it has been exposed to at least two frosts. It is then stored in a single layer, eye downwards. It will be a fortnight or more before it is ready for eating, although its chief use is for making jelly.

Varieties
Nottingham; Royal.

Mulberry

The mulberry has been cultivated for its fruit in Europe and Asia for centuries. Although there are many ancient trees in old gardens, very few new ones are planted today. It is a hardy, deciduous tree, grown as much for its ornamental foliage as for its fruit. It needs a sunny position and protection from cold winds. Modern gardens do not always provide the sheltered situation the old walled or hedged garden did. Yet it can be grown as a specimen tree for both decorative and useful purposes where something unusual is wanted.

The mulberry makes a tree up to 9-10 m (30 ft) high and can be propagated by cuttings of semi-ripe wood taken in August and September. These are rooted in peat and sand in a frame. It also roots readily from layers but it is often difficult to find shoots near enough to the ground, unless it has been grown as a bush. Seeds germinate readily and can be grown on in pots until large enough

to plant out. Plant the tree in October in deep moist soil. In the north it is better planted as a bush. At one time, straw was always laid under the tree to catch the ripe fruit when it fell, leaving it clean and undamaged. The modern equivalent is a polythene sheet.

The vine

The vine is a plant of great antiquity. A native of the eastern Mediterranean regions, it originated in Armenia and Turkey. It quickly spread over the whole area and was one of the trees that dominated the literature and religion of Greek, Roman and Christian cultures for centuries. It was not only grown for wine but for shade in hot countries. '*To Sit under one's own vine and fig tree*' was a Jewish expression for peace and prosperity.

Gradually the vine moved westward to most European countries, but it was in France that it found its real home, producing some of the world's most famous wines. Why

Above *Grape vines in summer trained by the Guyot system along horizontal wires strained between supporting posts.*

Below *Vines—initial pruning (left); first summer training (centre); first autumn pruning (right).*

Inset above *The sight of a juicy bunch of ripe grapes will tempt any gardener to become a home wine-maker.*

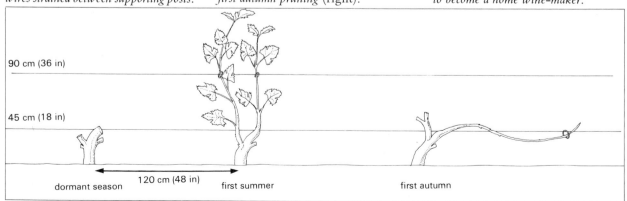

90 cm (36 in)

45 cm (18 in)

120 cm (48 in)

dormant season   first summer   first autumn

it produces better wine in France than in the country of its origin is perhaps due to a combination of soil and climate.

The vine will grow in all temperate regions and will withstand winter frost and cold. If grown in too warm a climate, it has to be defoliated to give it an enforced resting period. It has a tremendously long tap root which was probably developed to tap the under-ground water of the poor limestone soil of the Mediterranean. Vines do not require a rich soil and too much nitrogen only produces lush leaf growth and poor quality grapes.

The vine has been grown in England for many centuries. The coming of Christianity created a need for sacramental wine, and traces of old terraced vineyards have been found in many parts of the country. These have all disappeared over the centuries and the vine has been consigned to the greenhouse for growing high quality dessert fruit. During the last thirty years the number of commercial vineyards in Britain has increased, and the enthusiastic home winemaker has now turned to growing his own.

Cultivation
Vines can be grown outdoors for dessert purposes. They are best grown against a south wall although they can be left to climb over the house for decorative purposes but

Vines—second summer training (left); *second autumn pruning* (right).

the bunches of grapes produced will be small. Also they can be trained up the house, using the rod system to produce good dessert fruit.

They can be planted in the spring if purchased in pots. The plants are taken out of the pots and the roots washed free of soil so that they can be spread out evenly. In the first year the main shoot only is allowed to grow to its full length, while other shoots are removed. The laterals growing from the main rod are pruned to within one bud of the base to form spurs. These are cut back annually and as only one shoot is needed from a spur, only the most vigorous shoot is retained. If rods are planted singly they should be 35 cm (18-20 in) apart, but two shoots can be taken up to make a double rod. No grapes should be taken off the first year. A good variety for growing outdoors is Muscat D'Hamburgh.

Vines for wine making
Where vines are to be grown for wine making, quite a different system is used. Situation is very important. A south-west position is ideal and if the vines are on a slope they will each have the maximum amount of sunshine. Terraces were used extensively for this reason. Frost is always a danger to crops. The sun shining on frost-covered vines can destroy the crop if some protection from the east is not provided. Vines do better in the south, preferably in a limestone soil, at an altitude not exceeding 100 m (350

ft) above sea level. Unlike most fruit, vines prefer a deficiency of humus and a thin soil.

Training and pruning
The young plants are planted out any time during the dormant season. The soil, though not necessarily good, must be very well cultivated to ensure good drainage. The rows should be 105-120 cm (3½-4 ft) apart. Posts are driven in at each end of the row and two strands of galvanised wire strained between them. The lower wire should be 45 cm (18 in) from the ground and the second one 90 cm (3 ft). Plant the vines 120 cm (4 ft) apart and water in after planting, and again during the summer until they are established. Prune back after planting to two buds. The vine fruits on wood made the previous year.

It will fruit the second year after planting. The two buds to which the shoot was cut back will grow out the first summer. In the autumn the strongest of these will be bent down and tied along the 45 cm (18 in) wire while the other rod is cut back to two buds. In the following year the shoot tied to the wire will produce flowers and fruit and the two buds on the other shoot will grow out into two rods.

In the second autumn the rod tied to the wire which has fruited is cut back to two buds, but the strongest of the two rods is tied into the wire to fruit the following summer. The weaker of the two shoots is cut away. This is the Guyot system of pruning. It is carried out year after year, the root system and stock becoming gradually stronger.

Where necessary, cloches may be placed over the rod tied to the wire to protect it from frost in a late season. In the summer, when the flower has developed, the shoot should be stopped three leaves beyond the flower bunch. Only rods that have ripened well will stand the winter. A ripened rod can be identified by its brown colour, while an unripened rod will still be green.

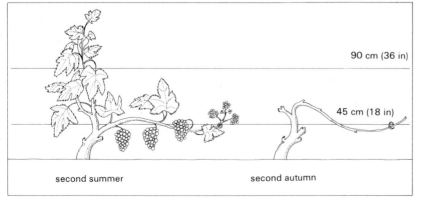

90 cm (36 in)

45 cm (18 in)

second summer   second autumn

Propagation

Propagation can be done either by cuttings or eyes. Eyes are best taken during the autumn, after the leaves have fallen. If they are taken in the spring there is a tendency to bleed. Take a piece of stem just over 5 cm (2 in) long with a bud in the centre. Place the cutting horizontally about 1 cm ($\frac{1}{2}$ in) deep in a mixture of peat and sand in a 7·5-cm (3-in) deep pot. The eyes should be kept moist and warm. Cuttings may also be taken at the same time from wood pruned after leaf fall.

Varieties

The vine most widely grown in Europe and one of the most popular in English vineyards is the Müller Thurgau. It was bred by a Professor Müller from Thurgau in Switzerland and is reputed to be a cross between a Riesling and a Sylvaner. It makes a very pleasant white wine and the vine itself grows well in any fairly well-cultivated soil, although it is very prone to vine mildew.

Other varieties include Madeleine Sylvaner, which crops well; Seyve Villard is a black grape with large bunches of very sweet fruit.

Pests and diseases

Powdery mildew This is the most common disease to attack the vine. This powdery substance attacks leaves, stems and fruit and causes the young fruit to drop off. Dust young shoots in the early stage with sulphur.

Downy mildew The grapes, and eventually the vine itself, can be destroyed completely by this mildew. To control it spray with Bordeaux mixture or captan.

Glossary

alkaloids   nitrogenous bases mostly bitter tasting.

alopecuroides   like a fox tail (Greek).

Anethum   anise (Latin).

angustifolius   narrow leaf (Latin).

Anthriscus   chervil (Greek).

aromatic   pleasantly fragrant.

basilicus   kingly (Latin).

biennial   plant that germinates one year, then flowers, fruits and perishes the next.

to blanch   to make white by depriving plant of light.

to bolt   to run to seed.

bonemeal   slow-acting organic phosphate.

borago   from burra, meaning rough hair (Latin).

bouquet garni   a bunch of herbs tied together to be used in cooking.

brassica   vegetable of the cabbage family.

broadcast   seeds scattered freely rather than planted in drills or rows.

bulb   swollen part of plant such as onion, for storing food, sending roots downwards and leaves upwards.

Carum   from Caria in Asia Minor.

cerefolium   waxy (Latin).

citrata citrus   a citron or lemon (Latin).

clamp   a covered mound for storing root vegetables out of doors.

cordon   a single-stem tree kept to a restricted height and trained along wires strained between posts.

culinary   for use in the kitchen.

cultivar   variety produced by cultivation.

dormancy period   period of inactivity during winter.

dracunculus   a small dragon (Latin).

dwarf   plant much below ordinary size of species.

espalier   a flat shape with pairs of opposite branches growing at right angles to the stem.

evergreen   having leaves all the year round.

F1 hybrid   first-generation seeds resulting from crossing of selected parents.

Foeniculum   fennel (Latin).

foliar feed   liquid fertiliser sprayed on to foliage and absorbed by leaves.

folius   a leaf (Latin).

to force   to speed the growth or maturity of a plant artificially.

frost pocket   low-lying area bordered by hedge or wall trapping cold air.

fruit cage   large wire mesh structure to protect fruit trees from attack by birds.

fungicide   chemical for the control and destruction of fungus diseases.

garni   from garnier, to strengthen (old French).

to germinate   to sprout, bud or put forth shoots.

graveolens   strong smelling (Latin).

growbag   bag filled with compost in which plants can be grown with added nutrients and water.

Guyot system   method of training vines.

hardy   robust plant able to grow in the open air all year round.

hortensis   from hortus, an enclosed place for plants, a garden.

hot bed   a bed of strawy stable manure used for forcing certain plants.

hybrid   plant or tree cross-bred from different species or varieties.

insecticide   chemical for the control and killing of insect pests.

Laurus   laurel (Latin).

Lavendula   from lavo, to wash (Latin). Lavender, for example, was added to soap.

levisticum   from ligusticum, either from Liguria a place in Italy or from liguria, dainty (Latin).

maiden   a one-year-old tree with a single stem; with side shoots this is called a feathered maiden.

majorana   from major, bigger (Latin).

melissa   a bee (Greek).

minimum   small (Latin).

ocymum   an aromatic herb (Greek).

officinalis   from officina, a shop (Latin).

origanum   from oros, a mountain; ganos, beauty (Greek).

pelleted seed   seed encased in a pellet for ease of handling and sowing.

petroselinum   petro, a rock; silinam, parsley (Latin).

to pollinate   to fertilize or sprinkle with pollen.

propagate   to increase a plant by vegetative means.

propagator   covered tray for the propagation of plants.

to prune   to cut back or remove wood to encourage the growth of vegetative

	shoots and fruit buds.
pulegium	from pulex, a flea (Latin).
pyramid	a shape in which branches radiate from the main stem in the shape of a pyramid.
ring culture	method of building up a secondary root system to absorb water so that more concentrated feeding can be given to the plants in the pot or ring.
rootstock	root system on to which can be grafted the scion of a chosen variety.
runner	creeping stem issuing from main stem of plant which takes root.
salvia	from salve, good health (Latin).
sativus	cultivated (Latin).
Satureia	savory (Latin).
schoenoprasum	from schoinospa, a rush; prason, a leek (Greek).
scion	the shoot or bud of the cultivar which is grafted on to a rootstock.
self–fertile	plant or tree which requires no outside pollinator.
Serpyllum	thyme (Latin).
shoot	young branch, sucker or new growth.
spicata	from spica, a point (Latin).
suaveolens	sweet scented (Latin).
sulphate of potash	potash fertilizer (potassium sulphate).
sulphur cone	used for fumigating the greenhouse.
superphosphate	inorganic source of phosphate used on the seed bed.
systemic	(of insecticides etc.) entering the plant via the roots or shoots and passing through the tissues.
to syringe	to sluice or spray.
tisane	an infusion of herbs in boiling water.
to train	to encourage a plant to grow in a certain way e.g. cordon, espalier etc.
to transplant	to move a plant from one station to another.
tuber	short, thick, rounded part of stem, usually underground.
vulgare	common, from vulgus, a crowd (Latin).
wigwam	group of three or more poles tied at the top for supporting beans.
yield	the quantity of edible fruit or vegetables produced by a plant or tree.

Index